高等院校专业英语系列教材

实用英语口语(第4版)

房玉靖 主 编
高海燕 刘晓春 副主编

清华大学出版社
北京

内容简介

本书充分借鉴和吸收了国内外优秀教材,语言知识与语言技能并举,为英语口语的学习营造了真实丰富的语言环境;在提供生动多元的文化背景知识的同时,设计了形式多样的教学活动,寓教于乐,极大程度地调动了课堂气氛与学生的学习兴趣。

本书共分两部分,各包含16个单元,每单元中包括课前热身(学习导入问题)、语音知识(分为元音、辅音和字母组合的读音规则、句子重读等)、精选对话(7个不同方面的对话对章节进行全覆盖)、词汇、口语短句(近百条日常口语表达句式)、口语练习(着眼于对章节内容的复习和常用口语的操练)、文化背景知识和课堂游戏(游戏方法新颖,适合课堂操作)等9个模块。

本书可供高职高专公共英语教学使用,也可供希望提高英语口语交际能力且具有一定英语基础的自学者、专业技术人员、出国人员以及涉外工作者学习使用。

本书封面贴有清华大学出版社防伪标签,无标签者不得销售。
版权所有,侵权必究。举报: 010-62782989, beiqinquan@tup.tsinghua.edu.cn。

图书在版编目(CIP)数据

实用英语口语 / 房玉靖主编 . --4版 . --北京: 清华大学出版社, 2025.5.
(高等院校专业英语系列教材). -- ISBN 978-7-302-68957-7
Ⅰ. H319.32
中国国家版本馆CIP数据核字第2025C27D50号

责任编辑: 张文青　陈立静
装帧设计: 杨玉兰
责任校对: 常　婷
责任印制: 刘海龙

出版发行: 清华大学出版社
网　　址: https://www.tup.com.cn, https://www.wqxuetang.com
地　　址: 北京清华大学学研大厦A座　　邮　编: 100084
社 总 机: 010-83470000　　邮　购: 010-62786544
投稿与读者服务: 010-62776969, c-service@tup.tsinghua.edu.cn
质量反馈: 010-62772015, zhiliang@tup.tsinghua.edu.cn
印 装 者: 三河市少明印务有限公司
经　　销: 全国新华书店
开　　本: 185mm×260mm　　印　张: 19.75　　字　数: 450千字
版　　次: 2009年10月第1版　　2025年6月第4版　　印　次: 2025年6月第1次印刷
定　　价: 59.00元

产品编号: 099138-01

PREFACE

  本书是为了满足高职高专英语教学改革的需求，根据教育部颁发的《高职高专教育英语课程教学基本要求》以及《高等职业教育专科英语课程标准（2021年版）》而修订的。在修订过程中，本书以习近平新时代中国特色社会主义思想为指导，全面贯彻落实党的二十大精神，坚持立德树人的根本任务，以能力培养和学习成效为目标，在体例上充分考虑高职学生的特点，突出口头沟通及书面表达等语言输出能力的培养，着力将学生培养成具有中国情怀、国际视野，并能够用英语进行有效沟通的高素质技术技能人才。

  本书可供高职高专公共英语教学第一学年使用，也可供希望提高英语口语交际能力且具有一定英语基础的自学者、专业技术人员、出国人员以及涉外工作者学习使用。

  本书本着"实用为主，够用为度"的原则，力求教学内容新颖，突出实训演练和实际应用的特色。全书分为两部分，每部分设16个教学单元，每个单元由以下9个模块组成。

  （1）Lead-in 通过一些具有针对性和激发学生学习兴趣的问题，导入单元主题。在导入环节列举了主题相关惯用语和常用句型，以引导学生正确灵活地使用语言，同时培养学生发散思维能力。

  （2）Warm-up Activities 包括语音和阅读两部分。语音部分旨在强化学生的基本语音和语调知识，并通过列举和听读一些相近的音素来帮助学生改掉读音、重音和语调等方面易犯错误，培养学生的语感；阅读部分精选了与主题相关的短文或小故事，学生通过听读掌握阅读的技巧，同时也可作为背诵资料，丰富语言积累。

  （3）Dialogues 由7个围绕本单元主题的情景对话构成，对话按照由易到难的顺序或者是按照题材进行分类组织，旨在为学生提供广泛的语言材料，教师也可根据不同班级特点及学生水平有选择地使用。

  （4）Vocabulary 包括该单元的重要词汇和词组，供学生学习及查询。

PREFACE

（5）Useful Expressions 包括与该单元主题相关的惯用语，旨在为学生补充拓展语言资料。

（6）Exercises 分为 4~5 项。题目新颖，针对性和可操作性强，旨在帮助学生领会、掌握、复习和运用所学的语言素材。

（7）Culture Tips 为学生介绍了同该单元主题相关的一些西方风俗、文化及禁忌，旨在使学生了解文化差异，提高跨文化交际能力，避免语用失误。

（8）Class Activities 由小游戏组成，其中很多是英语国家的传统游戏，目的是活跃课堂气氛，使学生在游戏的同时，巩固本单元所学的知识并提高学习兴趣。

（9）A Dip into Chinese Wisdom 为课程思政专题模块，是此次修订过程增加的模块。既选取了体现社会主义核心价值观以及在中华民族伟大复兴过程中政治、经济、社会和文化发展等方面内容的双语金句，也增加了体现中华优秀传统文化的古诗词名句、经典谚语、格言等内容，让学生树立文化自信，培养学生用英语传播中国文化的能力。

本书的前三版受到广大师生的好评，在此对大家的认可深表感谢。在本书第四版的修订过程中，我们根据读者反馈，对各章节内容进行了有针对性的完善，更新并修正了部分内容，还特别对本教材体系进行了充实和完善，增加了第九部分内容——课程思政专题 A Dip into Chinese Wisdom。

本书配套资源丰富，教学音频、习题答案及电子课件可扫描本书正文第 310 页下方的二维码进行下载。

本书由房玉靖担任主编，高海燕、刘晓春担任副主编，参加编写的人员还有付玉梅、秦玉娜、刘慧、李韶辉等。由于编写水平有限，难免有疏漏之处，恳请大家不吝赐教。

编　者
2025 年 5 月

CONTENTS

SECTION I

Unit 1 Greetings and Introductions ··· 1
Unit 2 Talking About the Weather ··· 10
Unit 3 Asking the Way ·· 18
Unit 4 Making a Telephone Call ·· 26
Unit 5 Seeing a Doctor ·· 35
Unit 6 Shopping ·· 45
Unit 7 Food ··· 56
Unit 8 At the Restaurant ·· 65
Unit 9 Sports ··· 75
Unit 10 Travel ·· 84
Unit 11 At the Airport ·· 93
Unit 12 Hobbies ·· 103
Unit 13 Talking About the Past and the Future ························· 111
Unit 14 Offering Help ··· 120
Unit 15 Thanks and Gratitude ·· 129
Unit 16 Saying Goodbye ··· 137

SECTION II

Unit 1 Holidays ·· 145
Unit 2 Parties ·· 152
Unit 3 Entertainment ·· 162

CONTENTS

Unit 4 On Campus 174
Unit 5 Renting an Apartment 184
Unit 6 Making an Appointment 195
Unit 7 Making a Reservation 204
Unit 8 Making an Apology 214
Unit 9 Opinions 224
Unit 10 Advice and Suggestions 236
Unit 11 Instructions 246
Unit 12 Comparing and Contrasting 256
Unit 13 Banking 266
Unit 14 Advertisements 277
Unit 15 Computers and the Internet 286
Unit 16 Job Interviews 297

SECTION I

Greetings and Introductions
Unit 1

📖 Lead-in

How do you greet your friends on campus? Discuss it with your partner. You may use the following examples for help.

Student A: Hi. Nice to see you here.
Student B: Nice to see you, too.
Student A: Hello, Jack. Haven't seen you for a long time. How's everything going?
Student B: Not bad. How about you?

📖 Warm-up Activities

I. Read the following words and find the pronunciation rules for letter "a".

1.  shame   plate   chase   tape   trace
2. [æ]   back   sad   fat   lamp   fan

II. Read the story below and pay attention to your pronunciation and intonation.

The easiest way to introduce people is simply to mention their names, for example, "Mr. Brown", "Mr. Carter". Try to pronounce the names slowly and clearly. Usually, one should introduce the younger person first to the older, "Grandma, please meet Alice and Carlos Steward, my neighbors." Or introduce a male first to a female, saying "Mrs. Clark, I'd like you to meet Dr. Martin Slater, he works in General Motor. And Dr. Slater, Mrs. Wanda Clark teaches philosophy at Cambridge University." In the United States it's customary (习惯的) for men to shake hands when meeting each other. If not, he should simply bow slightly. Men always stand up when being introduced while women remain seated. However, a young woman should stand up when being introduced to a person much older than her or in a higher social position.

Dialogues

Dialogue 1

Doris: How's life these days?
Steve: Mmmm, just OK. And how are you?
Doris: Pretty good. Nice weather today, isn't it?
Steve: Yes, it's good for doing some exercises.
Doris: How about going jogging together?
Steve: Good idea! Let's enjoy the sunshine!
Doris: Let's go.

Dialogue 2

Mary: Hey, Helen. Haven't seen you for ages.
Helen: Oh, hi, Mary. Yeah, it has been a long time. How's everything going?
Mary: Not too bad, thanks, and you?
Helen: Pretty good, thanks.
Mary: I'm sorry I'm in a hurry right now.
Helen: OK. See you some other time, huh?
Mary: Yeah, let's get together sometime. Take care.
Helen: You too.

Dialogue 3

Jason: Hello, Thomas. It's good to see you. Have you ever met Mr. Li?
Thomas: No, I don't think so.
Jason: Mr. Li, I'd like to introduce Thomas. Thomas is our business partner. And Thomas, Mr. Li is our new sales manager. He is the General Manager of the Beijing branch.
Thomas: I'm very happy to meet you, Mr. Li.

Mr. Li: It's my pleasure, Thomas.

Dialogue 4

Wu Ping: Hi, Liu Yun, nice to see you here.

Liu Yun: Hi, good to see you! How are you?

Wu Ping: Not bad. May I introduce you to our manager, Mr. Smith?

Liu Yun: How do you do, Mr. Smith?

Mr. Smith: How do you do, Liu Yun? Nice to meet you!

Liu Yun: Nice to meet you, too. Welcome to China.

Mr. Smith: Thanks. Your oral English is very good!

Liu Yun: Oh, thank you for saying so. I am flattered! Here is my business card.

Mr. Smith: Thanks. This is mine.

Liu Yun: I hope you will enjoy your stay here.

Mr. Smith: I bet I will.

Dialogue 5

(On the first day of a new semester, the new English teacher, Susan, is asking the students to introduce themselves.)

Teacher: Who would like to introduce yourself first?

Jeffery: My name is Jeffery. I'm from Yantai, a beautiful coastal city in Shandong Province. There are three people in my family, my father, my mother and I. I like playing basketball very much.

Teacher: I think we've already known something about you. But I still wonder why you choose business English as your major?

Jeffery: Well, I love English and business English is a hot major, graduates can easily find decent and better-paid jobs. Besides, working as an international trade specialist has always been my ultimate career goal.

Teacher: Oh, great. Thank you for your introduction.

Dialogue 6

Host: Good evening, everyone. Welcome to Sunshine Cup English Contest. Our first contestant today is Peter Pan. Peter, would you please introduce something about yourself to us?

Peter: OK, thanks. Hello, everyone! My name is Peter Pan. I come from Beijing Vocational College of Electronics Science. It is really a great honor to have this opportunity to participate in this contest. I'm an active and smart boy. My favorite subject is English. I like it very much. I'll try my best to give you a good performance this morning. Hope you can support me! Thank you!

Host：Thank you, Peter. Wish you success!

Dialogue 7

Stella：This is our new employee, Morgan.

Morgan：Hi, everybody! I'm glad to meet you all!

Stella：Would you like to make a brief introduction about yourself?

Morgan：Sure. My name is Morgan. I am from Guangzhou, China. I graduated from Tsinghua University with a master's degree in Economics. I've heard so much about this corporation and I've been looking forward to working here. I hope we can get along well with each other. Thanks a lot.

Stella：Okay. Welcome to our company! I will show you around later.

Morgan：Thank you. What will be my job duties?

Stella：You will be in charge of the promotion of goods. What do you say?

Morgan：No problem. I will try my best. You can count on me!

Stella：And if you have any questions, please don't hesitate to ask Mark, who is in charge of the Personnel Department.

Morgan：Okay! I really appreciate it.

Vocabulary

jog [dʒɒg] *v.* 慢跑 branch [brɑːntʃ] *n.* 分公司 flatter ['flætə(r)] *v.* 奉承，阿谀 appreciate [ə'priːʃieɪt] *v.* 欣赏，感激，赏识 decent ['diːsnt] *adj.* 得体的，相当好的 ultimate ['ʌltɪmət] *adj.* 终极的；最后的 career [kə'rɪə(r)] *n.* 职业，事业	contest ['kɒntest] *n.* 竞赛，争论 smart [smɑːt] *adj.* 聪明的，漂亮的 corporation [ˌkɔːpə'reɪʃn] *n.* 公司 promotion [prə'məʊʃn] *n.* (某商品的)推销广告或宣传活动 personnel [ˌpɜːsə'nel] *n.* 人事

Useful Expressions

A. Introducing oneself

- How do you do? My name's Teresa.

- Allow me to introduce myself. I'm Susan Li, a freshman from International Trade Department.
- Excuse me. I don't believe we've met. I'm Michael Hanks.
- Excuse me. Haven't we met before? I come from China.
- Hi, I'm Mike. May I know your name please?

B. Introducing somebody

- I don't think you've met my classmate Mike. This is Mike. And Mike, this is Mary.
- Let me introduce you to each other.
- Meet my cousin, Bob.
- Jason, I'd like you to meet Edison Brown, the principal of our school.
- Have you met Chanel Jones, Laura?

C. Greeting people

- Good morning/afternoon/evening.
- How are you?
- How are you doing?
- Glad to meet you.
- Nice to meet you.
- Haven't seen you for ages. How are you?
- How's everything?
- How are things going with you?
- Anything new?
- What's up/new?
- What's going on?

D. Responding to greetings

- I'm very well. Thank you. And you?
- Fine. How about you?
- As usual.
- Can't complain, thank you.
- Couldn't be better, thanks.
- Just so-so.
- Pretty good, thank you.
- Not too bad, thanks.

 **Exercises**

I. Choose your appropriate response with the expressions given below.

1. Greet someone you've never met before.
2. Check someone's name if you didn't hear it very well.
3. Greet someone you often meet.
4. Greet someone you haven't met though you've had contacted with him/her by phone or email.
5. Greet someone you've met before.
6. Introduce yourself.
7. Introduce a colleague.
8. Ask about someone's name.

A. I'm David Brown, your new neighbor.

B. Nice to meet you at last.

C. This is Mrs. Davis. She's in charge of exports.

D. Hi! How are you?

E. Good to see you again!

F. I'm sorry I didn't catch your name. Can you say it again?

G. Good morning. Pleased to meet you.

H. I'm sorry, may I know your name?

II. Complete the short dialogues by translating Chinese into English.

1	**A**：_____ (最近过得如何)?	**B**：Great! Thanks. _____ (你呢)?
2	**A**：Hi, I'm very glad to see you again. Have you met my cousin, Linda?	**B**：_____ (我尚未有幸见过呢).
3	**A**：Let me introduce Linda to you. This is Linda, my cousin.	**B**：_____ (你好), Linda. Glad to meet you.
4	**A**：Hello. My name is Liu Yan. _____ (你是哪个系的)?	**B**：_____ (我是国际贸易系的). I'm from Beijing.
5	**A**：I'm lucky to have you as my desk-mate.	**B**：I feel lucky too. _____ (有需要帮忙的地方请尽管找我).

6	A: Hello. _____ (请允许我介绍一下我自己). My name is Sarah. I'm from America.	B: Oh, hello, Sarah. Nice to see you. I'm Lin Hua.
7	A: How do you do, Mr. Smith?	B: Pleased to meet you, Wu Ying. _____ (我从Mary那里得知您的很多情况).
8	A: _____ (请允许我介绍一下我的朋友), Mr. Lin.	B: Nice to meet you.
9	A: _____ (你们以前见过面吗)?	B: No, we haven't.
10	A: This is Mr. Grant. _____ (他是一个通讯员).	B: Oh, my sister is a journalist.

III. Imagine you are a new employee in a company. Mr. Anderson is the President of the Company. You meet him for the first time at the café. Fill in the blanks with the expressions given in the box. Then act the dialogue out with your partner.

> A. I'm very happy that I can work in this company
> B. Are you from Germany
> C. Are you a newcomer
> D. Excuse me
> E. And I love China very much

Tom: ____1____. Are you Mr. Anderson?

Mr. Anderson: Oh, yes, Thomas Anderson. ____2____?

Tom: How do you do? I'm Tom, a graduate from Peking University. My major is Mechanics.

Mr. Anderson: Very good. Welcome to our company.

Tom: ____3____.

Mr. Anderson: Have you got used to the new environment?

Tom: Yes, the colleagues have helped me a lot. By the way, ____4____?

Mr. Anderson: Yes. ____5____.

Tom: Chinese people are very kind and friendly.

IV. Pair work: make dialogues based on the following situations.

1. You are a freshman. One day you meet your new teacher, Professor Thompson, on campus. You greet each other and talk about the university life and study.

2. It's the first day of the new school. Introduce yourself to your new classmates.

3. Kate meets her old friend Michael at a restaurant. They greet each other, and Kate introduces Michael and her parents to each other.

V. Topics for discussion.

1. What's the most impressive thing when you first came to your college?

2. What do you think is the best way to make friends in the college?

 Culture Tips

When people meet someone for the first time, it is common to greet him or her by shaking hands. You can address a new acquaintance by his or her title or family name. You may use their first name when they ask you to do so. The simplest thing to say is "Hello" or "Hi," which is a very common way of greeting someone in both formal and informal situations. A variation of that, which you're probably more likely to hear, is "How are you?", "How are you going?" or "How's it going?". The typical response is "Fine, thank you." After you've answered that question, the most usual thing to do is to return the question and ask the other person if they are well. You can return the question with a simple sentence like "And you?" or "How about you?"

 Class Activities

Guess Who

1. Take out a piece of paper, and write down some personal information about yourself. You should write at least five complete sentences, e.g., "I was born in September", "I like Jay Chou", "I am a football fan", etc. You should make sure the information is true.

2. Then please fold your paper and pass them to the front of the class. The teacher will distribute them and make sure each student has personal information about another student.

3. After reading the personal information, please try to find whose information they have by asking others questions. You can also ask the whole class open questions, such as "Who was born in September?" or ask individuals, such as "Do you like Jay Chou?"

4. The game ends when everybody finds out whose personal information they have got.

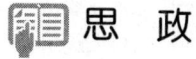 思 政

A Dip into Chinese Wisdom

1. 中国有独特的历史、文化和国情,决定了我国必须走自己的高等教育发展道路,扎实办好中国特色社会主义高校。

China, with its unique history, culture and conditions, has to follow its own path of higher education, and build institutions of higher education founded on socialism with Chinese characteristics.

2. 与君离别意,同是宦游人。

I feel on parting sad and drear,

for both of us are strangers here.

3. 随风潜入夜,润物细无声。

With wind it steals in night,

mute, it moistens each thing.

4. 来而不往,非礼也。

It is impolite not to repay, whatever it may be.

SECTION I

Talking About the Weather
Unit 2

Lead-in

What is the weather like today? What's the temperature inside/outside now? Do you happen to know what's the weather going to be like tomorrow? How can we get the above information? Discuss them with your partner. You may use the following examples for help.

Q: What is the weather like today?
A: It's stormy/awful/rainy/sunny/lovely/cozy/smoggy/chilly/humid today. I feel a little bit…

Q: What's the temperature inside/outside now?
A: The temperature is…

Q: Do you happen to know what's the weather going to be like tomorrow?
A: It will be clear/freezing cold…

Q: How can we get the weather information?
A: We usually get the information from…

Warm-up Activities

I. Read the following words and find the pronunciation rule for letter "e".

1. [iː]　　she　　be　　he　　evening　　piece

2. [e] pet   then   send   shed   chef
3. [ɪ] benefit   reduce   effective economy   eleven

II. Read the passage below and pay attention to your pronunciation and intonation.

Announcement

Attention, please.

It is six o'clock in the afternoon. I'm now giving the weather forecast as usual. From midnight to tomorrow morning there will be a strong north wind blowing across our town and the temperature will drop by 5~8 ℃. Also there will be showers tomorrow morning. Therefore be sure to close all the windows when you leave your classroom tonight and when you get up tomorrow morning, please put on more clothes in order to keep yourself from catching cold.

That's all. Thank you.

Dialogues

Dialogue 1

Kate: What a rain! It's terrible, isn't it, John?

John: You bet. It's raining cats and dogs!

Kate: And cows! The weather forecast says the wet weather is expected to continue towards the end of the week.

John: Too bad! Our barbecue on Sunday will be ruined again.

Kate: Then we'll have to take another rain check!

Dialogue 2

A: What's the weather forecast for today?

B: Cloudy in the morning, and overcast in the afternoon.

A: Any rain?

B: No, but I wouldn't be surprised if it rained tomorrow.

A: Neither would I. It has looked like rain for several days.

Dialogue 3

A: How's the weather in your hometown?

B: It's freezing cold in winter, sometimes the temperature drops to minus 15℃.

A: It must be terribly cold then.

B: Yes, but we've gotten used to it.

A: How about summer?

B: Rather hot and humid most of the time.

Dialogue 4

A: What a wind! It's really awful.

B: Yes, there's a sand storm blowing up.

A: You could get blinded if you go outside.

B: The weather forecaster recommends staying indoors.

A: Sure. Then let's just stay inside.

Dialogue 5

A: Fairly warm this morning, isn't it?

B: Yes, the weather is nice today. I hope it stays nice like this for a long period of time.

A: How about a walk in the park and enjoying the sunshine?

B: That sounds great. The sky is clear, and there's a nice cool breeze.

A: Sure. If the weather keeps up, we can have a picnic tomorrow.

B: Sounds great!

Dialogue 6

A: How terrible a day it is!

B: Yes. The weather is really awful!

A: Is this kind of weather common here? I almost can't stand it, you know, so hot and humid.

B: No. Actually, it is very likely to have a downpour tonight. After that, I think it will be cool.

A: I hope so. It's been so hot for several days.

B: Believe me, the weather like this never lasts long.

A: I began to miss the days in Kunming. It's neither too hot in summer nor too cold in winter.

B: The autumn will come in one or two months. That is the best season here, you'll enjoy it.

A: Well, I hope you are right. Would you like to go swimming with me?

B: All right. Let's go.

Dialogue 7

Mathew: Good morning, Li Yang. What's the weather like today?
Li Yang: It is still smoggy today. We'll have to go to school with face masks.
Mathew: What a pity! According to the news, PM2.5 pollution is the main problem.
Li Yang: Yes, and air pollution will do harm to people's health.
Mathew: So the Chinese government and Chinese people must take action to fight it.
Li Yang: Can you give some advice?
Mathew: Yeah. Since PM2.5 is mainly caused by factories and private cars, cars with high emissions should not be allowed to produce and factories should be closely watched.
Li Yang: I agree. I hope more people will join. And we suggest making the blue skies return for good.
Mathew: I hope so, too.

Vocabulary

you bet 当然，真的，的确 rain cats and dogs 倾盆大雨 weather forecast 天气预报 ruin ['ruːɪn] v. 破坏，损坏 take a rain check 改天 awful ['ɔːfl] adj. 糟糕的 sand storm 沙尘暴 smoggy ['smɒgi] adj. 雾霾的	recommend [ˌrekə'mend] v. 建议，推荐 final ['faɪnl] n. 决赛 thunderstorm ['θʌndəstɔːm] n. 雷暴雨（大雷雨） fair [feə(r)] adj. 晴朗的 sunny ['sʌni] adj. 阳光充足的，晴朗的，明媚的，和煦的

Useful Expressions

A. Asking about the weather

- What's it like outside?
- What's the weather like today?
- What's the weather going to be like tomorrow?
- What do you think of the weather there?
- How do you like the weather there?
- What's the temperature?
- What is the weather report?

B. Stating how the weather is or will be

- It is drizzling/raining/pouring/sunny/fine/cloudy/overcast/windy.
- It's cold/hot/warm/cool/mild/a bit chilly.
- The air humidity is 90%.
- There is a poor visibility.
- The PM2.5 concentration is...
- It'll clear up in the afternoon.
- The wind's getting up, but it may go down in the evening.
- The maximum/minimum temperature is 22℃.
- It looks as if there is a sandstorm.
- We couldn't ask for a better day than this.

Exercises

I. Do you know the symbols below? Write down the words on the lines. Then make dialogues with your partner using the following examples for help.

Example: A: What's the weather like today?   B: It's sunny.

A: What was the weather like yesterday?   B: It was cloudy.

II. Complete the short dialogues by translating Chinese into English.

1	A: _____ (你听天气预报了吗)?	B: Yes, they said it would be cloudy and rainy tomorrow.
2	A: Take your coat, it's freezing cold outside.	B: OK, I will. _____ (外面温度都达到零下10摄氏度了).
3	A: You'd better take your umbrella with you. _____ (看起来好像要下雨).	B: You may be right. Thank you for reminding me.
4	A: _____ (度假时天气如何)?	B: Not bad. It wasn't warm enough for swimming, but at least it didn't rain.
5	A: Is it hot enough for you?	B: Well, I don't mind the heat so much. _____ (最令我困扰的是潮气太重了).
6	A: What is it like outside today?	B: _____ (天气晴好，阳光明媚).
7	A: _____ (你认为今天会下雨吗)?	B: I don't know, but I hope so.
8	A: Do you like winter?	B: No, I'm afraid not. _____ (天气有点太糟糕了).
9	A: What did the weatherman say about today's weather?	B: _____ (他说将会是晴朗的一天).
10	A: _____ (你觉得家乡的天气怎么样)?	B: It's warm and fine in spring, but hot and muggy in summer.

III. Pair work: make dialogues based on the following situations.

1. You and your partner are planning to go picnic outside, but it becomes cloudy and is going to rain. You complain about the awful weather and suggest doing something else today.

2. Talk about the hot weather and invite your partner to swim and take a sunbath.

3. You and your partner talk about the first snow this year.

IV. Topics for discussion.

1. Do you think the weather will affect your mood? What can you do to avoid it?

2. What is your favorite season? And why do you like it best?

3. What causes global warming? What measures should be taken?

 ## Culture Tips

Native English speakers love to talk about the weather. It is an easy way of breaking the ice (starting a conversation) anytime and anywhere with anyone they meet. Whether on the phone or in person, from friends and families to co-workers and even strangers, people often discuss the weather before moving on to other topics. For example, friends and families may talk about the weather before they discuss what's new, and co-workers might chat about it before starting a hard day of work.

Weather patterns vary throughout the world and when we talk about the weather, we often use various phrases to describe it. For example, there are numerous ways to describe rainfall. "Drizzling" refers to rain that is very light, as does "spitting". "Showers" is used when we talk about rain that is average in strength.

There are also many phrases you can use to describe how hot the weather is. "A scorching day" is a day that is very, very hot and sunny, while "a freezing day" is one that is fairly cold.

Occasionally, you may experience rarer types of weather. "Hail" is when small to medium-sized balls of ice fall. A "rainbow" is bands of color that are seen across the sky following rain.

 ## Class Activities

Memory Game

Students are divided into two teams. While one team waits outside the classroom, the other has to make changes in the classroom, such as moving desks and chairs or rearranging objects. After five minutes, the other team returns and tries to detect as many changes as possible. One point is given for each correct response. Afterwards, the teams change roles and the game continues. In the end, the team with more correct responses is the winner.

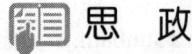 ## 思 政

A Dip into Chinese Wisdom

1. 冲出迷雾走向光明，最强大的力量是同心合力，最有效的方法是和衷共济。

For us to break through the mist and embrace a bright future, the greatest strength lies in united efforts, and the most effective approach is through concerted cooperation.

2. 停车坐爱枫林晚，霜叶红于二月花。

I stop in the maple woods, loving the late view;
Frost-bitten leaves outshine February flowers.

3. 空山新雨后，天气晚来秋。

After fresh rain in mountains bare,
Autumn permeates evening air.

4. 弘扬气象精神：准确、及时、创新、奉献。

Uphold meteorological professionalism: accuracy, timeliness, innovation and dedication.

SECTION I

Asking the Way
Unit 3

Lead-in

What do you usually ask when you've lost your way in a new place? Do you know some expressions used to ask or give directions? Discuss them with your partner. You may use the following examples for help.

1. Excuse me, is there a… around here? / Can you tell me how to get to…? / What's the best way to…?

2. Go straight down this street for… / Turn left when you get to… / Stay on… / It's on the right hand side.

Warm-up Activities

I. Read the following words and find the pronunciation rule for letter "i".

1. [aɪ]   bite   site   pipe   slide   quite
2. [ɪ]   bit   sit   pip   slid   quit

II. Read the story below and pay attention to the stress and intonation.

A guy went to a grocery store which sold goods on sale and asked the clerk behind the counter for two cans of dog food. "Do you have a dog?" asked the clerk. "Yes, I do," replied the puzzled customer. "I'm sorry, sir," the clerk replied, "but you're going to have to prove to me that you have a dog before I can sell you the dog food." The customer felt rather frustrated.

Two days later, the same guy returned to the store with a white shoe box with a small hole on its cover. He approached the clerk and placed the shoe box on the counter. "Yes, sir," asked the clerk, "What can I do for you?" "Put your finger in the hole," said the guy. "I beg your pardon?" asked the clerk. "Just do as I said. It won't bite." Cautiously the clerk put his finger in the hole. "So, sir, could you tell me what do you want now?" "Yes, I want to buy two rolls of toilet paper."

Dialogues

Dialogue 1

A: Excuse me, could you tell me the way to Tianjin College of Commerce, please?

B: Sure. You can take Metro Line 3 to Yingkoudao Station, and transfer to Metro Line 1 to Fuxingmen Station. Then, you can take Bus No. 220 which goes straight there. The college is just around the terminal. You can't miss it.

A: Thanks a lot. Have a nice day.

B: OK, you too.

Dialogue 2

A: Xiao Li, I just got off from Bus No. 703 at the final stop. How can I get to your house?

B: Well, can you see a flower shop on your left?

A: Yes, sure, I've seen it!

B: Turn left there, and just go straight ahead about 100 meters, you will find a neighborhood, and I'll wait for you at the gate.

A: OK, see you soon.

Dialogue 3

A: Excuse me, could you please tell me where the nearest coffee bar is?

B: Go straight along Station Road, continue pass the zebra crossing until you reach a crossroads with Market Street. The coffee bar is facing you on the right corner.

A: OK, many thanks.

Dialogue 4

A: Excuse me, will you tell me how I can find Miss Green's office?

B: Take the elevator to the eleventh floor. When you come out, go along the corridor.

A: The eleventh floor and go along the corridor, and then?

B: Then just go straight ahead and turn left on the corner, it will be right in front of you.

A: I got it! Many thanks.

Dialogue 5

A: Excuse me. Can you tell me where the nearest chemist's is?

B: A chemist's? Oh, yes. There is one on West Street. When you leave the station, turn left, and go along North Street until you get to the traffic lights. Take the right turning there, and walk straight on until just before a left hand turning called South Street. The chemist's is on the left, on the corner of these two streets.

A: Thank you very much.

Dialogue 6

Mrs. Smith is asking a policeman about the nearest ATM (Automatic Teller Machine).

Mrs. Smith: Excuse me, sir.

Policeman: Yes, madam? What can I do for you?

Mrs. Smith: I want to draw some money with my card. Do you happen to know where I can find an ATM around here?

Policeman: An ATM? Let me see. Oh, yes, there is one in this neighborhood. Please go down this street to the intersection, turn right, and then go straight for one block, you'll find a big supermarket on your right hand. There's an ATM on the first floor. You won't miss it.

Mrs. Smith: Yes, I got it. Thank you.

Policeman: Anytime.

Dialogue 7

A: Could you help me out? I'm going downtown. Which bus should I take?

B: Well, it depends on where you want to go in the downtown exactly.

A: Oh, yes, sorry, I want to go to the Golden Commercial Street there.

B: I'm afraid you have to change buses. You can't get there directly.

A: All right. Then which buses should I take?

B: First, you can take Bus No. 65 or Bus No. 87. Get off at the Lijiang Road, and then change to take Bus No. 96, which terminates at the Golden Commercial Street.

A: OK, first No. 65 or 87, then No. 96. Thank you very much. Well, do you know how long it may take to get there?

B: It's hard to say. It may take you one and a half hour if there isn't a traffic jam, but, you know, around Golden Commercial Street, at rush hour, cars always get jammed. So it may take you much longer.

A: I see. Many thanks.

B: You're welcome.

 Vocabulary

commercial [kə'mɜːʃl] *adj.* 商业的 *n.* 商业广告	intersection [ɪntə'sekʃn] *n.* 交集，十字路口，交叉点
frustrated [frʌ'streɪtɪd] *adj.* 泄气的	terminate ['tɜːmɪneɪt] *v.* 终止，结束
corridor ['kɒrɪdɔː(r)] *n.* 走廊	rush hour 高峰时间
cautiously ['kɔːʃəsli] *adv.* 慎重地	

Useful Expressions

A. Asking directions

- Excuse me, is this the way to the Bird's Nest?
- Is there a post office near here?
- I'm looking for National Olympic Stadium. Can you help me?
- How do I get to China Grand Theatre?
- Could you tell me the way to the city library?
- Could you tell me how I can get to the nearest Bank of China?
- Where is the railway station?
- What's the best way to the art gallery?

B. Giving directions

- Turn back.
- Take the road to…
- Cross…
- Take the first/second road on the left/right.
- It's next to/near/opposite/between/on the corner/in front of/behind/at the end of…

- (First,) go down/up/along this street (for… blocks).
- (Then,) turn left/right at the traffic light/into… street.
- (After that,) go straight on… Street until you get/come to the…
- (When you get to the…,) turn left/right again.
- There is a junction but there aren't any signposts.
- It's on your left, next to the… You can't miss it!
- Sorry, I don't know.
- I'm not sure, sorry.
- Sorry, I'm new here.
- Sorry, I'm just a passer-by.

 Exercises

I. What kind of transportation do you often use?

 coach	 helicopter	 bus	 subway
 bicycle	 motorcycle	 taxi (cab)	 boat
 train	 ship	 light railway	 car
 plane	 yacht	 cruise ship	 cable car

II. Fill in the blanks according to the following maps.

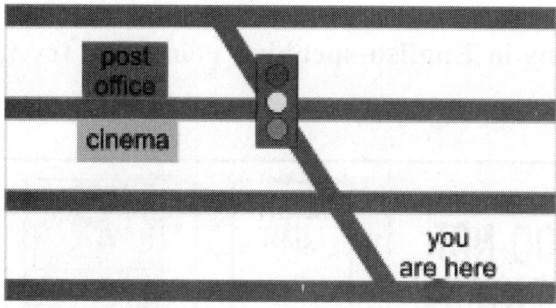
Map 1

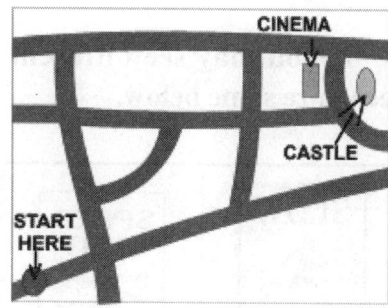
Map 2

1. (Map 1)

A: Excuse me, where is the post office, please?

B: _____ at the next corner. Then _____ until you come to the traffic lights. Turn _____ there. The post office is _____ the cinema. You won't _____ it.

2. (Map 2)

A: _____ me, how do I _____ to the cinema?

B: Go _____. Turn _____ at the corner. Then take the _____ road on your _____. _____ to the _____ of the road. _____ left there. The cinema is on your _____, _____ the castle.

A: Thank you very much.

B: You're _____.

III. Pair work: make dialogues based on the following situations.

1. Jeffery asks Kate the way to go to the nearest bank.
2. Jane asks a student how to go to the canteen on campus.
3. Ben asks the receptionist where Mr. Li's office is.

IV. Topics for discussion.

1. Talk about an experience of getting lost.
2. Describe the route from your home to the nearest shopping mall.

 Culture Tips

I. You may see different signs in English-speaking countries, try to recognize some below.

SLOW SCHOOL	SPEED LIMIT 50	DO NOT ENTER	WEIGHT LIMIT 10 TONS	AHEAD
STOP	NO DUMPING VIOLATORS WILL BE PROSECUTED	NO TRUCKS	AUTHORIZED PERSONNEL ONLY	STAFF ONLY
Dressing Room	ENTRANCE →	EXIT ←	FIRE STAIRS	NO U TURN
PRIVATE DRIVE NO TRESPASSING	RESERVED PARKING	RIGHT TURN ONLY	NO PARKING	ROAD WORK AHEAD

II. Driving in the United States.

It's not that there's no public transportation in the United States. Many cities have taxis, buses and subways to help commuters get to and from work. Some large universities even have buses to take students to classes across campus. But most people find it much more convenient to drive, even if they do have to deal with traffic. Nowadays, many busy families own more than one vehicle. Many people view owning a car as a status symbol. But no matter what their status is, people without wheels feel tied down.

Young people in the United States often get their driver's licenses around age 16 by passing a written test and a driving test. In many cases, before they can get their licenses, they have to take a driver's education course. This course gives students hands-on practice with driving and helps to reduce the high cost of insurance. For teenagers, being able to drive—and in some cases, having their own car—is a big deal. It gives them a sense of power and freedom.

Many young Americans consider a driver's license a right, not a privilege. It's rare to find an American teenager without a driver's license.

 Class Activities

Hangman

Divide the class into two groups. On the blackboard, draw spaces for the number of letters in a word. Have the players guess letters in the word alternating between the groups. If a letter in the word is guessed correctly, the teacher writes it into the correct space. If a letter that guessed is not in the word, the teacher draws part of the man being hanged. The team which can guess the word first receives a point, and then start the game.

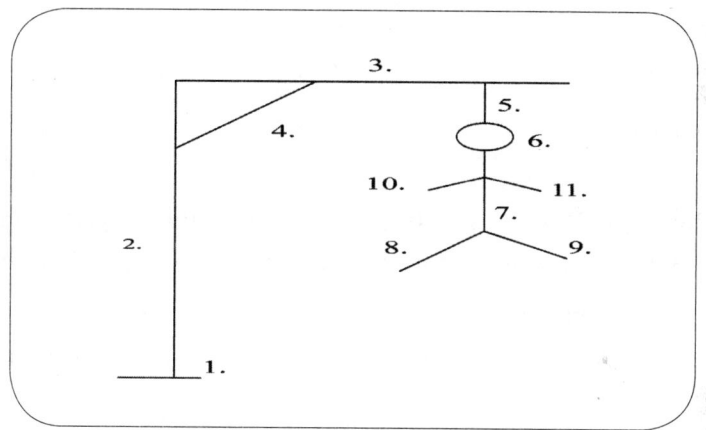

 思 政

A Dip into Chinese Wisdom

1. 全党要坚定道路自信、理论自信、制度自信、文化自信。

The whole Party should be confident in our path, theory, system and culture.

2. 会当凌绝顶，一览众山小。

I will ascend the mountain's crest,

It dwarfs all peaks under my feet.

3. 路漫漫其修远兮，吾将上下而求索。

For the road ahead is so far and so distant is my journey,

And I want to go up and down, seeking my heart's desire.

4. 日日行，不怕千万里。

Keep walking and one will not be daunted by a thousand miles.

Making a Telephone Call
Unit 4

Lead-in

On what occasions do you think you must make a phone call instead of a short message? Give your opinions with the help of the following examples.

A: If it is an emergency, I think we'd better make a phone call.
B: If it is your boss, you'd better call him instead of sending short messages. That will be more polite.

Warm-up Activities

I. Read the following words and find the pronunciation rules for letter "o".

1. [əʊ]   note   pope   hope   cope   code
2. [ɒ]   not   pop   hop   cop   god

II. Read the story below and pay attention to your pronunciation and intonation.

Wrong Number

A man joined a big foreign company as a trainee. On his very first day of work, he dialed the pantry and shouted into the phone, "Get me a coffee, quickly!"

The voice from the other side responded, "Sorry, but you've dialed the wrong extension! Do you know who you're talking to?"

"No." replied the trainee.

"It's the CEO of the company!"

The trainee shouted back, "I am sorry, but do you know who you are talking to?"

"No." replied the CEO.

"Good!" replied the trainee, and put down the phone.

 Dialogues

Dialogue 1

Man: Hello. 8613-1076.

Woman: Hello. May I speak to Sandy, please?

Man: Just a minute, please.

Woman: Thanks.

Man: I'm sorry, but she's not in at the moment. Would you like to leave a message?

Woman: Well, please tell her to call me back when she gets home. My name is Mary, and my number is 300-1963.

Man: 300-1963, right?

Woman: Yes. Thank you very much.

Man: You're welcome.

Dialogue 2

Garry: Garry Arnold speaking.

Bob: Hi, Garry. This is Bob. I need to talk to you about the report you sent me last week.

Garry: Uh. Bob. I was expecting your phone last night.

Bob: I kept calling your office last night, but only got a busy signal.

Garry: When did you call?

Bob: At about nine o'clock.

Garry: Oh, my mobile phone ran out of battery. I'm sorry about that. I thought you would call at eight o'clock.

Bob: I wasn't free until nine o'clock.

Dialogue 3

Ann: Was that the telephone ringing?

Frank: I didn't hear anything.

Ann: I thought I heard it ring two or three times.

Frank: Sometimes when the windows are open, you can hear the neighbors' phone.

Ann: Well, I'm expecting an important phone call, and I don't want to miss it.

Frank: Is it anything I should know about?

Ann: Not really. It has something to do with work and doesn't really affect us here at home.

Frank: Well, why don't you go and relax for a while? I'll call you if the phone rings for you.

Ann: Thanks. I've been waiting so long. I need to relax.

Dialogue 4

Operator: Hello! Overseas operator. May I help you?

Carl Marx: Yes. I'd like to make a collect call to the USA.

Operator: Your name, please?

Carl Marx: It's Carl Marx.

Operator: Who would you like to talk to?

Carl Marx: I'd like to talk to Ms. Jane Hanks.

Operator: Is that Ms. Jane Hanks?

Carl Marx: That's right.

Operator: What number are you calling from, please?

Carl Marx: From code 0632, 2610-1344.

Operator: And the number in the USA, please?

Carl Marx: Country code 1, area code 212, and the number is 334-2786.

Operator: Hold the line, please. I'll put you through.

Dialogue 5

George: Hello! 8647-5089.

Kim: Hello, can I speak to Brant, please?

George: Who do you want to speak to?

Kim: Brant Smith.

George: I'm sorry. You must have the wrong number. This is 8617-5098.

Kim: Oh, I'm sorry to disturb you.

George: That's alright, goodbye.

Kim: Goodbye! (*Murmuring to herself*, "let me try again!")

Brant: Hello, 8617-5089.

Kim: Hello, Kim speaking. May I speak to Brant, please?

Brant: Speaking.

Kim: Oh, hi, Brant, this is Kim. I just want to tell you that there is a meeting tomorrow at nine o'clock in the meeting room. Please be there on time.

Brant: OK. I see. Thanks for calling.

Kim: My pleasure.

Dialogue 6

Receptionist: Hello. Novas Company. May I help you?

David: Hello! This is David Jones. May I speak to Mr. Wright?

Receptionist: I'm sorry but he's in Beijing on business.

David: Do you have any idea when he'll be back?

Receptionist: Probably sometime next week?

David: I have a question about the computer we bought from your company. Is there anyone else who can help me?

Receptionist: Of course. Mr. Lin is the export manager. Would you like to speak to him?

David: Yes, please.

Receptionist: OK. I'll just put you through.

Mr. Lin: Hello! This is Lin speaking. Can I help you?

David: Sure. I want to ask you some questions about the computer we bought from your company.

Dialogue 7

Receptionist: Hello, GM Company. How may I direct your call?

Alice: Could I have extension 251, please?

Receptionist: I'm sorry the line is engaged now. Would you wait for a moment, please?

Alice: Sure.

(A few minutes later.)

Receptionist: The line is free now. I'll put you through.

Bill: Hello. This is Bill. Whom am I speaking to, please?

Alice: It's Alice!

Bill: Oh, Alice.

Alice: Where were you last night, Bill? I waited for you for almost an hour.

Bill: Oh! I'm sorry. I completely forgot.

Alice: You forgot! What did you do last night?

Bill: Oh, I'm so sorry, I…

Vocabulary

affect [əˈfekt] v. 影响，作用	export [ɪkˈspɔːt] v. 输出，出口
overseas [ˌəʊvəˈsiːz] adj. 海外的；adv. 在海外	receptionist [rɪˈsepʃənɪst] n. 接待员
	manager [ˈmænɪdʒə(r)] n. 经理
disturb [dɪˈstɜːb] v. 扰乱，妨碍	extension [ɪkˈstenʃn] n. 分机
probably [ˈprɒbəbli] adv. 大概，或许	

Useful Expressions

A. Answering the phone

- Good morning/afternoon/evening, Susan's speaking.
- Hello, who's calling, please?
- Hi, this is Lambert White speaking.
- Hello, this is Lambert White from BBA Company.
- Could/May I speak to Jerry Lincoln, please?
- I'd like to speak to Jerry, please.
- Could you put me through to Robert Johnson, please?
- Could I speak to someone who…
- I'm afraid Mr. Hilton isn't in at the moment.
- I'm sorry. He's in a meeting at the moment.
- I'm afraid he's on another line at the moment.
- Just a moment, please.
- Could you hold the line, please?
- Hold the line, please.
- Just hold the line for a second, please.
- I'm sorry. I can't hear you very well. Could you speak up a little, please?
- I'm afraid you've got the wrong number.
- You must have dialed the wrong number.
- I've tried to get through several times but it's always engaged.
- Could you spell that, please?
- Pardon? It's not clear. Could you speak a little louder?

B. Putting someone through

- One moment, please. I'll see if Mr. Jones is available.
- Would you hold the line, please?
- I'll put you through.
- I'll connect you.
- I'm connecting you now.
- Sir, you are through.
- Sorry, nobody is answering.
- The line is busy/engaged.

C. Leaving/Taking a message

- Would you like to leave a message?
- Can I take a message?
- Can I give him/her a message?
- I'll tell Mr. Jones that you called.

 Exercises

I. Fill in the blanks with the words or phrases given in the box.

| dial tone | answering | a phone booth | busy signal | ringer |
| payphone | call back | receiver | cell phone | dial |

1. When you pick up the phone to call someone, you hear a _____.
2. If I'm not at home, leave a message on my _____ machine.
3. Sally must be talking to her mom because I have been getting a _____ for two hours.
4. I never answer my _____ while I'm driving.
5. Mark always turns his _____ off when he is studying.
6. I'm busy right now. Can you _____ later?
7. You have to _____ "0" for the operator.
8. I have a _____ so I can do the dishes and chat at the same time.
9. You will need a quarter or a phone card if you want to use the _____.
10. Excuse me, is there _____ there?

II. Complete the short dialogues with the expressions given in the box.

> A. Could you spell your name
> B. he won't be back
> C. Could I have your telephone number, please
> D. Would you like to leave a message
> E. May I ask who's calling
> F. she's out for lunch

1. — _____?
   — This is Thomas Edward.

2. — I'm sorry, but _____ right now.
   — I'll call her after lunch.

3. — _____?
   — Yes. It's 2051-2658.

4. — _____?
   — No. I'll call later.

5. — _____, please?
   — It's spelled T-O-M.

6. — I'm sorry, but _____ until next Wednesday.
   — All right. Please tell him Mike called.

III. Complete the short dialogues by translating Chinese into English.

1	**A**: Is Mary _____ (在家吗)?	**B**: No, she's just out for a moment. _____ (我可以帮你留言吗)?
2	**A**: Why didn't you call me yesterday?	**B**: I tried to call you, but _____ (打不通).
3	**A**: How are you going to pay?	**B**: I will _____ (我用电话卡付话费).
4	**A**: _____ (为什么电话总占线) when I called you this morning?	**B**: My mom was chatting with her friends.
5	**A**: I would like to speak with Laura Green _____ (如果她有空的话).	**B**: I'm sorry, but she is not in the office right now.

6	A: Do you need me to _____ (让他给你回电话吗)?	B: Sure. I will _____ (留下我的电话号码).
7	A: _____ (我得打个对方付费电话).	B: Just one second, I will connect you.
8	A: I'm busy, _____ (谁接一下电话)?	B: Okay. I got it.
9	A: Alright, _____ (请告诉他我打过电话).	B: Okay.
10	A: Do you want to leave a message?	B: Yes, please tell him _____ (我会在一个小时之后再打来).

IV. Pair work: make dialogues based on the following situations.

1. You want to call Dr. Smith, but you dial the wrong number. An old man answers, and he doesn't seem to be happy about this.

2. Tony wants to ask his friend Lisa to see a film with him this weekend. They talk over the phone about what to see, where to see it, and when and where to meet each other.

3. Ruby arrives at the airport. She calls her friend Wang Dan to pick her up. And her friend is surprised by her early arrival.

4. You are calling Mr. Miller, but he is at a meeting. Then you want to call Mr. Wilson, but he is on business in Shanghai. So you have to call back later.

V. Topics for discussion.

1. Have you felt annoyed when a mobile phone rings during the class? Should cell phone be permitted in class?

2. Phubber, or smartphone addict, refers to someone who is snubbing real social contact by frequently checking their phones and posting words and pictures on the Internet. Are you a phubber? Are you a victim of phubbing? Tell us your stories.

Culture Tips

There are three kinds of phone books in Western countries: the White Pages, the Blue Pages, and the Yellow Pages. The White Pages list people with phones by last name. The Blue Pages contain numbers of city services, government services and public services. Businesses and professional services are listed in a special classified directory—the Yellow Pages. It is generally very easy to find a public telephone in the developed countries. Public phones are located in railroad stations, airports, stores, hotels, restaurants, and gas stations, on street corners and in most office buildings. To make a pay call, you pick up the phone, listen for a dial tone, deposit a coin or coins (depending on the cost in the area), and then dial the number.

A person-to-person call can only be answered by the particular person you are calling. Consequently, if the person is not available, you will not be charged. However, person-to-person and collect calls are more expensive than directly dialed calls because they involve the additional cost of operator assistance. The person being called pays for a "collect" call rather than the person making the call. If you make a long-distance call and get a wrong number, call the operator and explain what happened. This means that you can make the call again to the right number without paying extra. Alternatively, you can have the phone company mail you a credit coupon that has the same value as the phone call.

Class Activities

Extreme Situation

The point of this activity is to create challenging scenarios that involve making difficult decisions in an extreme situation.

You find a wallet containing $60,000 and the owner's ID. That amount is exactly what you need to cover the cost of a major operation for your father, who needs it to survive. What would you do in this situation?

思 政

A Dip into Chinese Wisdom

1. 人类历史告诉我们，越是困难时刻，越要坚定信心，任何艰难曲折都不能阻挡历史前进的车轮。

A review of human history teaches us that the more difficult things get, the greater the need grows to stay confident. No difficulties could ever stop the wheel of history.

2. 长风破浪会有时，直挂云帆济沧海。

A time will come to ride the wind and cleave the waves;
I'll set my cloudlike sail to cross the sea which raves.

3. 寡言为智。

A still tongue makes a wise head.

4. 眼见为实。

Seeing is believing.

SECTION I

Seeing a Doctor
Unit 5

Lead-in

What is your impression when somebody mentions "doctor"? Discuss it with your partner. You may use the following examples for help.

A: I think they are kind-hearted and helpful.
B: Oh, I am afraid of doctors. Every time I go to the hospital, I'm scared.

Warm-up Activities

I. Read the following words and find the pronunciation rules for letter "u".

1. [juː]   cute   tube   amuse   abuse   repute
2. [uː]   rude   truce Bruce   flute   fruit
3. [ʊ]   puss   push   bush   pull   put
4. [ʌ]   cut   tub   plum   us   nut

II. Read the story below and pay attention to your pronunciation and intonation.

A man who didn't feel well walked into a doctor's examining room.

"Please stick out your tongue," the doctor said.

The man put out his tongue.

"OK. You can put your tongue back now, " the doctor said. "It's clear what's wrong with you. You need more exercise."

"But, doctor," the man said, "I don't think…"

"Don't tell me what you think," the doctor said. "I am the doctor, I know what you need. I see hundreds of people like you. None of them get any exercise. They sit in offices all day and in front of the television in the evening. What you need is to walk quickly for at least 30 minutes a day. "

"Doctor, you don't understand," the patient said, "I…"

"I don't want to hear any excuses," the doctor said. "You must find some time for exercise. If you don't, you will get fat and have health problems when you are older."

"But I walk every day," the patient said.

"Oh, yes, and I know what kind of walking that is. You walk to the bus station from your house, then from the station to your office, and walk from your office to a restaurant for lunch and back. That's not real walking. I'm talking about a walk in the park for thirty minutes every day."

"Please listen to me, doctor!" the patient shouted, getting angry with this doctor who thought he knew everything.

"I'm a mailman," the patient went on, "and I walk for eight hours every day."

For a moment the doctor was silent, and then he said quietly, "Stick your tongue out again, will you?"

 Dialogues

Dialogue 1

Doctor: What can I do for you?

Philips: I have a headache, a sore throat and I cough a lot. I also feel weak.

Doctor: Let me take your temperature. Hmm… you are running a temperature.

Philips: Anything serious?

Doctor: Nothing serious. You need to take some pills and have a rest.

Philips: OK, thanks a lot.

Dialogue 2

Doctor: What's wrong with you?

Cathy: I have a headache, a running nose and my voice is hoarse.

Doctor: How long has this been going on?

Cathy: It began last night.

Doctor: Well, let's take your temperature and see if you have a fever.

Cathy: All right.

Doctor: It is 38.5 ℃. You do have a temperature. I'll give you some medicine to take.

Cathy: How often do I have to take the pills?

Doctor: Three times a day.

Dialogue 3

Doctor: What's the matter with you?

Tom: I've had a terrible stomachache since last night.

Doctor: Any symptoms? Like diarrhea, nausea?

Tom: Yes, I also feel dizzy.

Doctor: What about your appetite?

Tom: I have no appetite for anything.

Doctor: Can you think of anything you ate last night?

Tom: All I can think of is the fish I had. It didn't taste right.

Doctor: Then that might be it. I'll give you an injection. After a good rest, you will be better.

Tom: Thank you, doctor.

Dialogue 4

(At the dentist's)

Doctor: How long have you felt like this? Is it the first time it's aching?

Lisa: No. It has been troubling me for several times.

Doctor: Does it hurt when you eat something?

Lisa: I can't eat anything. Anything, hot or cold, sweet or sour, hurts me.

Doctor: Open your mouth as wide as you can. Well, I think you'd better take an X-ray.

Lisa: Can't you see anything?

Doctor: You've got an abscess. It's too late. I'm afraid we'll have to pull it.

Lisa: Will it hurt?

Doctor: Not during the operation. I'll give you some pills. They can relieve the pain.

Lisa: That's great.

Doctor: By the way, you can't eat anything hard or sticky within three days. You can have some liquid food, such as milk and porridge.

Dialogue 5

Jim: Excuse me, where can I get a blood test?

Receptionist: On the third floor.

Jim: What procedures do I need to follow?

Receptionist: Just tell the nurse that you want a blood test. She will prepare a test sheet for you.

Jim: And then?

Receptionist: You need to go to the second floor to pay, and then go back to the first floor and have your blood test.

Jim: Thank you.

Receptionist: You're welcome.

Dialogue 6

A: Hi, Fang. I heard you were sick. How do you feel now?

B: Oh, thank you for coming, Ross. It was a very bad cold. But I feel much better today. My fever's gone and so has the cough. I'm almost myself again.

A: A bad cold almost gone in a few days' time? That's a quick recovery. Who's been treating you? And what medication are you on?

B: I went to a traditional Chinese doctor who prescribed some herbal medicine for me.

A: So you've been taking the magical herbal remedy.

B: Yes, I've always found Chinese medicinal herbs especially effective for treating bad colds.

Dialogue 7

Doctor: Good morning, Mr. Grant! How are you feeling today?

Mr. Grant: Much better, thank you! I can sit straight today. The acupuncture is really great.

Doctor: Yes, acupuncture is one of the most effective ways to treat diseases.

Mr. Grant: I also heard of something about massage and cupping. They are also very good therapies. I know a little about acupuncture and massage. But can you tell me what cupping is? Do people really use cups?

Doctor: Yes. Cupping is a kind of therapy using a vacuum cup sucked firmly on the skin.

Mr. Grant: But how can you make the cup become vacuum?

Doctor: Usually, the doctor lights fire on an alcohol sponge, and puts it inside the cup for a short while to vacuum out the oxygen, and then he places the vacuum cup instantly over the selected spot of the skin.

Mr. Grant: Is it as effective as acupuncture?

Doctor: Yes. But cupping therapy is especially good for pains.

Mr. Grant: That's really fantastic.

Vocabulary

sore [sɔː(r)] *adj.* 疼痛的，痛心的	schedule ['ʃedjuːl] *n.* 时间表
throat [θrəʊt] *n.* 喉咙	sour ['saʊə(r)] *adj.* 酸的
hoarse [hɔːs] *adj.* 沙哑的，嘶哑的	porridge ['pɒrɪdʒ] *n.* 粥，麦片粥
pill [pɪl] *n.* 药丸	procedure [prə'siːdʒə(r)] *n.* 程序，步骤
symptom ['sɪmptəm] *n.* 症状，征兆	recovery [rɪ'kʌvəri] *n.* 恢复，复原，痊愈
diarrhea [ˌdaɪə'rɪə] *n.* 痢疾，腹泻	medication [ˌmedɪ'keɪʃn] *n.* 药物治疗，医药
dizzy ['dɪzi] *adj.* 晕眩的	
appetite ['æpɪtaɪt] *n.* 食欲，胃口，欲望	prescribe [prɪ'skraɪb] *v.* 开药方
injection [ɪn'dʒekʃn] *n.* 注射	herbal ['hɜːbl] *adj.* 草药的
reservation [ˌrezə'veɪʃn] *n.* 预定，预约	magical ['mædʒɪkl] *adj.* 魔术的
available [ə'veɪləbl] *adj.* 可用的，空闲的	remedy ['remədi] *n.* 药物，治疗法，补救

Useful Expressions

A. Asking a patient about illness

- What can I do for you?
- May I help you?/Can I help you?
- What's the trouble/matter with you?/What's wrong with you?
- What hurts/is troubling you?
- What seems to be the matter/problem/trouble?
- When did the pain start?
- How long have you been like this?
- How're you feeling now?
- What did you eat yesterday?
- Do you cough?

- Did you have pains here before?
- Are you feeling well/sick?
- What medicine did you take?
- Have you taken any medicine?

B. Telling a doctor how you feel

- I feel sick/very bad/terrible.
- I have a headache/stomachache.
- I'm aching all over.
- I'm having some trouble in sleeping. / I can't sleep well.
- One of my teeth troubles me.
- It hurts here.
- I don't like eating.

C. A doctor's advice and diagnosis

- Now take off your coat and shirt.
- I'll have your temperature taken.
- I don't think it's anything serious.
- Please breathe deeply (normally).
- Please stick out your tongue.
- Let me take your blood pressure.
- Please open your mouth and say "Ah".
- It's nothing serious, but you'd better stay in bed and have a good rest.
- You need a thorough examination.
- You'll be all right/well soon.
- You should stay in bed for a few days.
- We think that you had better be hospitalized.
- You'll have to be operated on.
- Take this medicine three times a day/every four hours.
- Please take the medicine according to the instructions.
- Complete recovery will take a rather long time.
- You will have to come here for periodical check-ups.
- Nothing serious, but we'll take an X-ray just to be certain.

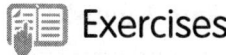 **Exercises**

I. Choose the best answer for each sentence on the left with the expressions on the right.

1. I've got itchy feet.
2. He's as right as rain now.
3. He's not right in the head.
4. I'm going to tell him what I think of him.
5. Mom's a bit off-color today.
6. Failing the exam was a bitter pill to swallow.
7. I've got a splitting headache.
8. The doctor gave me a clean bill of health.
9. How is your grandfather?
10. Tom's been feeling under the weather for several days.

A. Oh dear, I hope she's OK tomorrow.
B. Yes, but she'll soon get over it.
C. Where would you like to go?
D. That is a relief!
E. He is as fit as a fiddle.
F. I know, Jane told me he was off his rocker.
G. OK, I will turn the radio down.
H. I think he'd better go to see the doctor.
I. Good. Give him a dose of his own medicine.
J. Oh, good news!

II. Write down as many expressions as possible to express the Chinese meaning.

1. 我觉得难受。
   (1)_____.
   (2)_____.
   (3)_____.

2. 希望你早日康复!
   (1)_____!
   (2)_____!
   (3)_____!

3. 你怎么了?
   (1)_____?
   (2)_____?
   (3)_____?

4. 我背疼。
   (1)_____.
   (2)_____.
   (3)_____.
   (4)_____.

III. Complete the short dialogues by translating Chinese into English.

1	A: Well, what's wrong with you, Mr. Johnson?	B: It's... Well... I get tired very easily recently, and I often _____ ____(打瞌睡) during meetings, office hours, _____ (甚至吃饭的时候).
2	A: _____ (你背疼有多久了)?	B: I've been having pain for about two weeks.
3	A: Are you _____ (吃药) at the moment?	B: No, just an aspirin from time to time to _____ (止疼).
4	A: What's wrong with you?	B: I've got a headache and a cough, and _____ (浑身没劲).
5	A: I am sure that you got the flu. _____ (你需要打一针).	B: Oh, doctor. Do I have to? _____ (我害怕打针)!
6	A: Are you allergic to certain foods like prawns or shrimps?	B: _____ (我对所有海产食物都过敏).
7	A: Does it hurt?	B: _____ (我们会给你麻药的). If you feel any pain during the operation, just let me know.
8	A: _____ tomorrow (你就要出院了).	B: Is that so? I'm so happy.
9	A: To be on the safe side, _____ (你最好还是去照一张X光片).	B: OK. See you later.
10	A: Thank you very much. I have learned a lot from you today.	B: You're welcome. I hope _____ (祝你早日康复).

IV. Pair work: make dialogues based on the following situations.

1. You couldn't sleep last night, so you go to the doctor's and ask for some suggestions.

2. Mr. Lin was injured in a car accident. He goes to a hospital to see the doctor.

3. Lisa suffers from a backache for a long period, so she goes to the hospital. The doctor gives her an examination, and recommends her to take an X-ray.

V. Topics for Discussion.

1. What do you know about Chinese medicine?

2. Have you ever tried to lose weight? Which is more effective, doing exercise or going on a diet?

3. Should we get physical examinations every year? Why or why not?

 Culture Tips

Seeing a Doctor

The first time you visit a new doctor, you should discuss your medical history—the illnesses you have had, any surgeries you have undergone, and other relevant medical information. Your doctor may want to perform a check-up.

A check-up will include checking your blood pressure, as high blood pressure is a serious condition and can lead to life-threatening complications. Your doctor will probably also measure your pulse to ensure your heart rate is normal.

A doctor uses a stethoscope to listen to your breathing—particularly if you have a heart or chest infection, or a condition like asthma.

Of course, you can also visit the doctor for a wide range of other reasons. Children need to have their vaccinations, and if you are traveling abroad, you might need vaccinations against infectious diseases. In winter, you can also get a flu vaccine to prevent the flu.

If you need medication, your doctor will write you a prescription. You can get your prescription filled at a pharmacy.

For more serious medical conditions, you may receive a referral to a clinic or hospital. You might need blood tests, an X-ray, or a visit to a specialist.

 Class Activities

Fold-over Game

Give each row of students a blank sheet of paper. Write the following words on the board: WHO, WHAT, HOW, WHERE, WHEN, WHY. Explain that everyone will contribute one sentence to a story.

1. Tell them to write a person's name at the top of their paper. It can be the name of any person, such as a classmate, the teacher, or a famous person that everyone knows. Then, fold over the paper so that no one can see the name, and then pass the paper to the person on their right.

2. On the received paper, write what the subject did (suggest funny or outrageous actions). Fold the paper over and pass it to the right.

3. Continue by writing one line for each prompt: how the action was done (using adverbs), where it happened, when it happened, and finally, why it happened (starting with "because"). After each line, fold the paper and pass it to the right.

4. Have the students unfold the papers to reveal their stories. Ask one student at a time to read the stories aloud, or have them submit the stories for the teacher to read.

It is fun!

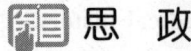 思 政

A Dip into Chinese Wisdom

1. "泰山不让土壤，故能成其大；河海不择细流，故能就其深。" 包容普惠，互利共赢才是人间正道。

As an ancient Chinese saying goes, "Constant piling up of earth makes Mount Tai great; ceaseless inflow of rivers makes the ocean deep." Inclusiveness, shared benefits and win-win outcomes is what we should pursue.

2. 万里悲秋常作客，百年多病独登台。

A thousand miles from home, I'm grieved at autumn's plight;

Ill now and then for years, alone I'm on this height.

3. 亲朋无一字，老病有孤舟。

No word from friends or kinsfolk dear;

A boat bears my declining years.

4. 时间是最好的良药。

Time is the best cure.

SECTION I

Shopping
Unit 6

 Lead-in

Do you enjoy shopping? How often do you go shopping? Discuss it with your partner. You may use the following examples for help.

A: Yes. I often go shopping on weekends. / I go shopping twice a month. / I often spend one hour buying things I want…

B: No, I don't like to go shopping, because… / I like shopping online.

 Warm-up Activities

I. Read the following words and find the pronunciation rules for letter "-s" or "-es".

1. [s]   months   cakes   grapes   roofs   ducks
2. [z]   plays   bars   smells   apples   congratulations
3. [ɪz]   brushes   catches   buses   places   chances
4. [ts]   cats   nuts   suggests   baskets   sheets
5. [dz]   birds   grades   sends   sounds   beds

II. Read the story below and pay attention to your pronunciation and intonation.

A young man was walking in a supermarket to buy some stuff when he noticed an old lady following him around. Thinking nothing of it, he ignored her and continued shopping. Finally he went to the checkout line, but she got in front of him.

"Pardon me," she said, "I'm sorry if my staring at you has made you feel uncomfortable. It's just that you look exactly like my son, who just died a few days ago."

"I'm very sorry to hear that," replied the young man. "Is there anything I can do for you?"

"Yes," she said, "as I'm leaving, can you say 'Good bye, Mom!'? It would make me feel so much better."

"Sure," answered the young man.

As the old woman was leaving, he called out, "Goodbye, Mom!"

The old woman smiled contentedly and left.

 Dialogues

Dialogue 1

Greengrocer: What can I do for you, Madam?

Woman: I'd like a kilo of apples, half a kilo of grapes, and a kilo of mangos.

Greengrocer: There you are. A kilo of apples, half a kilo of grapes, and a kilo of mangos. Anything else? The bananas are sweet and cheap these days.

Woman: OK, give me five bananas please.

Greengrocer: What about these ones?

Woman: Yes, I'll take them.

Greengrocer: Nineteen dollars fifty cents all together.

Dialogue 2

Saleswoman: Good afternoon, sir. May I help you?

Ted: Yes. I'd like to see the tie in the showcase.

Saleswoman: Which one, sir?

Ted: The green one.

Saleswoman: This one?

Ted: Yes, that one. Is it pure silk?

Saleswoman: Yes, sir, pure silk and hand-made.

Ted: How much is it?

Saleswoman: 80 yuan, sir.

Ted: I'm afraid it doesn't fit me very well. Have you got any other ones?

Saleswoman: How about this one? It's 55 yuan.

Ted: The price is all right, but it's a bit showy, isn't it?

Saleswoman: Oh, I don't think so, sir. I think it suits you well.

Ted: Then I'll take it.

Saleswoman: Thank you, sir. Will you wait a moment please? I'll have it wrapped.

Dialogue 3

Jane: What should I get for my mom for her birthday?

Rose: Well, you can buy her a bunch of flowers.

Jane: That's a cool idea. At least it would be a surprise. But I want something useful.

Rose: How much do you want to spend?

Jane: At least 75 dollars.

Rose: Alright, I have an idea. You know your mother has recently bought a new dress.

Jane: Yes.

Rose: Maybe we can buy her a hat, which can go well with her dress.

Jane: That's not a very easy task.

Rose: Okay, maybe you are right.

Jane: How about a pair of shoes?

Rose: I think that's a great idea. Where can we buy one?

Jane: Let's go to the department store.

Dialogue 4

Salesman: Good afternoon. Is there anything I can do for you?

Woman: Yes. Do you have sandals to match this skirt?

Salesman: Yes. We have quite a few different colors. And do you want high heeled or flat ones?

Woman: High, please.

Salesman: Do you like the red ones?

Woman: Yes. They're very nice.

Salesman: Please try them on.

Woman: They are a bit too large.

Salesman: How about this one?

Woman: They fit well. How much are they?

Salesman: 85 dollars.

Woman: Oh, they are too expensive. Any discount?

Salesman: We can give you a 5% discount.

Woman: All right. I'll take it.

Dialogue 5

Salesman: May I help you?

Woman: Yes. I would like to return these trousers.

Salesman: Alright. Do you have your receipt?

Woman: Yes. Here it is. I bought them last week.

Salesman: And why are you returning them?

Woman: I bought them to go with a blouse of mine. But they don't really match.

Salesman: Shall I show you some other colors?

Woman: Sorry, I just want to return it.

Salesman: No problem. Show me the receipt, please.

Woman: Here you are.

Salesman: Here's your money. Please sign your name here.

Woman: OK, thank you very much.

Dialogue 6

Mr. Allen: I'm afraid your prices are much too high.

Mr. Lu: Well, we can consider making some concessions in our price. But first, you'll have to give me an idea of the quantity you wish to order from us so that we may adjust our prices accordingly.

Mr. Allen: The size of our order largely depends on the prices. Let's settle that matter first.

Mr. Lu: Well, as I've said, if your order volume is large enough, we're ready to reduce our prices by 3 percent.

Mr. Allen: When I say your prices are much too high, I don't mean they are only 2 or 3 percent higher.

Mr. Lu: What kind of reduction are you expecting? Can you give me a rough idea?

Mr. Allen: To move forward with this deal, I should say a reduction of at least 10 percent would help.

Mr. Lu: Impossible. How can you expect us to make a reduction to that extent?

Mr. Allen: I believe you are well informed about the market situation. The supply of this product exceeds the demand at present. Well, would you mind checking with your home office and getting their feedback?

Mr. Lu: Very well, I will.

Dialogue 7

Mr. Stone: Look, Maggie. These tapestries are beautiful! Don't you think we could use one to decorate our room?

Mrs. Stone: All right. (Looking at the price tags) Oh, a bit too much!

Shop assistant: Artistic tapestry is an exquisite handicraft in typical Chinese style. Considering the fine craftsmanship, they are worth much more.

Mr. Stone: I agree. Is this the marvelous landscape in Shangri-la? What a lovely tapestry!

Mrs. Stone: I prefer to buy some embroidered tablecloths to match the tapestry.

Shop assistant: Which do you prefer?

Mrs. Stone: The brocade, please. How much is one piece?

Shop assistant: 280 yuan.

Mrs. Stone: Too expensive. Do you have anything cheaper?

Shop assistant: Yes, we have. Here, please have a look at the hand embroidered one with a new design of pine tree.

Mrs. Stone: What fine needlework! What's the price?

Shop assistant: One hundred and twenty yuan.

Vocabulary

grape [greɪp] n. 葡萄
greengrocer ['gri:ngrəʊsə(r)] n. 蔬菜水果商
showcase ['ʃəʊkeɪs] n. (玻璃)陈列柜, 陈列橱
hand-made adj. 手工裁剪的
bunch [bʌntʃ] n. 一串, 一束
sandal ['sændl] n. 凉鞋
discount ['dɪskaʊnt] n. 折扣 v. 打折扣
receipt [rɪ'si:t] n. 收据
slack [slæk] n. 松弛, 家常裤
exception [ɪk'sepʃn] n. 例外
adjust [ə'dʒʌst] v. 调整, 使……适于
settle ['setl] v. 安顿, 解决
reduce [rɪ'dju:s] v. 减少, 分解, 减低
extent [ɪk'stent] n. 长度, 大小, 范围, 程度
well informed [,wel ɪn'fɔ:md] adj. 消息灵通的, 见闻广博的

exceed [ɪk'si:d] v. 超过, 胜过
demand [dɪ'ma:nd] n. 要求, 需求
tag [tæg] n. 标签, 附属物
tapestry ['tæpəstri] n. 挂毯
exquisite [ɪk'skwɪzɪt] adj. 精致的, 细腻的
handicraft ['hændɪkra:ft] n. 手工艺品, 手艺
superb [su:'pɜ:b] adj. 极好的
artistry ['ɑ:tɪstri] n. 艺术作品
craftsmanship ['kra:ftsmən'ʃɪp] n. 手艺, 技艺
marvellous ['ma:vələs] adj. 惊奇的
landscape ['lændskeɪp] n. 风景, 山水
embroider [ɪm'brɔɪdə(r)] v. 刺绣
tablecloth ['teɪblklɒθ] n. 桌布, 台布
brocade [brə'keɪd] n. 织锦

Useful Expressions

A. Purchasing

- What can I do for you?
- Is there anything I can do for you?
- May I help you?
- I'd like a loaf of bread and two dozen eggs.
- Yes. I'd like to see some T-shirts.
- I want to buy a pair of shoes which can match my trousers.
- What kind are you looking for?
- What kind of material do you prefer?
- What make is it?
- What is it made of?
- What color do you like?
- May I try it/them on?
- It looks good on you.
- It fits me well.
- How about this one?
- Would you please show me another one?
- What size (do you want)?
- Do you have a yellow one? Yellow is my favourite color.
- What else do you want?
- Anything else?
- Where is the cashier?
- Here you are.
- I'll pack it for you.

B. Price and Bargaining

- How much does it cost?
- How much do you charge?
- What's the price?
- How much is this hat? / How much is it altogether?
- What price range do you have in mind?
- How much do you want to pay?

- Can I pay by credit card?
- Can I pay in cash?
- Here's the money.
- It's a real bargain.
- I'll take it.

C. Complaining

- What's wrong with the sweater?
- It's a nice dress, but it's too expensive.
- I want a coat, not a jacket.
- I don't think it is of good quality.
- It isn't long enough.

Exercises

I. Match each picture with the corresponding word.

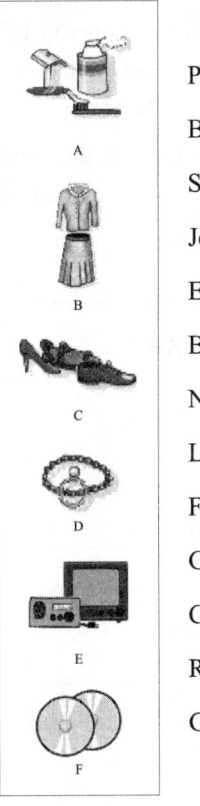

Post Office

Boutique

Shoe Shop

Jeweler's

Electrical Store

Bookshop

Newsagent's

Ladies' Clothing Store

Fishmonger's

Grocer's

Chemist's

Record Shop

Greengrocer's

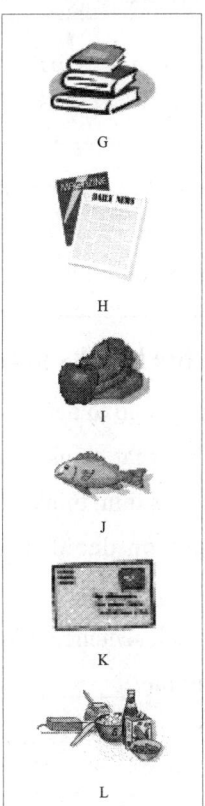

II. Complete the short dialogues by translating Chinese into English.

1	A: _____ (你方还打算购买多少)?	B: We're thinking... another 30.
2	A: _____ (你方可否给我们折扣)?	B: Well, as I've said, if your order is large enough, _____ (我方将会降价 1%).
3	A: _____ (你想要什么型号的)?	B: Size 40, please.
4	A: _____ (这裙子是什么面料的)?	B: It's made of cotton.
5	A: It's _____ (促销). It's only 30 dollars.	B: All right. _____ (我买这件了).
6	A: I want to _____ (我想买些纪念品).	B: _____ (你觉得这些银筷子怎么样)?
7	A: I'm sorry, but we are _____ (缺货了). We only have five at this time.	B: OK, I see.
8	A: Just as a matter of interest, _____ (你们可以给退款吗)?	B: Yes, of course. You can bring any clothing items back up to two weeks after purchase, but you must keep the receipt.
9	A: It's too small. I can't wear it.	B: I'll take it back to the supermarket and see _____ (是否能够更换一下).
10	A: Can I help you, sir?	B: Thank you, but _____ (我只是看看).

III. Fill in the blanks according to the situations.

1. Many people go to a shop to buy a jacket.

A person, who is fat, thinks the jacket is _____.

A person, who is thin, thinks the jacket is _____.

Finally, a person decides to buy it, he says that, "_____." Or _____.

2. Change each sentence into another way of expression.

The jeans suit me. _____

A six-month warranty. _____

That's a rip-off ! _____

The shoes fit me. _____

Valid for refund within three months of purchasing. _____

IV. Pair work: make dialogues based on the following situations.

1. Joe and Diana want to go shopping. They are discussing with each other about what to buy and where to buy them.

2. An American friend Tina is leaving for the US tomorrow. She asks her Chinese tour guide Miss Lin for suggestions about what to buy for her family members.

3. Sarah is discussing with her friend about the advantages and disadvantages of shopping online.

V. Topics for discussion.

1. Do you prefer going shopping in shopping malls or online? Why?

2. Do you know hands-chopping people? How do you comment on them?

3. If you have a chance to invest in a store, what kind of store do you want to choose?

Culture Tips

Clothing sizes in the USA and UK are different from those used in China. Here is a table to convert between the sizes used in these three countries. Please note that exact conversions are impossible since clothing sizes are not completely standardized even within a given country, and can vary slightly from one manufacturer to another. Furthermore, cuts of clothing vary among manufacturers and also among tailors. So when you want to buy clothes or shoes in the US and UK, please pay attention to the differences. It's better for you to try clothes on to confirm the sizes.

Women's Size

	Blouse/Dresses/Suits				
China (cm)	160~165/ 84~86	165~170/ 88~90	167~172/ 92~96	168~173/ 98~102	170~176/ 106~110
USA	2	4~6	8~10	12~14	16~18
UK	34	34~36	38~40	42	44

Men's Size

	Coats/T-shirts/Suits				
China (cm)	165/88~90	170/96~98	175/108~110	180/118~122	185/126~130
USA/UK	S	M	L	XL	XXL
	Shirts				
China (cm)	36~37	38~39	40~42	43~44	45~47
USA/UK	S	M	L	XL	XXL

Women's Shoes

Foot Length(cm)	22.5	23	23.5	24	24.5	25	25.5	26
China	35	36	37	38	39	39	40	40
USA	5	5.5	6	6.5	7	7.5	8	8.5
UK	4	4.5	5	5.5	6	6.5	7	7.5

Men's Shoes

Foot Length(cm)	24.5	25	25.5	26	26.5	27	27.5	28
China	39	40	41	42	43	44	45	46
USA	7	7.5	8	8.5	9	9.5	10	10.5
UK	6	6.5	7	7.5	8	8.5	9	9.5

Class Activities

Telling the Story

For this activity, the whole class can be divided into groups of 6 students. The teacher gives students a deck of cards with an imaginative theme that could be crafted into some sort of story, for example, "all those students will have a day off tomorrow." On the board, the teacher makes a list as follows:

- A-exciting
- B-depressing
- C-expensive
- D-heroic

- E-romantic
- F-sad
- G-almost fatal
- H-weird
- I-happy
- J-fantastic
- K-dramatic

The students are prompted to start telling the story, perhaps offer a beginning to the story. They then continue creating an oral story within their groups. By drawing one card, each student should continue the story according to the word he/she drew. For example, if he/she gets the letter "E", then there must be something romantic happening. If the students draw the letter "I" (or whatever card he/she draws), there should be something happy happen. Continue through all the cards until the story is concluded. The teacher can change the theme and make it more interesting.

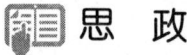 思 政

A Dip into Chinese Wisdom

1. 携手迎接挑战，合作开创未来。

Rise to challenges and build a bright future through cooperation.

2. 金樽清酒斗十千，玉盘珍羞直万钱。

Pure wine in golden cup costs ten thousand coins, good!

Choice dish in a jade plate is worth as much, nice food!

3. 五花马，千金裘，呼儿将出换美酒，与尔同销万古愁。

My fur coat is worth a thousand coins of gold,

And my flower-dappled horse may be sold,

To buy good wine that we may drown the woe age-old.

4. 非尽百家之美，不能成一人之奇。

Without achieving the good of one hundred various schools, the uniqueness of one individual cannot be achieved.

SECTION I

Food
Unit 7

 Lead-in

Do you know how to describe a dish? Discuss it with your partner. You may use the following examples for help.

Q: How do you like this dish?
A: It looks inviting.
A: It tastes good/nice.
A: It has a special flavor.
A: It's delicious/tasty.

 Warm-up Activities

I. Read the following words and pay attention to the pronunciation of "-ed".

1. [t]	asked	looked	watched	finished	passed
2. [d]	spelled	changed	answered	remembered	loaned
3. [ɪd]	rented	wanted	painted	needed	loaded

II. Read the story below and pay attention to your pronunciation and intonation.

Last Sunday at a dinner party, the hostess asked me to sit next to Mrs. Walker.

Mrs. Walker was a large, unsmiling lady in a tight black dress. She did not even look up when I took my seat beside her. Her eyes were fixed on her plate, and in a short time she was busy with her meal. I tried to make conversation.

"A new play is coming to the National Theatre soon," I said. "Will you go to see it?"

"No," she answered.

"Will you go traveling during your holidays this year?" I asked.

"No," she answered.

"Will you be staying in China?" I asked.

"No," she answered.

In despair, I asked her if she was enjoying her dinner.

"Young man," she answered, "if you ate more and talked less, we would both enjoy our dinner!"

Dialogues

Dialogue 1

Linda: Could you tell me something about the snacks in Xi'an?

Zhang Hua: There are quite a lot. The most famous snack is Pita Bread Soaked in Lamb Soup or "Yang Rou Pao Mo" in Chinese pronunciation.

Linda: I've heard of it. How does it taste?

Zhang Hua: It tastes good, and you should try some.

Linda: I think so. What else?

Zhang Hua: Persimmon cake, vegetable soup, cold noodles, etc.

Linda: Where can I taste all these snacks?

Zhang Hua: Nearly all restaurants have them.

Linda: I see. Let's go to that restaurant and try some.

Dialogue 2

Mary: Next Friday is my birthday. Would you come and celebrate it with me?

John: OK, of course. Happy birthday! By the way, how do you celebrate your birthday in China?

Mary: According to traditional ways, mothers would cook Longevity Noodles. And for old people, we'll prepare Longevity Peaches. Just for blessing.

John: Wow, Longevity Peaches! What's that? Real peach?

Mary: No. They are made of wheat flour and they look just like real peaches.

John: Why peaches? Is there any interesting tale behind it?

Mary: According to Chinese Mythology, if you eat peaches grown on magical trees in heaven, you will be immortal.

John: Oh, it's so interesting. In the United States, we just have a party with some friends. And if it's your birthday, then you don't need to pay a cent. Your friends take care of everything beforehand. We'll have a birthday cake, blow out the candles and open the gifts.

Mary: Oh, you can really have a lot of fun in a party, right?

John: Yes, that's true.

Dialogue 3

Kevin: It's 11:30. I'm hungry. Let's go for lunch.

Cathy: You have a good appetite… I'm still full from breakfast and you are already talking about lunch!

Kevin: That's the difference between you and me. What would you like, Chinese food, Western food or some fast food?

Cathy: Let me take you to a Chinese restaurant. There is a lot of food to choose.

Kevin: Like what?

Cathy: Steamed buns with stuffing, dumplings, fried noodles, stretched noodles, rice noodles, spring roll, and many other tasty dishes.

Kevin: OK, OK! Let's just go!

Cathy: Aha! Make your mouth water, huh?

Dialogue 4

Rachel: What kinds of meat are most popular in your country?

Joe: We usually eat chicken, pork and beef. You eat a lot of these kinds of meat in your country too, right?

Rachel: Yes, we do. We also eat mutton.

Joe: I've heard that people in your country like mutton chops.

Rachel: That's right. Mutton chops taste so good. We eat them with sauce. Have you ever tried?

Joe: Yes, I have. I tried once when I visited your country two years ago. I think they were very tasty. Can you cook them?

Rachel: Of course. I'll buy some from the butcher's and cook for you tomorrow.

Joe: That sounds great! We can eat them with a glass of wine.

Dialogue 5

Sophia: What are we having for supper today? Is there anything different?

Isabel: Oh, yes. I've prepared dumplings for supper. I made it myself. Have a taste, please. How do you like it?

Sophia: Hmm, it's delicious. Please tell me how to make it?

Isabel: First, mix the flour with water to make the dough. Then use meat such as beef or mutton, and some vegetables such as cabbages or carrots to make the filling.

Sophia: What else do you do next?

Isabel: You need to roll the dough into small, thin and round pieces, and fill and fold them to make dumplings. And finally boil them in water for about 5 minutes.

Sophia: How do I know when it can be eaten?

Isabel: When you see the dumplings floating in boiling water, you can put them in bowls or plates, and be ready to eat.

Sophia: Great! I'll have a try next time.

Dialogue 6

Shirley: Monica, do you like cooking?

Monica: I love it. I really enjoy creating a meal from various ingredients and watching my family enjoy it. It gives me a real sense of satisfaction. Do you enjoy cooking?

Shirley: I don't like it. It takes up too much time and I really hate having to clean up after the meal.

Monica: You can buy a dishwasher. It can save a lot of time.

Shirley: So, what kind of dishes do you usually make? I know you like Italian food.

Monica: Italian, Indian, and Chinese. I've just recently started cooking Indian meals and I need some more practice.

Shirley: Do you find it hard to get ingredients for Indian food?

Monica: Not at all. You can find most of them at the supermarket.

Dialogue 7

Helen: Hi, do you need some help with preparing dinner? What would you like me to do?

Alice: Thanks for coming over to help. I really appreciate it. First, could you clean the vegetables?

Helen: OK, I'll clean the vegetables and you chop them. I'm terrible at chopping vegetables. I always seem to chop them into pieces that are either too big or too small... Wow! You can chop vegetables really quickly, just like professional chefs on TV!

Alice: Thank you. After you've cleaned the vegetables, could you fry the meat in a little oil? Fry the meat until it is cooked.

Helen: Should I cook it over a low flame?

Alice: Cook it over a high flame, so that it will be ready quickly. Keep stirring the meat around the frying pan. Don't let the meat stick to the bottom of the pan.

Helen: OK, no problem.

Vocabulary

snack [snæk] n. 小吃，点心	spring roll n. (中国的) 春卷
lamb [læm] n. 小羊，羔羊肉	chop [tʃɒp] n. 厚肉片，排骨
persimmon [pə'sɪmən] n. 柿子	v. 剁碎，砍，切
reputation [ˌrepjuˈteɪʃn] n. 名誉，名声	dough [dəʊ] n. 生面团
appetite ['æpɪtaɪt] n. 食欲，胃口	ingredient [ɪn'griːdiənt] n. 成分，因素
stuffing ['stʌfɪŋ] n. 填塞物，填料	peel [piːl] n. 皮
stretch [stretʃ] v. 伸展，延伸	v. 削皮，剥落

Useful Expressions

Talking about Food

- Dinner is ready. Shall we go to the dining room?
- Just make yourself at home and help yourself to whatever you'd like.
- Would you like / Do you prefer…?
- I think our dish will be to your taste.
- Help yourself to / Have some more…
- I'm in the mood for something spicy/sweet/light/rich.
- I can't eat spicy food.
- I'm so sick of that junk.
- May I offer you the chicken?
- May I have just a little to taste?
- No more, thank you.
- No, I won't have any more.
- No, thank you. I've had enough/too much.

- This has been a great treat. Thank you.
- Here's to your health.
- Let's drink to / I'd like to propose a toast to your health, our cooperation/friendship, Mr. Greenwell!
- Cheers!
- No, thank you. I'm full.

Exercises

I. Fill in the blanks with measure words according to the Chinese translation and then take turns to ask and answer questions.

Example：A：Would you please pass me a bar of chocolate?
　　　　　B：OK, here you are.

1. a ____ of soda 一罐汽水
2. a ____ of honey 一罐蜂蜜
3. a ____ of coffee/tea 一壶咖啡/茶
4. a ____ of yogurt 一盒酸奶
5. a ____ of bread 一条(个)面包
6. a ____ of pastries 一盘馅饼
7. a ____ of olive oil 一瓶橄榄油
8. a ____ of water 一升水
9. a ____ of cider 一加仑苹果酒
10. a ____ of milk 一夸脱牛奶
11. a ____ of beer 一品脱啤酒
12. a ____ of salt 一茶匙盐
13. a ____ of butter 一大汤匙黄油
14. a ____ of cake/apple pie 一块蛋糕/一个苹果派

II. Match the Chinese dishes with their English version.

1. 西红柿炒鸡蛋	A. Mapo Tofu (Sautéed Tofu in Hot and Spicy Sauce)
2. 宫保鸡丁	B. Sweet and Sour Pork with Pineapple
3. 拔丝苹果	C. Dongpo Pig Knuckle
4. 菠萝咕噜肉	D. Sliced Beef and Ox Tongue in Chili Sauce
5. 醋熘白菜	E. Kung Pao Chicken
6. 鱼香茄子	F. Braised Pork with Preserved Vegetables
7. 麻婆豆腐	G. Scrambled Eggs with Tomatoes
8. 梅菜扣肉	H. Braised Fish with Soy Sauced
9. 东坡肘子	I. Yuxiang Eggplant (Sautéed with Spicy Garlic Sauce)
10. 夫妻肺片	J. Apple in Hot Toffee
11. 红烧鱼	K. Sautéed Chinese Cabbage with Vinegar
12. 红烧狮子头	L. Braised Pork Ball in Brown Sauce

III. Complete the short dialogues by translating Chinese into English.

1	A: It's very delicious. It is so _____ _____ (酥脆肉嫩).	B: I'm glad you like it. _____ _____ (一定多吃些).
2	A: Can't you eat the rest of the salad?	B: No, thanks. I'm supposed to be _____ (节食).
3	A: Why don't we have something for dessert?	B: I really shouldn't, but I'll _____ _____ (来一点冰激凌).
4	A: I find this dish _____ (特别合我的胃口). How do you like this dish?	B: I like this dish very much. It has _____ (味道很独特).
5	A: Do you want your fried egg _____ _____ (一面煎)?	B: No, I don't like to see my eggs staring up at me with big yellow eyes. I want two-fried eggs, _____ (两面煎，不要太老).
6	A: I want to have oatmeal first. _____ _____ (我自己来弄吧).	B: Good. I'll _____ (给你的面包抹上黄油) then.
7	A: _____ (看上去你似乎是位美食家).	B: I just like eating a lot.
8	A: I want it to be special. And _____ _____ (你知道我一直喜欢辣味的食物).	B: OK then. We shall ask them to put some red chili on it.
9	A: What would you like to eat? _____ _____ (你尝过北京的特色小吃吗)?	B: No, I haven't. What do you suggest?
10	A: I'm afraid _____ _____ (这肉臭了).	B: Well, I forgot to put it in the refrigerator.

IV. Pair work: make dialogues based on the following situations.

1. Lisa is talking with her deskmate Maria about their favorite dishes/beverage.

2. Sarah and Lily are talking about the dishes they are good at cooking.

3. Steve, an American student, is discussing with his classmate Xiao Hong about the differences between the breakfasts in two countries.

V. Topics for discussion.

1. How do you like the food in your school canteen? Do you have any suggestions to

the person in charge?

2. Do you like Chinese restaurant or western restaurant? Why?

Culture Tips

As you have probably noticed, western eating habits are very different from those of Chinese ones. Here is an introduction of the serving order in a Western-style formal meal.

1. Appetizers

The first course in a Western meal is the appetizer(开胃菜), which is designed to stimulate the appetite. It typically features unique flavors, often with salty and sour characteristics.

2. Soups

The second course in a Western meal is soup. Western soups are classified into clear broth, creamy soup, vegetable soup, and cold soup. Soup can stimulate the secretion (分泌) of gastric juices and enhance appetite.

3. Entrées

In a Western meal, fish is generally served as the third course, before meat dishes, due to its fresh and tender nature. Entrées serve as the main course and help to stimulate the appetite.

4. Main Courses

The main course in a Western meal is usually made of meat and poultry. The main ingredients for meat dishes include different parts of cattle, sheep, pig and calf, with beef and steak being typical examples. Dishes made of poultry in the main course mainly come from chicken, duck, goose, and other wild birds.

5. Vegetable Dishes

Vegetable dishes, often served as salads, are an important part of a Western meal. Western people pay particular attention to health, and vegetables are a favorite among many Westerners, ensuring a balanced nutrition intake.

6. Desserts

Dessert in a Western meal follows the main course and can be regarded as the sixth course. Essentially, it includes all food served after the main course, such as pudding, cake, ice cream, cheese, and fruits.

7. Coffee and Tea

The final part of a Western meal is the beverage, usually coffee or tea. A cup of coffee or tea after dinner is the best way to conclude a meal.

 Class Activities

Describer and Guesser

1. Divide the whole class into pairs;

2. In each pair, student A describes a kind of fruit, and student B will guess by asking questions;

3. The pair that can guess the most words correctly within 5 minutes will be the winner.

You can use the following word list as an example:

Fruits: watermelon, cucumber, mango, banana, peach, apple, kiwi fruit, pear, tomato, orange, etc.

Other foods (optional): hamburger, sandwich, candy, potato, chocolate, etc.

 思 政

A Dip into Chinese Wisdom

1. 粮食安全是"国之大者"。悠悠万事，吃饭为大。

Food security is among a country's most fundamental interests. Of all things, eating matters most.

2. 春种一粒粟，秋收万颗子。

Each seed when sown in spring,

will make autumn yields high.

3. 西塞山前白鹭飞，桃花流水鳜鱼肥。

In front of western hills white egrets fly up and down,

Over peach-mirrored stream, where perches are full grown.

4. 手中有粮，心里不慌。

Having food in hand,

You would not be flustered.

SECTION I

At the Restaurant
Unit 8

 Lead-in

What factors will you consider when you choose a restaurant? Discuss it with your partner. You may use the following examples for help.

A: I think environment is important, because…
B: I don't like a restaurant with too many people.
C: In my opinion, price and food are both very important.
D: I prefer restaurants with delicious food.
E: Tasty food is more important than environment.

 Warm-up Activities

I. Read the following words and pay attention to the pronunciation of [f] and [v].

1. [f]   fine   five   fifteen   finally   find
2. [v]   leave   of   very   achieve   save

II. Read the story below and pay attention to your pronunciation and intonation.

A guy walks into a lunch counter, asks for a menu, and the waiter tells him, "We don't have menus here. Our kitchen is well-stocked and our chef knows every recipe in the world. Order anything you like, and if we can't serve it, we'll give you one thousand dollars."

The man sees a chance to make some money, so he thinks of something impossible. "Bring me an order of hummingbird (蜂鸟) tongues on rye toast," he tells the waiter.

"Coming right up, sir," the waiter says. He disappears into the kitchen and returns moments later, with a plate. "One order of hummingbird tongues on rye toast. Will there be anything else?"

The man thinks for a second, and then says, "Yes... bring me an elephant ear sandwich."

"Coming right up, sir," the waiter says. He disappears into the kitchen and returns moments later, with a thousand dollars in cash, which he presents to the man. "Well, you did it, sir. You stumped us."

With a broad smile, the man puts the money into his pocket. "Didn't you have any elephant ears back there, huh?"

"Oh, no," the waiter says. "We have plenty of elephant ears. We just ran out of those giant rolls."

Dialogues

Dialogue 1

George: Let me pay the bill today.
Sylvia: Oh, no! Let's go Dutch this time. We're both students after all.
George: OK. It's 20 dollars altogether. So 10 dollars each. Right?
Sylvia: That's right. Waiter, bring the bill, please.

Dialogue 2

Waitress: Have you had time to look over the menu?
Wayne: Yes. I would like the beef steak.
Waitress: How would you like it cooked?
Wayne: Well done, please.
Waitress: Would you like a salad?
Wayne: No.
Waitress: Anything else to drink?
Wayne: Yes. A glass of red wine, please.
Waitress: Very good. I will bring your appetizer back immediately.

Dialogue 3

Waitress: Good evening. Do you have a reservation?

Mr. Scott: Yes. The reservation is under Scott.

Waitress: Very good, Mr. Scott. Do you prefer smoking or non-smoking area?

Mr. Scott: Non-smoking, please.

Waitress: If you follow me, I will show you to your table.

Mr. Scott: Thank you.

Waitress: You're welcome. Your server will be with you right away to take your order.

Dialogue 4

Waiter: Are you ready to order now, sir?

Jack: I'd like something typically Chinese.

Waiter: We serve a range of typical Chinese food here.

Jack: Great! Do you have something to recommend?

Waiter: Our specialties are Beijing Roast Duck and fried duck in soy sauce.

Jack: Good. I know Beijing Roast Duck is popular in China. I'd like to try it.

Waiter: OK. What would you like to drink?

Jack: I've heard about Moutai. Can I try just a small glass of it?

Waiter: Yes, of course. Would you like to use chopsticks or fork and knife?

Jack: I'd like to use chopsticks.

Waiter: OK. Wait for a moment, please.

Dialogue 5

Waiter: Good evening, sir. Are you ready to order now?

Steven: Yes, are there any dishes that the chef recommends today?

Waiter: The seafood is very good today. We just got the delivery this morning, so it is very fresh.

Steven: Sounds good. I'd like to have some white wine with my meal. What do you suggest?

Waiter: For seafood, a white wine, of course. Our house wine is quite good.

Steven: Good. I'll have a glass of the house white wine then.

Waiter: Would you like some dessert, sir?

Steven: No, thanks. But I would like some coffee, please.

Waiter: Very well. Is the meal satisfactory?

Steven: Very good. Could you get me some napkins?

Waiter: Sure, I will be right back.

Dialogue 6

Waiter: Hello, can I help you?

Lucy: Yes, I'd like to have some lunch.

Waiter: Would you like a starter?

Lucy: Yes, I'd like a bowl of chicken soup, please.

Waiter: And what would you like for a main course?

Lucy: I'd like a grilled cheese sandwich.

Waiter: Would you like something to drink?

Lucy: Yes, I'd like a glass of orange juice, please.

(After lunch)

Waiter: Can I bring you anything else?

Lucy: No, thank you. Just the bill.

Waiter: Certainly.

Lucy: That's $15.5, isn't it?

Waiter: Yes, it is.

Lucy: Here you are. Thank you very much.

Waiter: You're welcome. Have a good day.

Lucy: Thank you, the same to you.

Dialogue 7

Waiter: Hello. Can I take your order?

Jack: Yes. I'd like a large pepperoni pizza with mushrooms and green peppers.

Waiter: Would you like something else?

Jack: Well, wait. Uh, can I make that a half-and-half pizza?

Waiter: Sure. What would you like on each half?

Jack: Uh, what toppings do you have?

Waiter: Well, we have Italian sausage, ham, mushrooms, onions, pineapple, black olives, green peppers, bacon, tomatoes, shrimp, clams, and squid.

Jack: Uh, I'll try the "Italian Flavor" special, but I'll have pepperoni and mushrooms on one half and green peppers and Italian sausage on the other. Oh, and could I get extra cheese on that pizza?

Waiter: Alright. Would you care for any bread or beverage with your order?

Jack: Huh, sure, why not? I'll take orange juice.

Waiter: Okay. Your total comes to 20 dollars.

Vocabulary

go Dutch AA 制	delivery [dɪ'lɪvəri] *n.* 递送，交付
steak [steɪk] *n.* 牛排	seafood ['si:fu:d] *n.* 海产食品，海味
appetizer ['æpɪtaɪzə(r)] *n.* 开胃食品，开胃菜	dessert [dɪ'zɜ:t] *n.* 甜品
typical ['tɪpɪkl] *adj.* 典型的，有代表性的	pepperoni [,pepə'rəʊni] *n.* 意大利辣香肠
specialty ['speʃəlti] *n.* 专门，特别，特性	pepper ['pepə(r)] *n.* 辣椒，胡椒粉
roast [rəʊst] *adj.* 烘烤的，烤过的	mushroom ['mʌʃrʊm] *n.* 蘑菇
soy sauce *n.* 酱油	beverage ['bevərɪdʒ] *n.* 饮料
chopstick ['tʃɒpstɪk] *pl.*（中国的）筷子	napkin ['næpkɪn] *n.* 餐巾

Useful Expressions

A. Asking about a restaurant

- Could you recommend a nice restaurant near here?
- Is there a Chinese restaurant around here?
- I want a restaurant with reasonable prices.
- Are there any inexpensive restaurants near here?
- I'd like a quiet restaurant.
- I'd like to have some local food.
- Where is the nearest Italian restaurant?

B. Ordering food

- May I have a menu, please?
- May I order, please?
- May I take your order?
- Do you have a menu in Chinese?
- What is the specialty here?
- Do you have today's special?
- Would you like something to drink before dinner?
- What kind of drinks do you have for an aperitif?
- May I see the wine list?

- May I order a glass of wine?
- Could you recommend some good wine?
- I'd like to have French red wine.
- What kind of wine do you have?
- Can I have the same dish as that?
- I have to avoid food containing fat (salt/sugar).
- I'd like to have some local wine.
- Do you have vegetarian dishes?
- How do you like your steak?
- Well done (medium/rare), please.

C. Having dinner at a restaurant

- Could you tell me how to eat this?
- Could you pass me the salt/pepper?
- May I smoke?
- I'd like a glass of water, please.
- May I have a bottle of mineral water?
- My order hasn't come yet.
- This is not what I ordered.
- May I have some more bread, please?
- I'd like a dessert, please.
- What do you have for dessert?
- May I have some cheese?
- May I have just a little of it?
- Can I have some fruit instead of the dessert?

D. Paying bills

- Can we have the bill, please?
- Can I pay here?
- We'd like to pay separately.
- I think there is a mistake in the bill.
- Could you check it again?
- Can I pay with this credit card?
- May I have the receipt, please?
- It's my treat.
- It's all on me.

- Let's go Dutch.
- Let's pay separately.
- Let's go fifty-fifty on this meal.

E. Eating at a fast food restaurant

- Will you be eating here or is this to go/take out?
- I'll eat here.
- Take out, please.
- I'll have a small hamburger, milk, and one large order of French fries/potato chips.
- Can I sit here?/Can I take this seat?
- Can I have a hot dog, please?
- With ketchup or mayonnaise?
- With ketchup, please.
- How about onions or mustard?
- Yes, please.
- A sandwich, please.
- Which would you like for bread? White or whole wheat?
- Whole wheat, please.
- I'd like roast beef with cheese, tomato, and lettuce.
- Where can I get a knife and fork?

Exercises

I. Match the menu items with the menu sections they belong to.

A	B
1. Dessert	A. Hamburger with fresh cut fries
2. Starters	B. Homemade iced tea
3. Specialties	C. Junior spaghetti and meatballs
4. Refreshments	D. Peach pie a la mode
5. Seafood	E. Mouth-watering garlic cheese toast
6. Sides	F. Loaded mashed potatoes
7. Kids menu	G. Chef Brian's home-style chili
8. Sandwiches	H. Lemon and herb glazed salmon
9. Spirits	I. Seasonal tossed greens
10. Salads	J. 1/2 liter house white

II. Use this menu to practise ordering food in a restaurant.

Starters	
Chicken Soup	$2.50
Salad	$3.25
Main Course	
Ham and Cheese	$3.50
Tuna	$3.00
Vegetarian	$4.00
Grilled Cheese	$2.50
Piece of Pizza	$2.50
Cheeseburger	$4.50
Hamburger	$5.00
Spaghetti	$5.50
Dessert	
Apple Pie	$2.00
Blueberry Pie	$2.00
Drinks	
Coffee	$1.25
Tea	$1.25
Soft Drinks—Coke, Sprite, Juice, Milk, etc.	$1.75

III. Complete the short dialogues by translating Chinese into English.

1	A: _____ (今天我们出去吃饭如何)?	B: OK. I want to eat steak.
2	A: Do you have in mind which restaurant we can go to?	B: How about a restaurant _____ (有地方特色的)?
3	A: _____ (你们准备好点菜了吗)?	B: Wait for a moment, please.
4	A: _____ (你的牛排要几分熟), Sir?	B: I'll have it medium rare, please.
5	A: _____ (你想现在要咖啡还是一会儿再要)?	B: Later, please.

6	**A**: _____ (我今天没带足够的钱).	**B**: I'd like to _____ (这次由我来请你).
7	**A**: OK, _____ (我们 AA 制吧).	**B**: _____ (如果你坚持，我同意).
8	**A**: What kind of beer would you like?	**B**: _____ (你可以给我推荐一下度数低的啤酒吗)?
9	**A**: What do you call these?	**B**: They are called Jiaozi. Please mix a little soy sauce and sesame oil on this plate and _____ (在里面蘸一蘸再吃).
10	**A**: We have a daily chef's special of fried chicken.	**B**: _____ (这个特色餐中包括什么配菜)?

IV. Pair work: make dialogues based on the following situations.

1. Lisa is talking with Mary about the best restaurant they have ever been to.

2. You are talking with your foreign friend about the different table manners between your two countries.

3. You want to dine out with your friend Xiao Wang. You are discussing which restaurant to go and what to eat.

V. Topics for discussion.

1. Nowadays, people like to have family reunions at a restaurant during the Spring Festival. What do you think are the possible reasons?

2. Do you like Chinese food or Western food? Why?

Culture Tips

In western countries, if you have dinner in a restaurant, it is a custom to give a tip to the waiter or waitress. The tip is normally a percentage of the pre-tax amount of the bill. The exact percentage is up to you, depending on the quality of service and your own generosity. However, 10%~15% of the pre-tax amount is usually considered an appropriate amount. No matter what kind of restaurant it is, tipping a few percent more is always a good idea when the server has worked particularly hard for your table or gone out of his/her way to make your meal especially pleasant.

However, tips are generally not required at these eating places like cafeterias, where you serve yourself. At snack bars or drugstore restaurants, most people leave some small change under their plates.

 Class Activities

Make up a Story with the Given Opening Sentences

Work together in groups to create stories. One student begins by giving a sentence as the opening of the story. Then the next student continues the story, and so on. After a few sentences, tell the story to the whole class. How long can you keep the story going? Is the story logical and interesting?

You can start your story using one of the following sentences:

1. Once upon a time, in a far-off land…
2. It was about midnight…
3. One day, I went shopping, suddenly…
4. I was walking home the other night when I saw a person really strange…
5. Do you know the story about a mouse who can speak?

 思 政

A Dip into Chinese Wisdom

1. 历览前贤国与家，成由勤俭败由奢。

Looking at the former virtuous countries and families, success results from diligence and frugality, and failure from extravagance.

2. 谁知盘中餐，粒粒皆辛苦。

Each bowl of rice, who knows?

Is the fruit of hard toil.

3. 一粥一饭，当思来之不易；

半丝半缕，恒念物力维艰。

With each meal of porridge and rice,

Consider the difficulty of its origins;

With every half of silk, every half of thread,

Always remember the scarcity of resources.

4. 民以食为天。

Food is the first necessity of the people.

SECTION I

Sports
Unit 9

Lead-in

Do you like sports? What is your favorite sport? Discuss it with your partner. You may use the following examples for help.

A: I like… best. I prefer… to…
B: I'd rather watch it than play.
C: My favorite sport is…

Warm-up Activities

I. Read the following words and pay attention to the pronunciation of [ʃ] and [ʒ].

1. [ʃ]   sure   beneficial   conscious   luxury   shine
2. [ʒ]   occasion   usually   leisure   luxurious   pleasure

II. Read the story below and pay attention to your pronunciation and intonation.

A fan arrived at the sports ground one Sunday, but only to find the place completely empty. He went to the office and asked an official.

"What time does the match start?"

"There's no match today," replied the official.

"But there must be!" insisted the fan. "It's Sunday."

"I'm telling you there's no match today," repeated the official.

"But there's always a match on Sunday afternoon," said the fan.

"Watch my lips," shouted the indignant official. "There is no M-A-T-F-C-H today!"

"Well, for your information," the would-be spectator shouted back, "there's no F in match."

"That's what I've been trying to tell you!" yelled the official.

Dialogues

Dialogue 1

Lisa: Are you interested in playing badminton?

Beth: Yes. I like it very much. It's a nice sport. Why?

Lisa: A poster on the noticeboard says there will be a badminton tournament this weekend.

Beth: Really? Let's go to see it together. It'll be a great way to spend the weekend.

Lisa: Yeah, let's go together.

Dialogue 2

Nathan: Hi, Martin. You look so tired.

Martin: Yes. We had a football match with School of International Logistics.

Nathan: Really? What was the result?

Martin: Two to nil. We won!

Nathan: That's fantastic! Who scored the two goals?

Martin: Jack and Danny. Will you join us next time?

Nathan: But I can't play football well.

Martin: It doesn't matter. You can be the goalkeeper, right?

Nathan: Well, I don't know...

Martin: Come on, don't let me down.

Nathan: OK. But what's your position?

Martin: I'm a defender.

Nathan: I thought you were a striker. You run so fast.

Martin: Sometimes I also play as a midfielder.

Dialogue 3

A: Well, Shirley, it's really been interesting to talk to you. It'd be fun to get together sometime.

B: I'd like that. What kinds of things do you like to do?

A: I like getting out of the city when I can.

B: What do you do when you go out of the city?

A: I like lying around in the sun, doing nothing! Especially on the beach in summer. Do you enjoy the beach?

B: Well, no. It takes so long to get to the beach, and it's always so crowded.

A: Oh, I see. Then how about sports? I like ping-pong. And you?

B: I like mountain biking. It is very popular among young people.

A: That sounds great! I'd like to try!

B: OK. We can do it together sometime.

Dialogue 4

A: Hi, how do you keep yourself in such a fantastic shape, Li Hua?

B: I get plenty of exercise. I try to exercise every day.

A: Oh, what do you usually do? I suppose you have all sorts of expensive equipment.

B: No, I don't use any equipment actually.

A: Do you jog?

B: No. I don't like jogging much. It makes me feel bored.

A: So what sports do you play?

B: I swim a lot. I go to the pool about three times a week.

A: Good for you. How long does that take you each time?

B: About forty-five minutes.

A: What other sports do you play?

B: Well, I also play basketball.

Dialogue 5

A: When I was at school, I was quite good at track and field events.

B: Really? What were you good at?

A: I was on the school team for the high jump, the 100-meter sprint and the javelin. What about you?

B: I was quite good at hurdles and the discus.

A: I was terrible at hurdles. I could never jump over them!

B: I thought you were good at long jump!

A: No, I was not good at long jump. I liked sprints best.

B: Did you ever win any competitions?

A: I was the champion in the 100 meters at our school. How about you?

B: Well, I never won a competition.

Dialogue 6

A: Do you know the results from the Olympic Games today?

B: Yes, we got gold medals in three events.

A: That's great. Those athletes must train for years to get into peak physical condition. They must be terribly disappointed if they don't win.

A: Did they break the records?

B: Yes, the woman who won the 1,500 meters broke the world record by 3 seconds.

A: That's amazing! Were any other records broken?

B: A Jamaican man broke the 100 meters sprint record by 0.02 seconds. Our best athlete broke his personal best in the long jump, but it only got him the third place.

A: Did you see the final of the women's 200 meters? It was very exciting. One competitor made two false starts.

B: Was she disqualified?

A: Yes, she was. What a pity!

Dialogue 7

A: Don't you think it is very interesting to watch the Olympics? There have been some excellent performances by athletes from all over the world.

B: I don't think so.

A: I think it's wonderful to see people around the world come together and take part in such a great event.

B: As far as I can see, it's just a way to show which country is more powerful.

A: I think the Olympics helps to promote world peace.

B: I'm not so sure about that. Despite the Olympics, we still have many wars in the world. While the idea behind the Olympics is noble, the reality often falls short. True cooperation and friendliness between people seem rare.

A: You are being a bit pessimistic! The Olympics is a great opportunity for athletes to demonstrate their speed, skill, endurance, and strength. Most people also feel happy to see the amazing performances of athletes from other countries.

B: Well, I think the most amazing performances are by athletes who participate in the Paralympics.

A: Now there we are in agreement!

Vocabulary

defender [dɪ'fendə(r)] *n.* 后卫，防卫者	champion ['tʃæmpiən] *n.* 冠军
midfielder [ˌmɪd'fiːldə(r)] *n.* 中锋	peak [piːk] *n.* 山顶，顶点
badminton ['bædmɪntən] *n.* 羽毛球	Jamaican [dʒə'meɪkən] *adj.* 牙买加的 *n.* 牙买加人
tournament ['tʊənəmənt] *n.* 比赛，锦标赛	disqualify [dɪs'kwɒlɪfaɪ] *v.* 使……丧失资格
fantastic [fæn'tæstɪk] *adj.* 极好的，难以相信的	athlete ['æθliːt] *n.* 运动员
track [træk] *n.* 跑道	reality [ri'æləti] *n.* 现实，实际，真实
field [fiːld] *n.* 地，田地	cooperation [kəʊˌɒpə'reɪʃn] *n.* 合作，协作
track and field 田径	pessimistic [ˌpesɪ'mɪstɪk] *adj.* 悲观的
javelin ['dʒævlɪn] *n.* 标枪	demonstrate ['demənstreɪt] *v.* 示范，演示
hurdle ['hɜːdl] *n.* 障碍，跨栏	endurance [ɪn'djʊərəns] *n.* 忍耐，忍耐力，耐性
discus ['dɪskəs] *n.* 铁饼	Paralympics [ˌpærə'lɪmpɪks] *n.* 残疾人奥运会
sprint [sprɪnt] *n.* 短距离赛跑	

Useful Expressions

A. Expressing curiosity

- Can someone tell me the results of the match?
- Does anyone know what's going on?
- Do you happen to know when the next race begins?
- I'd like to know how they managed to win the World Cup.
- I hope you don't mind me asking, but are they from Brazil?
- If only I knew about that!
- I wish I knew more about the marathon.
- What I'd really like to find out is the result of that competition.

B. Expressing excitement about sports event

- Fantastic!
- Great!
- How wonderful!
- Oh, that's marvelous!
- Super!

- Terrific!
- That's good news!
- That's the best news/thing I've ever heard about!

C. Asking others about the match

- Are you going to the rowboat match?
- Between which teams? / Who are competing?
- What time does it start?
- What time is the match and where (is it)?
- Where can I get a ticket?
- What's your favorite sport?
- What do you usually do on weekends?
- Are you interested in playing table tennis?
- What do you feel like doing?
- How about a bicycle ride to the seaside?
- It's a healthy sport.
- We need some fun and relaxation on weekends.

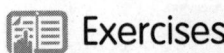 Exercises

I. Do you know the following lingo about playing volleyball? Please write down the Chinese meaning according to the English explanation.

	Volleyball Lingo	English Explanation	Chinese Meaning
1	ace	a serve that is so good that your opponent cannot reach the ball	
2	side out	when the team that served the ball makes a mistake, causing the ball to go to the other team	
3	roof	when a player jumps above the height of the net, and blocks the ball	
4	stuff	when a player jumps about the height of the net, blocks the ball, and the ball goes back at the person who attacked (spiked) the ball	
5	dig	when a player makes a save from a very difficult spike	
6	kill	when a team spikes the ball and it either ends in a point or a side out	

II. Do you know these sport idioms? Match the meanings with the idioms, and then fill in each of the blanks with the appropriate one.

A.

Idioms/Origin of sport	Meaning
1. get off the hook (fishing)	A. have a burst of energy after tiring
2. get a second wind (sailing)	B. break
3. give it your best shot (hunting)	C. start too early
4. hot shot (big shot) (hunting)	D. do something risky, take a chance
5. jump the gun (track)	E. accept at a later time
6. skate on thin ice (skating)	F. a person who thinks he is the best
7. take a rain check (baseball)	G. try your hardest
8. time out (any sport)	H. escape, get out of one's difficulties

B.

1. Even though Luke only placed 20th in the ski race, he thinks he's a _____.

2. You're _____ by not sending in your college application before now.

3. _____ and you may just make it to the finals.

4. I guess I _____ by buying Pam and Steve a wedding gift. They called off the engagement.

5. The child _____ for stealing because the security camera was broken.

6. Sorry, I can't go to the movies today, but I'd love to _____.

7. I was exhausted after 3 kilometers of running, but I _____ after I passed the beach.

8. Let's take some _____ and grab a coffee.

III. Complete the short dialogues by translating Chinese into English.

1	A: Do you know _____ (今天奥运比赛的结果吗)?	B: Yes, we got gold medals in three events.
2	A: You know that? _____ (我们取得了1500米比赛的冠军).	B: Great! _____ (你们打破纪录了吗)?
3	A: Look! _____ (在那边的布告牌上有一张彩色的海报).	B: Yes. It says there will be a chess game at the Students' Center on Sunday.
4	A: _____ (比赛在哪两方中展开)?	B: The International Trade Department versus the English Department.
5	A: You are really a basketball fan. _____ (比赛什么时间开始)?	B: It's at 10:00 a.m. on Oct. 26.

6	A：_____ (我们还是能赢得这场比赛).	B：Really? Do you think so?
7	A：_____ (我想他出界了).	B：Yes, I saw it, too.
8	A：_____ (你为什么不去滑雪啊)?	B：I'm afraid I'd break my leg!
9	A：_____(极限运动是对人的耐力和智力的测试).	B：Maybe you're right.
10	A：_____(你的脚步非常轻快). I cannot even follow you.	B：I feel strong.

IV. Pair work：make dialogues based on the following situations.

1. Mike invites Jim to join him in a sports activity.

2. Invite your partner to attend a sports event.

3. Pretend one of you is a famous athlete, and another is a journalist. Make an interview with your partner.

4. Mary asks Tom about his plan for the weekend and suggests playing a certain kind of sport. They talk about the need for people to play sports.

5. Peter and Kevin are talking about the position they ever played in a basketball game.

V. Topics for discussion.

1. Who is your favorite sports star? Do you like Yao Ming? Why or why not?

2. Which is more important in sport—winning or taking part in?

 Culture Tips

Modern Olympic Games

The French Baron Pierre de Coubertin was the initiator of the modern Olympic Games. He wanted to bring nations closer together and have them compete in sports rather than fight in wars. Thanks to the efforts of Coubertin and his supporters, the first modern Games took place in 1896—in Athens, the actual birthplace of the Olympics.

Coubertin's idea of bringing the nations closer together is symbolized in the Olympic flag：its rings represent the five continents of the world, and the colors (blue, black, red, yellow and green) and the white background were chosen to represent the colors of the flags of all participating nations.

Months before the Olympics, the Olympic Flame is lit in Olympia and relayed to the host city. At the opening ceremony, the last runner lights the Olympic cauldron. Another highlight of the opening ceremony is the parade of the competitors.

There are Summer Olympic Games, Winter Olympic Games and Paralympic Games. The Winter Games take place two years after the Summer Games. The Paralympic Games are an event for athletes with physical disabilities. They are held shortly after the Olympic Games, at the same venues.

Class Activities

Making Words from Letters in a Long Word

This game is a good activity for you to learn new words and get some word knowledge.

The class is divided into 4 or 5 groups. The teacher writes a long word on the board. You should try to compose different words using the letters in the given word. Each letter can be used only as many times as it appears in the word. Only valid English words are accepted, and each word can only be used once. Words must be at least 3 letters long. The group that has composed the most words wins.

For example, your teacher gives the word "circumstance", and then you can compose words such as: circuit, certain, curtain, meat, meet, mess, mean, measure, neat, stir, sea, turn, tire, cut, eastern, sit, star, start, sum, summit, aunt, ant, stun, tame, nurse, near, name, nut…

思 政

A Dip into Chinese Wisdom

1. 实现中国梦是一场历史接力赛，当代青年要在实现民族复兴的赛道上奋勇争先。

The realization of the Chinese Dream is a relay race. Young generations should strive for their best to help realize national rejuvenation.

2. 流水不腐，户枢不蠹。

Running water is never stale and a door-hinge never gets worm-eaten.

3. 耳闻之不如目见之，目见之不如足践之。

Seeing is better than listening, while practice is the best.

4. 人生万事须自为，跬步江山即寥廓。

Everything in life must be experienced by oneself;

it is the minor steps that take one to a wider world.

SECTION I

Travel
Unit 10

 Lead-in

I. How many places of interest can you name? Here are several names for your reference.

Sahara Desert	撒哈拉大沙漠
Pyramids, Egypt	埃及金字塔
Eiffel Tower, France	法国埃菲尔铁塔
The Himalayas	喜马拉雅山
The Great Wall, China	中国长城
The Palace Museum, Beijing, China	中国北京故宫
Mount Fuji, Japan	日本富士山
Taj Mahal, India	印度泰姬陵
Bali, Indonesia	印度尼西亚巴厘岛
Disneyland, California, USA	美国加利福尼亚迪士尼乐园
Niagara Falls, New York State, USA	美国纽约州尼亚加拉大瀑布
Hawaii, USA	美国夏威夷
Arch of Triumph, France	法国凯旋门
Leaning Tower of Pisa, Italy	意大利比萨斜塔

II. If you have money and time, where will be your first choice to travel around? Discuss it with your partner. You may use the following examples for help.

1. I've always dreamed of going to… / I can't wait to visit…
2. I ever heard about this place from…
3. It is famous for…

Warm-up Activities

I. Read the following words and pay attention to the pronunciation of "gh".

1. [/]   eight   neighbor   daughter   through   caught
2. [f]   laugh   cough   tough   enough   clough

II. Read the passage below and pay attention to your pronunciation and intonation.

The Great Wall, like the Pyramids of Egypt, the Taj Mahal in India and the Hanging Gardens of Babylon, is one of the eight great wonders of the world.

Starting out in the east on the banks of the Yalu River in Liaoning Province, the Wall stretches westwards for 12,700 kilometers to Jiayuguan in the Gobi desert, and is thus known as the Ten-Thousand-Li Wall in China. The most imposing and best-preserved sections of the Great Wall are at Badaling and Mutianyu, both of which are located in the suburbs of Beijing and open to visitors.

As a cultural heritage, the Wall belongs not only to China but also to the world. The Venice Charter says: "Historical and cultural architecture not only includes individual architectural works, but also the urban or rural environment that witnessed certain civilizations, significant social developments or historical events." The Great Wall is the largest of such historical and cultural architectural works, and that is why it continues to be so attractive to people all over the world. In 1987, the Wall was listed by UNESCO as a world cultural heritage site.

Dialogues

Dialogue 1

A: Where do you plan to go on vacation?
B: I think I'm going back to my hometown to visit my parents.

A: That's a wonderful idea. When will you be back?

B: I'll be back in a month.

A: Have a nice vacation!

B: Thank you. See you then.

Dialogue 2

A: Hi. Finally back from your vacation.

B: What do you mean "finally"? I feel like I've only been gone for two days instead of two weeks.

A: Well, you know what they say—"Time flies when you're having fun." You did have fun, didn't you?

B: Oh, it was marvelou—the scenes were so beautiful. And it was so nice to get away from this cold, miserable weather. And those mountain views—they were absolutely breathtaking.

A: One of these days, I'll get there myself. In the meantime, I'd better get back to work. Maybe we can get together sometime and you can tell me more about it.

B: Sure, and I'll show you my pictures next time I see you.

A: Great. See you later.

B: Bye.

Dialogue 3

A: I've made up my mind. We're going to the United States for the vacation.

B: Oh, really! How exciting! I've never been there myself. When are you leaving?

A: Next week.

B: How long are you staying?

A: About two weeks.

B: Why did you choose America? Have you got friends there?

A: No, I've always wanted to go there, and see the Grand Canyon and Las Vegas.

B: Well, have a nice trip.

A: Thank you.

Dialogue 4

A: Let's have a look at the copy of the itinerary. Well, a three-day sightseeing and a half-day shopping.

B: Would you like to go to the details about the sightseeing now?

A: Sure. What interests me most is the Great Wall. It is one of the Eight Wonders of the World.

B: So, we'll climb the Great Wall on the first day of our sightseeing.

A: Great!

B: Do you have anything special in mind you'd love to see?

A: I've always liked to see the Tian'anmen Square. I've seen it on the Internet. But I want to see it in person.

B: What else are you interested in?

A: I'm crazy about Beijing Opera shows. I hope I can have a chance to enjoy it.

B: No problem. I'll book the ticket for you in advance.

A: That's very kind of you. Thank you very much.

B: My pleasure. Do you feel like sightseeing the Temple of Heaven and the Summer Palace?

A: I'd be delighted to. As a matter of fact, I'm anxious to see everything you arrange for me.

B: You may come often and I'll be very glad to be your guide next time.

A: I'll come again, that's for sure.

Dialogue 5

(On the train, a Chinese meets a foreigner and talks with him.)

A: Excuse me, may I sit here?

B: Of course, please.

A: Thank you. Going to Shanghai?

B: Yeah, and you?

A: I'm going to Hangzhou. By the way, my name is Zhang Jie, nice to meet you.

B: Glad to meet you. I'm John, from America. So, what do you do, Zhang Jie?

A: I'm a sales manager in an import and export company. Do you come to China for sightseeing?

B: Half business, half sightseeing.

A: Um?

B: Well, I'm a reporter. I write news stories and reports. I go where there's news. In the meantime, I enjoy myself.

Dialogue 6

A: Where are you going to spend your holiday this year?

B: I'm not so sure, but we may go abroad. You know, my wife and I would like to go to Japan.

A: It's an interesting country to see.

B: Yes, but a round-trip ticket costs a lot. So we can't make up our minds yet.

A: But you may go by sea.

B: You're right. It's cheaper, isn't it?

A: You may save at least half of your money if you go by ship.

B: Don't you think it would take a long time?

A: But you can enjoy the scenery of the sea and the rising sun.

B: Yes, I'll talk about it with my wife.

A: You'll definitely enjoy yourselves, I'm sure.

B: Thank you for your terrific idea.

Dialogue 7

(*A*: *Tourist guide*)

(*B*: *Guest*)

A: Good morning, Mr. Smith. According to the traveling schedule, today we're going to visit the Palace Museum. Are you ready now?

B: Good morning, Miss Liu. I'm really anxious to go sightseeing there. But it looks like it's going to rain, so I want to bring my raincoat with me. Please wait for a moment.

A: No hurry. It is still early now.

B: All right. Everything is ready now. Let's be on our way.

(*After a while, they reach the Palace Museum.*)

A: Now, we are standing on the grounds of the Imperial Palace.

B: Oh! It is gorgeous and elaborate, indeed.

A: This is the world-famous Forbidden City where emperors, empresses and their families once lived.

B: Yes, it looks very lovely and picturesque.

A: Let's go ahead.

B: Shall we proceed to this hall?

A: OK. Let's go there. This is the Hall of Central Harmony, in Chinese, Zhong He Dian.

B: Oh, how splendid! What was it built for?

A: It was here that the emperors handled their daily affairs.

B: Yes, a peaceful and tranquil atmosphere permeates the place.

Vocabulary

itinerary [aɪ'tɪnərəri] n. 旅行路线 marvelous ['mɑ:vələs] adj. 了不起的，不可思议的 miserable ['mɪzrəbl] adj. 悲惨的，痛苦的 absolutely ['æbsəlu:tli] adv. 绝对地，完全地 round-trip ticket 来回机票 definitely ['defɪnətli] adv. 明确地，确切地 terrific [tə'rɪfɪk] adj. 极好的，非常的 gorgeous ['gɔ:dʒəs] adj. 华丽的，灿烂的	elaborate [ɪ'læbərət] adj. 精细的，详尽的，精心的 emperor ['empərə(r)] n. 皇帝 empress ['emprəs] n. 女皇，皇后 picturesque [ˌpɪktʃə'resk] adj. 生动的，如画的，独特的 tranquil ['træŋkwɪl] adj. 安静的，宁静的 permeate ['pɜ:mieɪt] v. 弥漫，渗透

Useful Expressions

A. Talking about travelling

- I wish you a good journey.
- I hope you have a good trip.
- Did you have a nice journey?
- How long would you be staying in China?
- What's the purpose of your visit?
- I have come to make sure that your stay in Beijing is a pleasant one.
- I can't wait to visit the Great Wall.
- I'm excited about going to Korea for the World Cup.
- I had a marvelous time. I'm thinking of going some time later on.
- I don't feel like taking a tour.
- I'm hoping to travel around the world.

B. Talking about business trip

- I'm going to London on business.
- You don't know how tight the schedule is for this business trip.
- We always discuss business matters. It's boring.
- Every time she gets back from a business trip, she gives a few small gifts to her colleagues.
- We'd like to send you to Beijing on a business trip this weekend.

- They scheduled the negotiation at nine.
- I like to take an occasional business trip.

Exercises

I. Do you know the names of the places below? Write down the names on the blank lines.

II. Match the English expressions with the Chinese equivalents.

1. International Flight		A. 单程机票
2. Business Class		B. 行李
3. Domestic Flight		C. 头等舱
4. One-Way Ticket		D. 国际班机
5. First Class		E. 男空服员
6. Economy Class		F. 经济舱
7. Lavatory		G. 盥洗室
8. Stewardess		H. 汇率

9. Steward	I. 商务客舱
10. Baggage/Luggage	J. 国内班机
11. Exchange Rate	K. 女空服员

III. Complete the sentences with the help of the Chinese translation.

1. — _____ (你是怎么去加拿大的)? Did you fly?

   — No，I was planning to, because it's such a long trip. But Tom decided to drive and invited me to join him. It _____ (花费了我们两天的时间).

2. — I'm thinking of going to Austin for a visit. Do you think it's _____ (值得一看)?

   —Yes, I wish _____ (我去过那儿).

3. — How about the tour to Hong Kong?

   — It was worth _____ (既不) the time _____ (也不) the money.

4. — This is my _____ (最喜欢的) time of year, the grass's getting green again and birds are singing in the trees.

   — I _____ (更喜欢) autumn. The colors of the leaves are so beautiful at that time.

5. — Are you _____ (赶 10:15 的航班) to New York?

   — No, I'll leave this evening.

IV. Pair work：talk about a place of interest you are familiar with by using the following questions and compose dialogues with your partner.

1. Where is it exactly?
2. What's it most famous for?
3. What're the features of it?
4. Is it still in good condition?
5. Why do you like it best?

V. Topics for discussion.

1. Do you prefer to travel alone or travel with friends? Why?
2. Have you ever met with any problems when you were on a trip? What were they? How did you overcome them?

Culture Tips

Learning about the culture of the country you want to visit before you travel is necessary. Dressing appropriately is especially important. Proper appearance will help you gain the respect and friendship of the locals easily.

In some places, you should be even more careful. In traditional Muslim countries, for instance, you'll find most women cover almost all visible flesh and wear a scarf over their hair. Perhaps it's not strictly necessary to follow suit, but it would be respectful to do so.

Be particularly respectful in religious buildings. For example, in Italy, you are not allowed to enter some of the most beautiful buildings in the world if you arrive with bare shoulders, arms or knees.

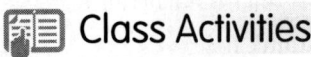 Class Activities

Knowledge Race

Work in groups of four and appoint one person to be the group leader. The teacher will name a country. You have one minute to write as many notes as you can about the people and the geography before your teacher names the next country, e.g. China—big, 1.4 billion people, the Great Wall, pandas, capital city Beijing.

> Britain, America, Australia, New Zealand, Russia, Sweden, India, France

You have five minutes to turn your notes into full sentences, e.g. China—It's a big country. There are over 1.4 billion people. The Great Wall is one of the greatest wonders in the world. Pandas are the national treasures of China. The capital city is Beijing.

Read out your sentences in class. You get one point for each sentence.

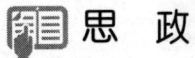 思 政

A Dip into Chinese Wisdom

1. 真理只有在实践中才能得到检验，真理只有在实践中才能得到确立。

Truth must be tested in practice and can only be established in practice.

2. 知者行之始，行者知之成。

Vision spurs action and is achieved through action.

3. 读万卷书，行万里路。

Read ten thousand books and travel ten thousand miles.

4. 踏遍青山人未老，风景这边独好。

We have trodden green mountains without growing old.
What scenery unique here we behold!

SECTION I

At the Airport
Unit 11

 Lead-in

I. Have you ever seen somebody off, met somebody or taken the plane at the airport? If so, please share the experience with your partner.

II. What are the boarding procedures if you want to take a flight? Here are some words and phrases for reference.

the Customs	海关
passport	护照
boarding pass/boarding card	登机牌
window seat	靠窗的位子
aisle seat	靠通道的位子
to board the plane	上飞机
ground hostess	地勤小姐
passenger	乘客
air-hostess	空中小姐
departure lounge	候机大厅
security check	安全检查
arrival time	抵达时间
visitors terrace	迎送平台
transit passengers	中转旅客
luggage retrieval	行李提取处

luggage lockers 行李柜
passport check 护照检查

Warm-up Activities

I. Read the following words and pay attention to the pronunciation of "th".

1. [θ]   thank   think   birthday   maths   tooth
2. [ð]   the   these   with   within   without

II. Read the announcement below and pay attention to your pronunciation and intonation.

In order to better safeguard the security of civil air transportation during the Beijing Olympics, the Civil Aviation Administration of China (CAAC) carried out special security check measures in certain airports. The announcement was as follows.

(1) Special security check measures will be carried out in most of the big airports in China.

(2) People entering the above-specified airports will be subject to security checks at the entrance to the terminals.

(3) Passengers entering those airports with explosives, flammable materials or explosive items will be subject to severe punishment in accordance with current laws and regulations. Passengers will be responsible for any resultant consequences, such as missing their flights.

(4) Passengers are encouraged to arrive at the airport in advance and allow sufficient time for security checks to avoid missing their flights.

Dialogues

Dialogue 1

A: Good morning.

B: Good morning. What can I do for you?

A: I'd like a ticket to Washington, please.

B: Round trip?

A: No. Just one way.

B: OK. That'll be 270 dollars.

A: 270? It was only 200 dollars I took this flight last time.

B: I know. The rates have risen this month.

A: Just like everything else.

B: Yeah.

A: Does the flight still leave at 10:30 a.m.?

B: Yes, that's right.

A: Fine. Thanks a lot.

B: You're welcome. Have a good trip.

Dialogue 2

A: Could you hear clearly, Jack?

B: I don't know. There's too much noise. What time does Tom's plane arrive?

A: I told you. At 9:30, Flight DF655.

B: Gosh, it's almost a quarter past ten now! The plane's probably landed. Why don't you go and ask at the Information Desk?

A: OK. And you go and wait by the exit over there.

B: Hey, wait a minute! What does Tom look like?

A: Oh, he's like me. But he's taller and thinner. And his hair's much darker. Anyway, don't worry. I'll be back in a minute.

Dialogue 3

A: Excuse me, would you please help me?

B: Yes. What can I do for you?

A: I'm looking for gifts to take back to my family.

B: Here's my favorite, a purse-sized perfume for a mother or sister.

A: This is a good price. I will take it for my mother. I also need gifts for my father and my sister.

B: Do you know that you will save even more because you do not pay taxes on your purchases?

A: That is wonderful. May I see this wallet, please?

B: You are lucky, there is an additional ten percent off the price today.

A: This is for my sister. She loves anything made of leather. And I have chosen one for my father. I will buy two bottles of this fine wine.

B: Excellent choices. Let me fill out the forms for customs. Thank you for shopping duty free.

Dialogue 4

A: Excuse me. Where can I check in?

B: Where are you going, sir?

A: I'm going to England by Flight ED859.

B: We are checking in here. May I have your ticket, your health certificate, and your luggage, please?

A: Here you are.

B: This is your luggage check, which you must show when you disembark at your destination. And here is your boarding pass and your ticket.

A: Thanks.

B: Now could you wait until your flight is called? There are about twenty-five minutes to go.

A: I'm a little nervous. I have never flown before.

B: There is nothing at all to worry about. Once you're up in the air, it's just like sitting in your own living room. It's going to be a very pleasant flight.

A: All right, thank you.

Dialogue 5

Customs: May I see your passport, please?

Passenger: Here you are. It is not a good picture of me. I've lost weight.

Customs: What's the purpose of your visit?

Passenger: I'm on a trip.

Customs: Do you have any fruit or vegetables to declare?

Passenger: If you mean fresh fruit and vegetables, no.

Customs: Do you have anything else to declare?

Passenger: I don't know what's dutiable. Do I have to pay duty on things for my own use?

Customs: No, you don't have to pay duty on personal belongings.

Dialogue 6

(*Announcer: Last call for Flight 520 for Shanghai, leaving from Gate 5.*)

A: Got all your bags, honey?

B: I suppose so.

A: Where're your ticket and your passport?

B: Here in the pocket. Oh, I've got to hurry up. That's the last announcement. Take care of the children.

A: No problem. Take good care of yourself. Don't forget to phone me when you settle in. Just let me know you've arrived safely.

B: I will. Don't worry.

A: Oh, I put a book of detective stories in your handbag. I guess it'll be boring to fly over the ocean. It can help you kill time.

B: It's sweet and thoughtful of you. Thank you, honey.

A: Have a nice trip. See you next week.

B: See you.

Dialogue 7

(At the Information Counter)

A: Welcome to San Francisco. May I help you?

B: I would like some information on ground transportation.

A: Would you like to rent a car or find another means of travel?

B: I need to get to my hotel, I have a car waiting there for me.

A: Which hotel are you staying at?

B: I will stay at the Downtown Courtyard.

A: You are in luck. That property has a free shuttle that will pick you up at the airport.

B: Oh, that's great. How do I get them to do that?

A: The bulletin board on the wall shows each shuttle service.

B: Once I find the hotel, do I just call them from that phone?

A: Yes, it's just that easy. Just go to the south curb and wait.

B: Thank you for your help.

Vocabulary

round trip 往返旅行 rate [reɪt] *n.* 价格 noise [nɔɪz] *n.* 喧哗声，噪声 land [lænd] *n.* 陆地，土地 *v.* 登陆 the Information Desk 问讯处 perfume ['pɜ:fju:m] *n.* 香水，香气 purse [pɜ:s] *n.* 钱包 tax [tæks] *n.* 税 *v.* 课税 wallet ['wɒlɪt] *n.* 皮夹，钱包 additional [ə'dɪʃənl] *adj.* 附加的，另外的 leather ['leðə(r)] *adj.* 皮革制的 *n.* 皮革 detective stories 侦探故事 kill time 消磨时间	customs ['kʌstəmz] *adj.* 海关的 *n.* 海关 duty free 免税 check in 办理登记手续，报到 health certificate 健康证明书 luggage check 行李票 disembark [ˌdɪsɪm'bɑ:k] *v.* 下（车、船、飞机等） destination [ˌdestɪ'neɪʃn] *n.* 目的地 boarding pass 登机证 declare [dɪ'kleə(r)] *v.* 申报，宣布，声明 belongings [bɪ'lɒŋɪŋz] *n.* 所有物，财产 the bulletin board 公告牌 curb [kɜ:b] *n.* 边石，路缘

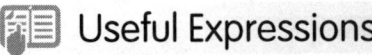 Useful Expressions

A. Asking for information about traveling at the airport

- Where do I pick up the ticket?
- I'd like to change this ticket to the first class.
- I'd like to buy an excursion pass instead.
- I'd like to have a seat by the window.
- We will wait for… in the lobby of the airport.
- What time should I be at the departure gate?
- By what time should I check in?
- Where is the Customs?
- Where can I get my boarding pass and have my luggage weighed?
- Excuse me, which way should I go?
- Is this seat non-smoking?
- Do you have any pills/medicine for airsickness?
- Will the flight be canceled?
- What time does the plane take off?
- When is the boarding time?
- Will this flight leave on time?
- Where is Gate 6?
- Where is the boarding gate for this flight?

B. Information from the clerk

- You'd better have your passport ready.
- Do you have anything to declare?
- Here is a Customs Declaration Form for you to fill in.
- Let me examine your luggage and check it with your form.
- Which seat do you prefer, a window seat or an aisle seat?
- Please put your suitcase on the scale.
- You will have to show the boarding pass on your way to board the plane.
- I wish you a pleasant journey/flight.
- Would you please produce your passport?
- What is your seat number?

 **Exercises**

I. These are some signs you may see at the airport. Try to identify them, and tell their functions in your own words.

II. Complete the short dialogues by translating Chinese into English.

1	A：Welcome to Scotland. Your passport, please. _____ (你会在此地停留多长时间), Miss?	B：Four months. I'll be staying with my grandmother.
2	A：Excuse me, my luggage hasn't appeared.	B：_____ _____ (请出示你的行李收据).
3	A：How was your flight? You must be quite tired after flying all the way from the U.S.	B：I have done quite a lot of long-distance flights going back and forth. _____ _____ (感谢你来接我).
4	A：Is there a problem, officer?	B：_____ _____ (只是常规检查). Would you care to open your luggage yourself?
5	A：_____ (飞机上的食物如何)? Are you hungry now?	B：Well, a little bit. You know the food was so bad.

6	A: I'm sorry, but the 8:30 flight to Chicago just left.	B: Oh, my God! _____ _____ (我错过了航班)!
7	A: _____ (请出示您的飞机票和护照).	B: Yes, here they are.
8	A: You have to hurry, _____ _____ (您的航班将在20分钟后起飞).	B: Yes, the traffic was quite heavy on the freeway.
9	A: _____ (这是您的登机牌).	B: Thank you very much.
10	A: _____ _____ (您有什么要申报的吗)?	B: No, nothing.

III. Complete the dialogues with the words and expressions given in the box, and then role-play with your partner.

Dialogue 1

> put your luggage on this scale   hand luggage   check in

A: Is this the right counter to ___1___ for this flight?

B: Yes, it is. Please ___2___.

A: OK. Is the plane on schedule?

B: Yes, it is. How many pieces of ___3___ do you have?

A: Two.

Dialogue 2

> right back   keep an eye on   but will it take long

A: Excuse me. Will you please ___1___ my suitcase? I just want to make a phone call.

B: Certainly, ___2___?

A: No, I'll be ___3___.

B: OK. I'll look after it then.

Dialogue 3

> leaves from Gate No. 8   I'm a transit passenger for this flight   don't worry

A: May I help you?

B: Yes, ___1___. Can you tell me where to go?

A: Let me see. Oh, you're at the wrong gate. Your plane ___2___.

B: Really? I hope it hasn't left without me.

A: No, ___3___. Just follow me.

IV. Pair work: make dialogues based on the following situations.

1. You and your friend are picking up your brother at the airport. You are complaining about the late flight.

2. You want to change your ticket from economy class to first class. Make a dialogue between you and the officer.

V. Topics for discussion.

1. Which procedure do you think is the most important when you take a flight? Why?

2. Share one of your experiences at the airport with your classmates.

 Culture Tips

Checking in

Check-in desks are found in the majority of commercial airports. Their main function is to take in luggage that passengers wish to, or are required to, place in the aircraft's cargo hold.

However, there is an increasing trend towards more automated check-in processes. Many passengers now have the option to check in online before arriving at the airport (often several days before their flight), or use an airline's self-service check-in kiosks at the airport, to avoid queues at the main staffed check-in desks. After the luggage is weighed and tagged, it is placed on a conveyor that usually feeds into the main baggage handling system.

Going through Security

You need to put your hand luggage through the X-ray machine. Some items cannot be taken on board as hand luggage (such as knives, aerosol cans, etc.). As you pass through security, you may set off the alarm. When this happens, airport personnel will search you or your belongings.

In the Departure Lounge

After you pass through security and before you board your flight, you can wait in the departure lounge. At international airports, there is duty-free shopping, where you can buy goods without paying taxes.

Travel Documents for Flying

Passports are becoming increasingly essential, even in countries where you once just needed proof of residence. Visas, too, are often additional requirements to enter a country. Regardless of the requirements, it is important to have your documents in order.

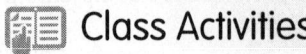 Class Activities

Role-play

The following is an advertisement.

Two-week South China Tour

Suzhou   See traditional Chinese gardens.
               Shop for silk.
Hangzhou   West Lake tour.
               Visit Ling Yin Temple and Tianmu Mountain.
Nanjing   Visit the scenic area in the eastern suburbs.
               Explore the Old City Wall and Confucian Temple.
               Visit Southeast University.

Student A role-plays an agent at a travel agency; Student B role-plays a customer who wants to travel in the south of China. They talk about the details, including the cities, activities, hotels, weather, etc., of the tour.

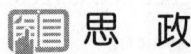 思 政

A Dip into Chinese Wisdom

1. 安而不忘危，存而不忘亡，治而不忘乱。

One should be mindful of potential danger in times of peace, the risk of downfall in times of rise, and potential chaos in times of stability.

2. 山川异域，风月同天。

Lands apart, sky shared.

3. 欲穷千里目，更上一层楼。

You will enjoy a grander sight,
By climbing to a greater height.

4. 小心驶得万年船。

Better safe than sorry.

SECTION I

Hobbies
Unit 12

Lead-in

What are your hobbies? What do you usually do in your spare time? Discuss them with your partner. You may use the following examples for help.

Q: What are your hobbies? / What do you usually do in your spare time?
A: I have lots of hobbies. I love to keep myself busy. I like/enjoy… / I'm keen on… / My favorite hobby is…
B: I like coin collecting/reading/jogging/traveling/being an amateur photographer/ playing chess/playing the piano/going shopping…

Warm-up Activities

I. Read the following words and pay attention to the pronunciation of "wh".

1. [w]   what   which   where   when   wheel
2. [h]   who   whoever   whom   whose   whole

II. Read the passage below and pay attention to your pronunciation and intonation.

I often hear the P.E. teacher say that sports are good for one's health and will make one live longer. So, I like sports very much. I go jogging at five o'clock in the morning; and after class in the afternoon, I play ping-pong with my friends. These sports have kept me healthy.

At home, I like to sing and play the violin. I hope to be a singer or a violinist in the future. In order to attain these goals, I go to my teacher's home for a lesson every Saturday and practice singing and playing the violin every day. Busy as I am, I am quite happy.

Of all my hobbies, I like reading books best. There are nearly six hundred books in my bedroom. There are story books, textbooks, magazines, and others.

Dialogues

Dialogue 1

A: What do you do in your free time?

B: I have many hobbies. I like almost all kinds of sports and I also like listening to classical music.

A: What kinds of sports do you like?

B: I like playing football. Football is a very exciting game because it keeps you alert and I also enjoy its team spirit.

Dialogue 2

A: Do you have any special hobbies?

B: Well, nothing special. I just like reading whenever I'm free.

A: So, what kinds of books do you like best?

B: I enjoy reading biographies, especially those of well-known statesmen, military leaders, scientists, and artists. I can learn a lot from their life stories.

A: Who are your favorite authors?

B: I like Dickens very much. I've read almost all Chinese versions of his novels. I wish I could read the originals—it is said they're even better.

Dialogue 3

A: What are you doing?

B: I'm catching butterflies.

A: How many butterflies do you have now?

B: There are several of these.

A: Do you usually catch them in your free time?

B: Yeah! But sometimes I catch bugs. By the way, what do you do in your free time?
A: I usually play basketball.
B: Do you have any other hobbies?
A: Yes, I like hiking over the weekend.
B: That sounds really nice.

Dialogue 4

A: You got carried away by the music from your walkman. You must be a music lover.
B: Yes, you bet. There's nothing I enjoy more than music.
A: What kind of music do you enjoy most? Do you like rock & roll?
B: Yes, I'm crazy about it. Listen to it, how exciting! I can't express how much I enjoy it.
A: I'm afraid I don't like it. It's too noisy. Sometimes I can't stand it.
B: How can't you! Almost every youngster likes rock & roll. Don't you just like music?
A: Yes, I'm fond of music, too. But I prefer classical music. I often read while listening to music.
B: I like all kinds of music. Would you please tell me who your favorite singer is?
A: Celine Dion.
B: She's really very, very popular with the song *My heart will go on*.
A: Yes, the theme song of the movie *Titanic*. Don't you like her songs?
B: She's Okay, but I prefer music with strong beat and rhythm.
A: I should say we have different tastes.

Dialogue 5

A: What are your hobbies?
B: I play chess, and I like taking pictures. What do you like to do in your spare time?
A: I'm fond of fishing and hiking. In summer, I like swimming best.
B: Do you play tennis?
A: Yes, but I'm not very good at it. Just for fun.
B: Shall we have a game together some day?
A: Yes, that'd be very nice. Let's fix it for next week.
B: You've got it.

Dialogue 6

A: What do you usually do in your spare time? I often feel exhausted after a day's work, and I'm too tired to do anything but dinner and TV.

B: Well, I'm free most of the week. I have my fitness class on Tuesdays and Thursdays.

A: Fitness class? What kind of class is it?

B: Aerobics—it's fun, a lot of kicks and dance-type steps.

A: Dance? I can't dance. My poor heart will beat like crazy and I'll be out of breath pretty soon.

B: Don't worry about it. When I first started, I was breathing hard and couldn't follow, but everybody was too busy jumping and stepping to notice anyone else. One has to take care of oneself. Why don't you come and have a try?

A: I suppose I might try it out.

Dialogue 7

A: What's the matter? You look tired.

B: I feel awful. I sit in my office all day. I'd like to go to a health club, but I can't find the time.

A: Yes, you can. Everybody can.

B: How about you? You look great! How much exercise do you get?

A: A lot. I like rowing, sailing and diving. I jog a few times a week and I go to a health club three times a week. In fact, I'm going after work today. Why don't you come with me?

B: I wish I can, but I have too much work and I'm too tired.

A: You can come for half an hour. It's just across the street.

B: I can't exercise in these clothes!

A: I have an extra sweat suit with me. The only problem is shoes.

B: I have a pair of sneakers in my desk.

A: Great! We can go together after work. We can work out together. Then you can decide if you want to join or not.

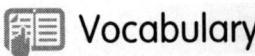 Vocabulary

classical ['klæsɪkl] *adj.* 古典的 alert [ə'lɜːt] *adj.* 警觉的，灵敏的 biography [baɪ'ɒgrəfi] *n.* 传记 statesman ['steɪtsmən] *n.* 政治家	military ['mɪlətri] *a.* 军事的 original [ə'rɪdʒənl] *n.* 原文，原著，原件 *adj.* 原始的，最初的，独创的 hiking ['haɪkɪŋ] *n.* 徒步旅行，远足

walkman 随身听 rock & roll 摇滚乐 stand [stænd] *v.* 忍受 youngster ['jʌŋstə(r)] *n.* 年轻人 rhythm ['rɪðəm] *n.* 节奏	exhausted [ɪɡˈzɔːstɪd] *adj.* 筋疲力尽的 sneakers ['sniːkə(r)z] *(pl.) n.* 胶底运动鞋 aerobics [eəˈrəʊbɪks] *n.* 有氧运动法，健身操

 ## Useful Expressions

A. Talking about someone's hobbies

- Do you go for/enjoy/like…?
- What do you like to do in your spare time?
- What kind of things are you interested in?
- Is there anything that attracts you?
- Do you find… interesting/fascinating/exciting?
- Do you have any special hobbies?
- What hobbies do you have?
- Are you interested in anything in particular?

B. Introducing your own hobbies

- I like… very much.
- I'm crazy about/over…
- I'm brilliant in…
- I'm rather keen on…
- I really adore…
- I love all kinds, especially…
- My favorite is…
- I get interested in…
- I'm obsessed with…
- I like… better than…
- I like… best/most.

 ## Exercises

I. Give possible answers to the following questions.

1. **A**: Do people like classical or rock music more?

B：_____

2. A：Which sport is more popular, swimming or jogging?

   B：_____

3. A：Which is true for most people: they never exercise in their free time, or they like to be active?

   B：_____

4. A：_____

   B：I read everything I can get my hands on, but I like stories best.

5. A：Do you have any hobbies?

   B：_____

6. A：_____

   B：I often play volleyball with friends.

7. A：_____

   B：Ice-skating? Yes, I like it very much. I play it in the winter.

8. A：My hobby is taking pictures. _____

   B：I go in for a lot of sports—basketball, volleyball, tennis and ping-pong of course.

9. A：_____

   B：I'm interested in realistic literature and biography of eminent persons.

10. A：_____

    B：I have lots of hobbies. I love to keep myself busy.

II. Complete the short dialogues by translating Chinese into English.

1	A：So, Jeffery, _____ (空闲时间你做什么)?	B：Well, I love sports.
2	A：_____ (你对什么样的事情感兴趣)?	B：I love music and dancing.
3	A：_____ (你有什么特别的爱好吗)?	B：I have lots of hobbies. I love to stay busy.
4	A：_____ (把你的兴趣和爱好告诉我).	B：Hmm. Hockey, baseball, and skiing are my favorites.
5	A：My hobby is collecting stamps. _____ (你有爱好吗)?	B：I read when I have the chance.
6	A：I enjoy camping.	B：Really? I'm not much of _____ (喜欢户外活动的人).

7	A: Have you got any hobbies?	B: _____ (我喜欢拍照), but I haven't got a digital camera.
8	A: I like going to the cinema and the theatre. And I like reading books and I play the guitar in a band.	B: Wow! _____ (你有这么多的业余爱好啊).
9	A: _____ (你还有什么别的爱好)? Do you collect anything?	B: Yes, I collect stamps and I've got quite a big collection of records and tapes, but I don't buy many now.
10	A: _____ (晚上你都喜欢做些什么)? Do you watch much TV?	B: Yes, quite a lot of television.

III. Pair work: make dialogues based on the following situations.

1. Talk about what you do in your free time with one of your classmates.

2. Find out what hobbies your partner has. Then write five questions about the hobbies. Take turns asking the questions.

3. Both partners discuss each other's hobbies at length and try to decide whose hobbies are best.

IV. Topics for discussion.

1. There are several societies on campus, such as the English Corner, photography, singing and dancing, etc. Which one do you want to join? Why? Discuss with your group members.

2. Do you think you can tell one's personality by his/her hobbies? Discuss it with your group members.

3. Do you like to be with a group of people or alone when you're free?

Culture Tips

What do you usually do after school? Continue to study? Have you ever heard of the proverb "All work and no play makes Jack a dull boy"? Therefore, you may agree that hobbies are a common and great topic for you, your classmates, and friends to learn more about each other. In English, there are several words that have similar meanings to "hobby", like "interest" or "pastime".

Different people have different hobbies, but "music" and "sports" are the most common topics to talk about. When it comes to "music", the questions might be "Do you play any musical instrument?" or "What musical instrument do you play?" You might answer, "I play the piano." When someone asks, "What kind of music do you like?", the answer might be "I like classical/pop/light/folk music" or "I enjoy listening to classical/pop/light/folk music." For "sports", we're familiar with basketball, football, tennis and volleyball, etc. However, in some other countries, you may also hear of hockey, baseball, golf or curling. You might ask, "What sports do you do?" or "What is your favorite sport?"

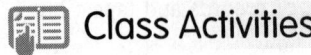 Class Activities

Abilities and Talents

1. Divide the students into groups. Have the students sit in a circle. Take turns asking about the abilities and talents listed in the word map.

2. Complete the word map by adding abilities and talents from the list.

3. Tell the class about the people in your group. Who is musical or artistic? Who is athletic? Who has technical or mechanical skills? Who has other talents?

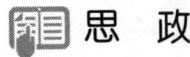 思 政

A Dip into Chinese Wisdom

1. 志合者，不以山海为远。

Even mountains and seas cannot distance people with common aspirations.

2. 予独爱莲之出淤泥而不染，濯清涟而不妖。

My favorite is the water lily. How stainless it rises from its slimy bed! How modestly it reposes on the clear pool—an emblem of purity and truth!

3. 道不同，不相为谋。

Those whose courses are different cannot lay plans for one another.

4. 有志者，事竟成。

Where there is a will, there is a way.

SECTION I

Talking About the Past and the Future
Unit 13

 Lead-in

Talk about one thing which gave you the deepest impression. What do you think you will do after graduation / after this class / in the winter vacation? Discuss with your partner. You may use the following examples for help.

Q: What gave you the deepest impression?
A: One Sunday morning... I first visited..., and then, I went to... That was really terrible/wonderful!
Q: What do you think you will do after graduation / after this class / in the winter vacation?
A: I can't wait to... / I'm hoping to...

 Warm-up Activities

I. Read the following words and pay attention to the pronunciation of "ar".

1. [ɑ:]	star	park	garden	dark	large
2. [ɔ:]	quarter	wharf	ward	war	warm
3. [ə]	dollar	collar	scholar	molar	polar

II. Read the passage below and pay attention to your pronunciation and intonation.

Do you blame yourself for things which you did—or failed to do—in the past? Everyone does this at some point. However, if you want to lead a successful and productive life, you have to let the past go and do not regret events that cannot be changed.

The successful person takes this approach: learn a lesson from past mistakes and make adjustments in future behavior. If you just indulge in the negativity, you will create a vicious cycle where negative experiences and negative feelings are reinforced, which leads to more negative outcomes and feelings.

If you insist on dwelling in the past, I suggest that you focus on your past successes. When you find yourself starting to dwell on past negative experiences, immediately halt and remind yourself, "There is nothing I can do now that will change what happened." Regardless of what you have done—or failed to do—the only sane approach is to accept it and move forward.

Dialogues

Dialogue 1

Tom: Hi, Jane. Long time no see. I heard you went to Hangzhou last month.

Jane: Hi, Tom. Yes, I went there during the summer vacation. I had a very good time.

Tom: Great! How was the weather there?

Jane: It was great. Though it rained sometimes, I enjoyed it very much.

Tom: Did you live in the hotel?

Jane: Yeah, I booked the hotel online before I went there. It was very clean and the price was reasonable.

Tom: Oh, good for you! How about the food? Did you like it?

Jane: Yes, the local food was very tasty.

Tom: What was your deepest impression of your trip?

Jane: The people there were kind and the ancient city was gorgeous. It was a wonderful place to go!

Dialogue 2

Dad: Do you often recall our wedding?

Mom: Yeah, and our wedding photos always remind me of the most exciting moment.

Dad: Sure. We looked so young at that time, right?

Mom: Well, but the pictures were black and white, and we seemed so outdated.
Dad: Come on, honey, though outdated, they are our precious memories.
Mom: New technology really takes wedding photos into a new era.
Dad: I have an idea. Why don't we have some more photos taken?
Mom: Can we? But who can take photos for us?
Dad: That's not a problem. I heard there is a popular photo gallery on this beach.
Mom: Really? Let's get the children together.

Dialogue 3

A: Did you go back to your hometown to have a family reunion during the Spring Festival vacation?
B: Yes, I did. My parents were so glad to see me back home again.
A: What did you do while you were together?
B: Well, first of all, I told them what college life was like, how I felt about my studies, and how well I actually did in my lessons. And I was so glad to find that both my parents were good listeners.
A: What else did you do then?
B: Then it was their turns to tell me all about the changes that had taken place in my family and the town during the months of my absence. Thus we talked and talked without knowing that my vacation would soon be over.

Dialogue 4

Kate: How time flies! We had already left this college for 30 years!
Anne: Yes, we had so many sweet memories here, right?
Kate: I remember that there used to be a bridge here.
Anne: Yes, that was the only pass to the canteen.
Kate: Well, the campus is much larger than before. The flowers are very beautiful.
Anne: What a wonderful scenery!
Kate: Look! A new teaching building is under construction there.
Anne: Well, that is the new laboratory. It will be finished next year.
Kate: That means the students can have their training courses on campus.
Anne: Sure. They are so lucky.

Dialogue 5

A: Have you made up your mind about what you'll do after graduation?
B: Yes, I have thought much about it.

A: What do you intend to do?

B: I'd much prefer going into business for myself.

A: What do you hope to do exactly?

B: I do hope to open my own real estate business. I've had this idea for a long time. How about you?

A: Me? I expect that I'll start taking courses for a diploma in business.

Dialogue 6

A: What are you going to do after the final examination?

B: I'm going to stay with my family.

A: What will you do all day?

B: I'm going to work with my father at the store. In the evening, I'll read books. On weekends, I'll go to the beach with my family.

A: Have you ever worked?

B: No, but I will try. What's your plan for the summer vacation?

A: I'll make some money and then go to the mountains.

B: How will you make your money?

A: I have no idea up to now. But I hope I can get a job in a Wallace's.

B: Sounds great. Well, so long. Have fun.

A: The same to you.

Dialogue 7

(M=Man; W=Woman)

M: Well, could you describe the two people who robbed the bank for which report we're filling out here? Now, anything you could remember would be extremely helpful to us.

W: Well, just, I can only remember basically what I said before.

M: That's all right.

W: The man was tall—about six feet, and he had dark hair.

M: Dark hair.

W: And he had moustache.

M: Do you remember how old he was, by any chance?

W: Eh, well, I guess around thirty.

M: Around thirty. Anything else that strikes you at that moment?

W: I remember he was wearing a light shirt under the sweater, a cotton one with dark, I think, dark stripes. It looks like a good brand.

M: Ah, very good.

W: I remember it specifically because I was then near the counter, next to the bank manager, and my little daughter started to cry.

M: Ah.

W: This is really all I can remember.

M: All right, Mrs. Harrison. I really appreciate what you've told us. I'm just going to ask you to look at some photographs before you leave, if you don't mind. It won't take very long. Can you do that for me?

W: Ah, all right.

M: Would you like to step this way with me, please?

W: OK, sure.

M: Thank you.

 ## Vocabulary

online [ˌɒnˈlaɪn] *adj.* 联机的，在线的 *adv.* 在网上 impression [ɪmˈpreʃn] *n.* 印象 ancient [ˈeɪnʃənt] *adj.* 古代的，古老的 outdated [ˌaʊtˈdeɪtɪd] *adj.* 旧式的，过时的 gallery [ˈgæləri] *n.* 美术馆，画廊	pavilion [pəˈvɪliən] *n.* 楼阁 under construction *adj.* 在修建中 diploma [dɪˈpləʊmə] *n.* 文凭 moustache [məˈstɑːʃ] *n.* 小胡子 strike [straɪk] *vt. & vi.* 给……留下印象

 ## Useful Expressions

A. Inquiring about a person's past experience

- Have you ever...?
- Didn't you once...?
- Tell me about it, will you?
- Tell me about the time... / your first visit to...
- What happened next?
- What did you do then?
- What did you hear/see/notice/find when…?
- How did you feel when...?
- What were you doing while that was going on?
- What did you do after that?

- Why didn't you...?
- What made you...?
- Why didn't you decide to...?
- Did you find it an exciting experience?
- Have you ever visited Britain?
- Have you seen Mrs. Smith lately?

B. Talking about past events

- I heard that...
- I met her yesterday as a matter of fact…
- I'll never forget...
- The next thing I did was to…
- I remember quite clearly that...
- That reminds me of the time I…

C. Inquiring about a person's future plan

- What are you going to / hoping to / planning to / intending to / proposing to / aiming to do (when you leave school)?
- What do you think you'll do (when you grow up)?
- What are you thinking of doing (when you grow up)?

D. Talking about plans

- I'm going to / hoping to / planning to / intending to / proposing to / aiming to go to university.
- I'm going to study abroad.
- I plan to / intend to / propose to / aim to / mean to work for a big company.
- I'll study medicine.
- She is expecting a baby. / She's going to have a baby.
- They're getting married. / They are going to get married.
- He is leaving for Beijing. / He leaves for Beijing tomorrow.
- He'll be here in thirty minutes. / He's expected to be here in thirty minutes.
- There's been a delay and the plane won't get in until 10.
- There will be showers in Shanghai and the temperature is expected to drop below normal.

 Exercises

I. Talk about past activities with your partner with the help of the following questions.

Did you read any books last weekend?	Did you have dinner at a restaurant?
Did you write any letters?	Did you see any movies?
Did you have a part-time job?	Did you go dancing?
Did you play any sports?	Did you meet any interesting people?
Did you go shopping?	Did you talk on the phone?
Did you buy any clothes?	Did you sleep late?
Did you see any friends?	Did you study hard?

Examples:

A: Did you read any books last weekend?

B: Yes, I did. I finished *Harry Potter II*, and I really enjoyed it! Did you go shopping?

A: No, I didn't. I didn't have any money.

II. Complete the short dialogues with the expressions given in the box.

A. What are you planning to do after your graduation?

B. I didn't use to be so heavy.

C. There won't be any help in crying over split milk.

D. Great! I will take the fish! And you?

E. I remember quite clearly that you played the guitar and sang for me.

1. **A:** Exercise is really important.
   B: I know. I'm getting a little fat. _____
2. **A:** Oh, take a look at the menu!
   B: _____
   A: I will probably order the fish, too. I do not know yet!
3. **A:** _____
   B: To be honest, I do not have interest in my major now. I am quite interested in learning about customs. I want to become a civil servant in the customs field.

4. A: Hi, Lucy! It's been such a long time since we last saw each other! Look at you, you are still as charming as you were in the past.

   B: _____

5. A: You can't always live in the past.

   B: Yes, I see. _____

III. Pair work: make dialogues based on the following situations.

1. Student A asks Student B about his/her past educational experience.
2. Student A asks Student B about where he/she lived in the past.
3. Student A asks Student B about his/her future career plans.
4. Student A and Student B describe the jobs they want to pursue in the future.

IV. Topics for discussion.

1. What are your plans for the next ten years?
2. What is the first thing you will do when you arrive at a new place?
3. Do you plan to study abroad? Why? What do you plan to study?

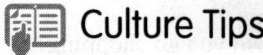
Culture Tips

Generally speaking, Western people have a strong sense of time. If you have a date with a foreign friend from Western countries, they will confirm the specific time. At the same time, they like to arrive on time for the meeting. Especially in business situations, they are likely to be very punctual. To be kept waiting is often considered impolite and irresponsible. They hold the opinion that every minute of life is precious and should not be wasted. Just as the saying goes, "Time and tide wait for no man".

Class Activities

Guess a Famous Person

The class will be divided into 10 groups, with one member of each group thinking of a famous person. The other members of the group can ask up to twenty questions, such as the ones below. The member who thinks of the famous person answers with "Yes" or "No".

e.g.

Is the person a man or a woman?

Does the person live in China?

Is the person a singer, an actor or something else?

Does the person wear glasses?

Is the person young, middle-aged or old?

When you think you know the person's name, speak loudly, "Is the person's name…?"

 思 政

A Dip into Chinese Wisdom

1. 只争朝夕，不负韶华。

Seize the day, and live it to the fullest.

2. 年年岁岁花相似，岁岁年年人不同。

The flowers of this year look like those of last year;

But next year the same people will not reappear.

3. 花开堪折直须折，莫待无花空折枝。

Gather sweet blossoms while you may,

And not the twig devoid of flowers!

4. 机不可失，失不再来。

Opportunity knocks but once.

SECTION I

Offering Help
Unit 14

Lead-in

What do you usually say when you need help or offer help to others? Discuss it with your partner. You may use the following examples for help.

Q: What do you usually say when you need help?
A: Excuse me, could you tell me how to…
Q: What do you usually say when you offer help?
A: May I help you? / What can I do for you?

Warm-up Activities

I. Read the following words and pay attention to the pronunciation of "er".

1. [ɜː]   term   herb   germ   serpent   perfect
2. [ə]   worker   alter   chapter   after   brother

II. Read the joke below and pay attention to your pronunciation and intonation.

The Drive Thru (得来速)

Tony just finished his training session at the local McDonald's, so he was a little nervous being behind the register for the first time.

His first customer ordered a Milkshake. "Tony," his manager said, "remember to say 'Welcome to McDonald's' to each customer before they order." His second customer ordered a Cheeseburger. This time, the manager approached Tony again, and said, "Remember to ask each customer if they want fries with their order."

At this point, a man came in wearing a ski mask. He approached Tony at the register and pointed a gun in his face. "Give me all the money you have got in that register!" Tony took one look at his manager, thought for a moment, and quickly said, "Welcome to McDonald's. Do you want fries with the money?"

 Dialogues

Dialogue 1

A: Hey! What's the rush?

B: The bank closes in half an hour and I need to cash a check.

A: Let me help you with it. I can lend you some money.

B: I appreciate your concern and help, but I need to cash a check because I'm going on a trip this weekend. Actually, I want to buy some traveler's checks.

A: Hmm. Can I help in any way?

B: Well, you can drive me to the bank if you have time. My car's out of gas.

A: Yeah. Glad to. Let's go.

B: Thank you for everything.

Dialogue 2

A: What's the trouble, Mike? Need a hand?

B: I've got a headache, a sore throat and I'm coughing and sneezing constantly.

A: Do you feel a bit tired?

B: Not a bit tired but exhausted. My whole body feels weak. I really feel terrible.

A: Do you have a temperature?

B: I think so. I feel feverish.

A: I'm sorry to hear that. What can I do for you?

B: It's very kind of you. Could you help me to call Mr. Lee for a sick leave? I'm afraid I can't go to his class today.

Dialogue 3

A: Sorry to trouble you, but could you do me a favor? I want to borrow your laptop this afternoon to check some information.

B: I'm sorry, I'd like to, but I have to finish my term paper today.

A: Oh, I see. That's OK. Thanks anyway.

B: I wish I could help you. Say, what about tomorrow morning? I think I can finish the paper tonight.

A: Really? It's very kind of you. Thank you very much indeed.

Dialogue 4

A: Excuse me, Mrs. Johnson. May I ask you a question?

B: Yes, of course.

A: I didn't quite follow you when you were talking about the requirements of the paper. Could you please explain them again?

B: Sure. You are expected to write a reaction paper to one of the books you have been reading. The paper should be typed in double space. It should not exceed four pages in length, and the due date is next Wednesday.

A: Oh, I see. Thank you. I appreciate your help so much.

Dialogue 5

A: Good afternoon.

B: Hello. I want to know if you can help me. I've just arrived here and I'm looking for somewhere to stay.

A: Pardon?

B: Can you tell me where I can find a cheap hotel?

A: Certainly. There are a few around here, but the nearest and one of the nicest is just around the corner. It's called the Euro Hotel. Would you like me to phone to see if they have a room?

B: No, that's OK. I'll go there myself. Ah! One more thing, I need to change some travelers' money, but I don't know what time the banks close. Could you help me with that?

A: Yeah, they close at 7 o'clock in the evening.

B: Right, thanks. This is a very small town, isn't it? It looks very old. Have you got any idea how old this town is?

A: Yes, it was built in 1726.

B: Really? As old as that? Well, I'd better go now. Oh, I'm not sure if we're near the centre of the town, because I've only just arrived.

A: Yes, it is just about the centre.

B: Thanks for your help. I'll go to… oh, sorry, I can't remember the name of the hotel.

A: The Euro Hotel.

B: The Euro Hotel. Thanks a lot. Bye!

Dialogue 6

A: Could you do me a favor?

B: Sure. What can I do for you?

A: Well, I want to send this parcel to a friend, but I've no idea how to mail in China. Could you please help me with that?

B: With pleasure. As a matter of fact, I can manage it for you right now. Give me the address of the recipient, please.

A: Here it is. Thank you very much.

B: By the way, do you want to send it by ordinary mail or by air mail?

A: How long does it take by air?

B: About a week.

A: And by ordinary mail?

B: A month or so.

A: Well, I'll send them by air. How much for it?

B: I'm not sure. I'll give you a receipt later.

A: Thank you for all your help.

B: I'm delighted to be of any help.

Dialogue 7

A: Good morning. May I help you?

B: I wonder if you can give me more information about this computer model you're showing.

A: I'd be glad to help. Would you like a packet of our promotional literature?

B: Thank you, that's really useful.

A: Yes, and this model can run any software.

B: These models seem to be quite small.

A: Yes, one of the problems our company was trying to solve when we worked on this model was to do away with the bulk of some desktops. Our computer is only 11 pounds.

B: Remarkable! There's nothing quite like seeing a problem and solving it to create a good product. Are all the components made here in Shenzhen?

A: Yes, we do some subcontracting, but only in Shenzhen. These computers are made here. May I ask what company you work for?

B: I represent ABC Computer and Supply Company. We're a high-volume, discount mail-order house.

A: Would you like to tour our factory and perhaps visit one or two of our subcontractors?

B: Yes, if it wouldn't take too long to arrange. I'm due to fly back to the States on Wednesday.

A: I'm sure we can arrange it before then. How about meeting the founder of our company? Would you be interested in talking with him about our ideas for the upcoming models?

B: Yes, that would be useful. Thank you for your help again.

 Vocabulary

rush [rʌʃ] n. 匆促 v. 冲进	receipt [rɪ'si:t] n. 收据
checkbook ['tʃekbʊk] n. 支票簿	promotional literature 宣传推广资料
sneeze [sni:z] n. 喷嚏 v. 打喷嚏	bulk [bʌlk] n. 容积，体积
feverish ['fi:vərɪʃ] adj. 发烧的	desktop ['desktɒp] n. 台式机
exceed [ɪk'si:d] v. 超过，越出	remarkable [rɪ'mɑ:kəbl] adj. 显著的，值得注意的
length [leŋkθ] n. 长度	
recipient [rɪ'sɪpiənt] n. 接受者，收信人	component [kəm'pəʊnənt] n. 元件，组件
ordinary mail n. 平信	subcontract [ˌsʌbkən'trækt] n. 转包合同
	upcoming ['ʌpkʌmɪŋ] adj. 即将来临的

Useful Expressions

A. Asking for help

- Excuse me, could you...?
- Would you please lend me a hand?
- Do/Would you mind...?
- I'm sorry to trouble/bother you, but would you..., please?
- I wonder if I could...
- I'd like to ask you to help me with..., if you don't mind.
- Please help me with this letter.

- Can you do me a favor?
- Could I trouble you to shut the door?
- May I invite some friends over?
- Please oblige me by closing the window.
- Would you be so kind as to...?
- May I trouble you to...?
- Is it all right if I...?
- I'd like to ask you to... if it's not too much trouble.
- Perhaps you'd like to help me with...

B. Offering help

- May I help you?
- Want any help?
- Need a hand?
- Can I give you a hand?
- Can I offer you some assistance?
- Would you like some help?
- Is there anything I can do for you?
- Is there any way I could be of help?
- Let me help you with it.
- Let me do it for you.
- I'd like to give a hand with...

C. Appreciating help

- I appreciated your concern and help.
- I appreciated everything you did for me.
- Thank you for everything.
- This is for all the things that you have done for me.
- Thank you for your time and consideration again.
- Thank you. I appreciate your help.
- I am truly grateful for all your help.
- Thank you very much indeed.
- I'd be most grateful for your help.

Exercises

I. Complete the short dialogues by translating Chinese into English.

1	A: George, _____ (不知道你能不能借给我50美元)?	B: Sorry, I'm afraid I can't. I'm living from hand to mouth these days.
2	A: I want to buy a used house with two bathrooms. _____ (从哪里可以得到这方面的信息呢)?	B: You can buy a newspaper.
3	A: Good morning. May I help you?	B: _____ (我想开个账户).
4	A: Good morning, sir. _____ (我能为你做些什么)?	B: I'd like to deposit some money.
5	A: Judy, _____ (能帮我沏一下茶吗)?	B: No problem. Mum, I can't find the tea. Where is it?
6	A: _____ (能帮我照张照片吗)?	B: No problem.
7	A: Would you mind taking the parcel to the post office for me now?	B: _____ (恐怕不行), because I'm not going anywhere near the post office.
8	A: Would you mind buying some apples for me?	B: _____ (不，当然不介意).
9	A: Could you do me a favor and _____ (把这些书拿到我的办公室)?	B: Yes, with pleasure.
10	A: Need a hand?	B: Yes, _____ (能帮我翻译一下这句话吗)?

II. Complete the dialogues with the expressions given in the box, and then role-play with your partner.

Dialogue 1

> How do you want to do it   Can you do me a favor
> I want to put up some new beautiful curtains

A: I want to redecorate my bedroom, Tom. __1__?

B: No problem. __2__?

A: I want to make it more colorful and attractive.

B: Do you plan to repaint the wall?

A: Yes. Besides, ___3___.

Dialogue 2

> what's the postage   can I help you   send this letter by airmail

A: Good morning. ___1___?

B: I want to ___2___.

A: Yes.

B: I also want to know ___3___.

A: Well, I'll have to weigh your letter first.

Dialogue 3

> What's up   It's OK with me   Will you be able to cover for me while I'm on leave

A: Hey, John. Will you be at work this Friday?

B: No. ___1___?

A: I have to go to the airport to pick up my parents. ___2___?

B: Let me think. I will be free that day. ___3___.

III. Pair work: make dialogues based on the following situations.

1. Joan lost her purse after taking the subway. She goes to a police office to ask for help.

2. Charlie lost his way when he first arrived in the downtown. He's asking the way from a policeman.

3. Tony missed several classes because of his illness, so he asks his classmate Jack to help him.

4. Xiao Hong wants to borrow a book from the library, but she cannot find it. Now she is asking the librarian to help her.

IV. Topics for discussion.

1. If you run out of money, and you have to borrow some from your friend, what will you say?

2. Did you have the experience of offering help to others? Could you share the experience with us?

3. Why do you think helping others is important in one's life?

Culture Tips

When you ask for help, it is important to be polite. The intonation you use in making your request is as important as what you actually say. If you think someone might refuse your request, phrase your question in a way that avoids embarrassment for both of you. However, when you offer something to a westerner, remember it is important to understand how they accept or decline offers. Generally speaking, when a westerner says "no" to your offer, he/she means it. If a westerner offers you something, like a seat, he/she may do so only once. So if you want it, say "Thank you" or "You're so kind" and accept it.

Class Activities

The class will be divided into 10 groups. Each group will be assigned a place by the teacher and prepare a dialogue based on the information about the place. Then, each group takes turns performing the dialogue, and the other groups guess the name of the place.

思 政

A Dip into Chinese Wisdom

1. 同舟共济克时艰，命运与共创未来。

Pulling together through adversity and toward a shared future for all.

2. 大道之行，天下为公。

A just cause should be pursued for the common good.

3. 春蚕到死丝方尽，蜡炬成灰泪始干。

Spring silkworm till its death spins silk from love-sick heart;
A candle but when burned out has no tears to shed.

4. 远亲不如近邻。

Close neighbors are better than distant relatives.

SECTION I

Thanks and Gratitude
Unit 15

Lead-in

Do you think it is important to be grateful to others? Why do you feel grateful? You may use the following examples for help.

Examples:

I'm grateful because…

I feel (truly/deeply/extremely/overwhelmingly) grateful to… because…

Warm-up Activities

I. Read the following words and pay attention to the pronunciation of "ir".

[ɜː]　　firm　　sir　　bird　　circle　　dirt

II. Read the passage below and pay attention to your pronunciation and intonation.

We automatically say "thank you" because we have been taught that it is right. What that automatic response lacks is the feeling that it is genuine. It is time for our own sake and the sake of others to start saying "thank you" with a deep sense of gratitude (感恩) for what has been given to us.

It's easy because, at first, you don't have to be embarrassed about expressing gratitude to the universe. There are no words to memorize or audience to please. You can express gratitude in just a few minutes—anytime, anywhere. Say "thank you" for what you have previously taken for granted, for the commonplace (寻常事), and for the growth of your insight (见识) and experience. Say "thank you" for having two sound legs to walk on, eyes that can see, and people who love you. Moreover, if you don't have anyone who loves you, say "thank you" for the possibility of change, for a new day and for the opportunity to attract respect and good people into your life. Express gratitude for the job you hate (it helps you pay the bills), and for the opportunity to start a business of your own with some of the finest teachers and future colleagues. Express gratitude for the ability to wake up, think coherently, and experience the day. You will be surprised by what this simple act can do—first for yourself, and then for others. As you radiate gratitude, more grace will flow into your life.

 Dialogues

Dialogue 1

A: I really don't know how to thank you.

B: I'm glad I was able to help.

A: I don't know what I'd have done without your help.

B: Don't mention it. It was the least I could do.

A: Thank you so much. I'm really very grateful to you.

B: It was a pleasure.

Dialogue 2

Passenger: Hi! Could you please help me out? I need to catch the next train to Beijing, but I've no idea where to go.

Passer-by: Don't worry. Take the escalator. It's over there, to the lower level. Then enter the platform area and go to Platform Number 8. It's on the left side. You'll see the time schedule there, too.

Passenger: I see. Downstairs, Platform 8, on the left side.

Passer-by: Yes, that's right. Also don't forget to keep your ticket stub to show the ticket collector.

Passenger: Thanks a million!

Passer-by: It's a pleasure to have been of some assistance.

Dialogue 3

A: What's the matter?

B: There's something wrong with my camera.

A: Do you want me to have a look at it?

B: It's very kind of you, but I think I can manage.

A: Oh, well, if you need any help, just let me know.

B: I will. Thank you very much.

A: You're welcome.

Dialogue 4

A: I really like the cross stitch you brought me the other day.

B: Oh, don't mention it. I'm glad you like it.

A: The design is just so delicate and beautiful. Everyone in my dorm likes it very much.

B: I'm happy you like it. It's the gift for Thanksgiving Day.

A: I'm most grateful. It must be expensive. I don't know how to express my thanks.

B: You deserve it.

Dialogue 5

Lily: Hi, Mary.

Mary: Hello, Lily. How are you doing?

Lily: Fine, thanks. You know, I'm planning to take Listening and Speaking this semester. Can you recommend a professor?

Mary: Sure. I would recommend Prof. Ryan. One of my roommates attended his classes last year, and she said that he was one of the best professors for that course.

Lily: Good! Thanks!

Dialogue 6

Tom: Congratulations, Mr. Pitt. I've got the news that you won the Best Actor.

Brad: Thank you, Mr. Hanks.

Tom: I really feel happy for you. I know you deserve the honor.

Brad: It's very kind of you to say so.

Tom: I have watched many of your movies and I am very much impressed.

Brad: I owe much to your kind help and support, Mr. Hanks.

Tom: I'm sure you will have more wonderful performance in the next movie.

Brad: Thanks for your kind words. I'm looking forward to our cooperation in the future.

Dialogue 7

Ann: Maggie. I've come to say goodbye. I'm leaving tomorrow.

Maggie: Why so soon? Can't you stay a few days longer?

Ann: No. And I just can't leave without thanking you for all you have done for me.

Maggie: It's so nice to have had you here. It's a shame that you are leaving.

Ann: I enjoyed myself immensely. You made everything so glorious. I hope I can do something in return for you someday.

 ## Vocabulary

passer-by [ˌpɑːsə ˈbaɪ] *n.* 过路人，经过者 escalator [ˈeskəleɪtə(r)] *n.* 自动扶梯 platform [ˈplætfɔːm] *n.* 平台，月台 assistance [əˈsɪstəns] *n.* 帮助，援助 dorm [dɔːm] *n.* (集体)宿舍 deserve [dɪˈzɜːv] *v.* 应该得到，应受，值得	semester [sɪˈmestə(r)] *n.* 学期 shame [ʃeɪm] *n.* 羞愧，遗憾的事 　　　　　　　　　 *v.* 使羞愧 immensely [ɪˈmensli] *adv.* 极大地，无限地 glorious [ˈɡlɔːriəs] *adj.* 光荣的，辉煌的 in return 作为回报，作为报答

 ## Useful Expressions

A. Expressing gratitude

- Thank you.
- Thanks a million.
- Thanks so much.
- Many thanks.
- I can never thank you enough.
- I really can't thank you enough.
- I'm extremely grateful to you.
- Thank you ever so much.
- Thank you very much indeed.
- Much obliged.
- Much appreciated.
- It's very kind of you.

- It's so sweet of you.
- It was ever so nice of you.
- I'm very much indebted to you.
- That was extremely good of you to…
- I do appreciate your…
- It's very good of you to…
- You're very kind.
- You're just wonderful.
- I should like to express how grateful I'm for…
- You're very thoughtful.
- It's most thoughtful of you.

B. Responding to thanks

- That's all right.
- That's OK.
- No problem.
- It's all right.
- Think nothing of it.
- Not at all.
- No bother at all.
- No trouble at all.
- You're welcome.
- My pleasure.
- It's a pleasure.
- Pleasure was all mine.
- Delighted I was able to help.
- Delighted to have been of some help.
- It's a pleasure to have been of some assistance.
- I'm glad to be of some assistance.
- At your service.
- I'm glad to have been of some service.
- Any time.
- I'm very glad you enjoyed it.
- It was the least I could do.
- You would have done the thing in my position, I'm sure.

 **Exercises**

I. Complete the short dialogues with the expressions given in the box.

A. Thanks. It's a birthday gift from my sister.
B. Thank you. I will try my best.
C. Thanks. I've already got two other guys. But thanks for offering.
D. It was my pleasure. Keep up the good work.
E. Not at all. I hope you'll come and see us again soon. Drop in anytime you feel like it.

1. —Good luck with your exam. I'm sure you will do great.
   —_____

2. —Do you need help cleaning this weekend?
   —_____

3. —Wow, your hat is so smart.
   —_____

4. —Thank you very much for the excellent tea.
   —_____

5. —I couldn't have done it without your help. I really appreciate it.
   —_____

II. Complete the dialogues by using the expressions of thanks learned in this unit.

1. **Mary**: You're a great dancer, Bob! I wish I could do half as well as you!
   Bob: _____.

2. **Peter**: Sam, your photographs are unbelievable! I really wish you'd give me some advice to help my pictures come out better.
   Sam: _____.

3. **A**: What a pretty necklace you have!
   B: _____.

4. **A**: Excuse me. Could you tell me the way to the library?
   B: Sorry, I'm new here, too.
   A: _____.

5. **A**: I'm looking for the recent edition of the Oxford Idioms by the Foreign Language Teaching and Research Press.

B: Let me see.... I'm sorry we don't have any more in stock.

A: _____.

III. Act out the following pictures with your partner(s). Use the expressions for expressing and responding to gratitude that you have just learned.

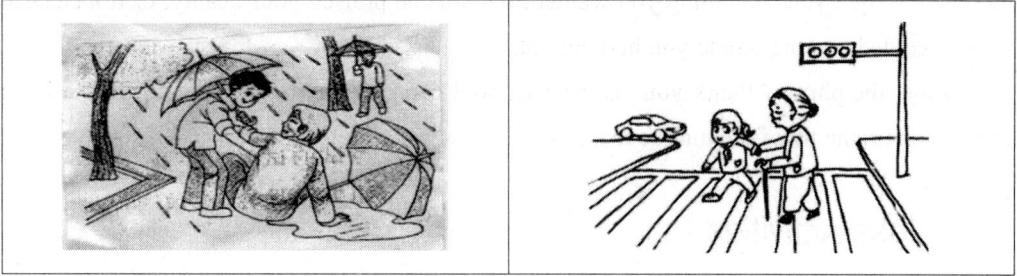

IV. Pair work: make dialogues based on the following situations.

1. Thank a librarian for his/her help in finding the book you want to borrow.
2. Thank your classmate for helping you with your studies.
3. Your mobile phone is powered off. Thank your friend for lending his/her phone to you.
4. Something dropped out of your pocket. Thank a stranger for reminding you to pick it up.

V. Topics for discussion.

1. There are many holidays that people use as opportunities to express gratitude. Can you list these holidays and identify who you should thank and how to do so?
2. Tell your classmates about the person you are most grateful to, and explain why.
3. Describe situations in which we need to express our gratitude.

Culture Tips

Expressions of gratitude and thanks are found in every culture. It is common to say "Thank you" for an invitation, a present, an offer of help, etc. Although some native English speakers have the reputation of being informal in their conversations, they are accustomed to using a set of behaviors and speech patterns that are culturally defined as polite.

Differences arise between the Chinese and English-speaking people in that we Chinese do not use "thank you" so frequently among family members or very intimate friends as westerners do. If one should do so in China, it might sound strange or suggest a remote relationship.

However, native English speakers say "thank you" in nearly every situation, no matter how minor or routine it is. When someone, no matter who he/she is, does something for you, however trivial it is, it is proper to say "thank you". For example, you would say "thank you" in any one of the following occasions: if someone picked up and handed to you something you had dropped; if a stranger showed you the way to go; if even a quite young family member brought you something you wanted; if someone praised your beauty; or if a clerk in a store handed you the article you had bought.

Often, the phrase "thank you" is used without carrying any deep meaning. It is a mere expression on the tip of the tongue to show courtesy.

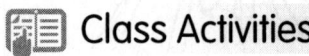 Class Activities

Thank You

Work in pairs. Take it in turns to thank each other for:

A lovely present

A timely warning

A kind invitation

A piece of good advice

A generous offer of money

A good book to read

 思 政

A Dip into Chinese Wisdom

1. 不忘初心，方得始终。

To accomplish our great mission, we must always remain true to our original aspiration.

2. 谁言寸草心，报得三春晖。

Such kindness as young grass receives

From the warm sun can't be repaid.

3. 滴水之恩，当涌泉相报。

Receiving drips of water when in need, and I shall return the kindness with a spring.

4. 最强大的力量是同心合力。

The biggest strength comes from cooperation.

SECTION I

Saying Goodbye
Unit 16

Lead-in

Do you think it's hard to say "goodbye" all the time? When you have to say "goodbye", how do you express it? Discuss with your partner. You may use the following examples for help.

Good luck and a pleasant journey to you. / Have a nice trip! / Take care! / See you then…

Warm-up Activities

I. Read the following words and pay attention to the pronunciation of "or".

1. [ɜ:]   world   word   work   worm   worse
2. [ɔ:]   born   torn   worn   dorm   formal
3. [ə]   forget   forbid   forgive   forsake   doctor

II. Read the English version of the famous poem by Xu Zhimo— *Saying Goodbye to Cambridge Again*, and pay attention to your pronunciation and intonation.

Saying Goodbye to Cambridge Again

Very quietly I take my leave
As quietly as I came here;
Quietly I wave goodbye
To the rosy clouds in the western sky.

The golden willows by the riverside
Are young brides in the setting sun;
Their reflections on the shimmering waves
Always linger in the depth of my heart.

The duckweeds growing in the sludge
Sway leisurely under the water;
In the gentle waves of Cambridge
I would be a water plant!

That pool under the shade of elm trees
Holds not water but the rainbow from the sky;
Scattered among the duckweeds
Is the sediment of a rainbow-like dream.

To seek a dream? Just pole a boat upstream
To where the green grass is more verdant;
Or to have the boat fully loaded with starlight
And sing aloud in the splendor of starlight.

But I cannot sing aloud—
Silence is my farewell melody;
Even summer insects keep quiet for me;
Silent is Cambridge tonight!

Very quietly I take my leave
As quietly as I came here;
Gently I flick my sleeves—
Not even a wisp of cloud will I bring away!

 Dialogues

Dialogue 1

A: Are you going away on holiday tomorrow?

B: No. I'm traveling on business.

A: How long will you be away?

B: About two weeks this time.

A: I wish you a pleasant journey.

B: Thank you. Goodbye.

Dialogue 2

A: I'm afraid I must be leaving now. It was nice to talk with you.

B: Why so soon? It's still early.

A: Well, I have to attend a meeting.

B: OK, in that case, I won't keep you. Goodbye.

A: Bye.

Dialogue 3

A: I really appreciate talking to you. It's time for me to say goodbye.

B: So soon. It seems as if you just got here.

A: Yes. So glad to be with you. I've had a delightful time and it was really fun for me.

B: I feel that too. It gave me a chance to get away from my routine and do something just a little bit different.

Dialogue 4

A: Thank you for seeing me off.

B: Don't mention it. It's my pleasure.

A: You really did me a great favor when I was working for you.

B: You're welcome. That is what I should do.

A: Anytime you drop by, please don't forget to call me. I'll do whatever I can for you.

B: Thank you. I'll be looking forward to that.

A: It's time to board the plane. Hope to see you again. Goodbye.

B: Goodbye. Have a good journey.

Dialogue 5

A: How time flies! I've been in China for almost a year.

B: Sure. I didn't even realize your departure was imminent.

A: Thank you very much for giving me so much help during my stay here. Without your help, I would never have achieved so much.

B: I've really done nothing. It is your own efforts that have made your stay so fruitful.

A: It's been a really amazing experience. I hope we will meet again some day in the future.

B: I hope so too. Let's keep in touch.

A: OK. Goodbye.

B: Goodbye, and have a safe trip!

Dialogue 6

A: Good evening, Mr. Smith. It's very kind of you to invite me to dinner tonight.

B: Good evening. Sit down, please.

A: Thanks. So you are leaving tomorrow?

B: Yes.

A: It's a pity you are leaving so soon.

B: Well, life is just like that.

A: We'll miss you after you leave.

B: Me, too. I could stay a few days longer with you.

A: I hope you'll come to China again.

B: I'm sure I will. Oh, here's a small gift for you. Thank you for everything you've done for me during my stay here.

A: It's very kind of you to say so. I hope you enjoyed your trip in China.

B: Oh, yes. It was excellent. I visited different places, which has helped me to get to know a lot more about China and Chinese people. I can see your country is growing fast. I'm sure I'll come back some day in the near future.

Dialogue 7

Jack: What a surprise! Fancy seeing you here! Where are you going?

Bill: We've just arrived here. Laura, look who's here! Jack, this is my wife, Laura.

Jack: How nice to meet you, Laura. I remember Bill writing to me about you.

Laura: Hello, Jack. I've heard a lot about you, too.

Jack: Never imagine seeing you here. I can't believe it. I can't help remembering the old days. Let's have a drink together.

Bill: OK, but we only have half an hour.

Jack: Where are you going?

Bill: We come here to attend a trade fair for a month.

Jack: That's wonderful! How's Beijing?

Bill: Changing all the time. But you'd still recognize it. What's new about you?

Jack: I'm married, and have two children. Mary is seven and John is five.

Bill: That's great.

Jack: Oh, I'm afraid it's time for me to board the plane.

Bill: We'll be flying back to Beijing in a week. This is my address. Come to see us then.

Jack: All right. See you two in Beijing.

Bill and Laura: Goodbye. Have a good journey.

Vocabulary

routine [ruːˈtiːn] n. 例行公事，常规 board [bɔːd] v. 登 (飞机、车、船等) imminent [ˈɪmɪnənt] adj. 逼近的，即将发生的	fancy [ˈfænsi] v. 喜爱，想要，爱好 trade fair 商品交易会 recognize [ˈrekəgnaɪz] v. 认出，认可

Useful Expressions

- I really must be leaving.
- I'd better be off now.
- I think I should be on my way now.
- I really got to go now.
- Well, I'd be getting on my way right now.
- It's been really nice seeing you again.
- I had a good time.
- Thank you for your hospitality.
- It's a pity that I am at the end of my trip.
- All the best.
- Be in touch.
- Have a nice and safe journey/trip (home).
- Farewell! I hope we will meet again soon.
- Give my love to your daughter.

- All the best regards to your family.
- Goodbye and see you again next time.
- Goodbye then, and all the very best.
- I'm really going to miss you.
- Look forward to seeing you again soon. Bye!
- Mind how you go. Bye!
- Regards to Mary.
- Say hello to your uncle.
- See you soon!
- Take care. Bye!

Exercises

I. Fill in the blanks with the words and expressions given in the box to make the dialogue complete and logical.

A. hospitality   B. are unable to   C. contact you   D. I must go now   E. see me off

A: It's very kind of you to ___1___.

B: My pleasure. I'm sorry you ___2___ stay in Guangzhou a little longer.

A: I feel sorry, too. Thank you for your ___3___.

B: It's my pleasure. What's your flight number?

A: Flight No. 810. Oh, they're announcing my flight. ___4___.

B: Goodbye. Have a good flight.

A: Goodbye. I'll ___5___ again.

II. Complete the sentences with the Chinese given.

1. —Well, I'm afraid I must be going now. I have to attend a meeting. But it was nice to talk with you.
   —I enjoyed talking with you, too. Come and see me again _____ (当你有时间的时候).

2. —I really think I should be going now. I had no idea it was so late.
   —Don't let me _____ (留下你). It was very nice of you to come to see me.

3. —Would you like some tea?
   —I'd like to, but I _____ (有个约会) at 5 o'clock.

4. —It's very kind of you to come and _____ (给我送行).
   —Happy journey and _____ (祝你好运).
5. —_____ (我现在要走了). Would you please bring down my suitcase?
   —Yes, just a moment. I'll take it for you right now.

III. Pair work: make dialogues based on the following situations.

1. Mr. Smith has stayed in Beijing on business for a week and he is now returning to New York. You, as his colleague in Beijing, are seeing him off at the airport.

2. Imagine you're going to graduate from college. You come to say goodbye to your teacher.

3. Your foreign teacher Juliet has taught you for one term and she is going back to the U.S. tomorrow. Say goodbye to her.

IV. Topics for discussion.

1. What kind of occasions do you think are really hard to say goodbye on?
2. Describe a moving goodbye scene you've ever experienced.
3. If you have a chance to go abroad to further your studies, who do you think is the first person you'll say goodbye to, and why?

Culture Tips

Saying goodbye in the West is a little bit conventionalized. Westerners tend to add some introductory remarks as a way to lead into the real farewell, like "I'd better be going now, as I don't want to get caught in the rush hour." or "I'm afraid I must be going now, since I've got a class." After these remarks, they may get ready to leave. This approach shows their politeness and avoids appearing rude. Moreover, when they say goodbye, they really mean it. In such cases, the hosts could respond with "Thank you for coming", "It was a pleasure meeting you", or "Hope to see you again soon".

Class Activities

Saying Goodbye

Work in groups. Every student expresses how happy he/she has been with his/her classmates and teachers throughout the term and then says goodbye to them one by one.

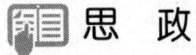 思 政

A Dip into Chinese Wisdom

1. 百年成就使人振奋，百年经验给人启迪。

The CPC's 100-year achievements provide a source of motivation and its 100-year experience a wellspring of inspiration.

2. 野火烧不尽，春风吹又生。

Fire tries to burn them up in vain,

They rise again when spring winds blow.

3. 故人西辞黄鹤楼，烟花三月下扬州。

My friend has left the west where the Yellow Crane towers

For River Town green with willows and red with flowers.

4. 莫愁前路无知己，天下谁人不识君。

Fear not you've no admirers as you go along.

There is no connoisseur on earth but loves your song.

SECTION II

Holidays
Unit 1

 Lead-in

What's the customary way to spend a special holiday? Discuss it with your partner. You may use the following examples for help.

It's customary to… in… holiday. / To celebrate the… holiday, we usually…

 Warm-up Activities

I. Read the following words and pay attention to the pronunciation of "ur".

1. [ɜː]   fur   blur   hurt   turn   purchase
2. [ə]   assure   pastureland   insure   resurrect   leisure

II. Read the passage below and pay attention to your pronunciation and intonation.

How Chinese Spend Their Holidays

People have adopted a new concept of rest and entertainment for their holidays. They now have a wide range of options to help them enjoy their time off to the fullest extent, from parties at home to travelling on organized tours.

In the past, most Chinese people chose to use their time off to strengthen their relationships by visiting families and friends. This is still a popular way to spend the holidays today. But growing numbers of people are packing their bags and setting off to explore the beautiful scenic spots scattered around the country.

Others are choosing to spend their time at the gym, a sign of the growing health consciousness across China. A number of women have flocked to take yoga classes at fitness clubs over the holidays. Some literary folk prefer to spend their holidays recharging their batteries through reading.

Besides all the above-mentioned, there are quite a few homebodies who prefer to stay at home and catch up on TV episodes or much-needed sleep.

 Dialogues

Dialogue 1

Monica: So, Dennis. What are you going to do on New Year's Day?

Dennis: I'm going to have dinner at my parents' house. What about you? Any plans?

Monica: Yeah. I'm going to Washington to meet my parents and friends there.

Dennis: Oh, that's a great plan.

Monica: Yes. And every year, my parents and I make some different food and take pictures together to celebrate the New Year.

Dennis: That sounds like fun. Well, Happy New Year!

Monica: Thanks. You too.

Dialogue 2

Amy: Do you know something about the Dragon Boat Festival? I heard it is coming.

Sue: Yeah. I got something from *China Daily*. The Dragon Boat Festival falls on the fifth day of the fifth month on the Chinese lunar calendar. This festival has a history of about 2,000 years and is said to commemorate a patriotic poet named Qu Yuan.

Amy: Oh, I didn't know that. Are there any activities held during this festival?

Sue: Yes, a dragon boat race is held every year, especially in Zigui County, Hubei Province. Besides, people made Zongzi, an indispensable and traditional food for Dragon Boat Festival.

Amy: Oh, that must be delicious. I really hope I can have a chance to try it.

Dialogue 3

Jason: Merry Christmas, Professor Li!

Prof. Li: Oh! Hi. Season's greetings!

Jason: There are a lot of people here.

Prof. Li: Yeah, every year is just like this. You know, I'm in a hurry. I've got to buy several gifts today. This is the season to be jolly.

Jason: Yes, but it's hard to be jolly in a crowded department store like this.

Prof. Li: That's true. Oh, sorry. I'm afraid I must be going now. Have a good holiday!

Jason: The same to you.

Dialogue 4

A: What do you usually do during the Lantern Festival?

B: We prepare Yuanxiao, which is a delicacy that resembles a miniature full moon. We also watch beautiful lantern displays at night and guess lantern riddles.

A: Guessing lantern riddles? That sounds interesting!

B: Yeah, there are also some folk performances, such as stilt walking.

A: That sounds difficult to perform.

Dialogue 5

A: What's the biggest holiday in China?

B: The Spring Festival. That's the Chinese Lunar New Year, about one month later than the Western New Year, you know, which is just as important as Christmas in your country.

A: That's fascinating. How do you celebrate it? Are there any special traditional customs?

B: Well, as it's the right time for family reunions, everyone stays at home with their family, having a big feast on New Year's Eve, watching the CCTV Spring Festival Gala, and setting off firecrackers, etc.

A: Amazing! It's really a great holiday.

B: Definitely! Especially for the children, because they all dress up in their best clothes and can get lucky money from the adults.

A: Well, sounds interesting!

Dialogue 6

(Elaine and Li Hong are talking about the coming of the Mid-Autumn Festival.)

Elaine: Hong, what holidays do you have in China?

Li Hong: Well, there are so many. We have holidays almost every month. For example, the Mid-Autumn Festival, also called the Moon Festival, is just in this month.

Elaine: Yes, I have heard a lot about it these days. I was told that mooncakes are traditional food for the festival, because they're round cakes shaped like a full moon.

Li Hong: Exactly! Chinese people enjoy mooncakes during this festival, just as they eat Zongzi during the Dragon Boat Festival.

Elaine: Oh, that sounds interesting!

Li Hong: Yep! It is believed that the moon is the brightest and roundest on that night, and that's why it is also called the Moon Festival.

Elaine: Oh, really poetic! I can't wait to enjoy the moonlight!

Dialogue 7

A: What's your favorite festival?

B: It's the Mid-Autumn Festival.

A: It's a very important festival for us Chinese.

B: Yes, it is. It is a special holiday for family reunions, and I can eat mooncakes and enjoy the moon with my family. What about you?

A: My favorite festival is the Spring Festival. You know, my hometown is far from here. During the Spring Festival, I can go back to my hometown and stay with my parents for several days.

B: How long is your Spring Festival holiday?

A: 7 days.

B: Oh, that's great. That's enough time for you to go back.

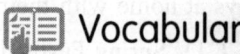

Vocabulary

Chinese Lunar New Year 中国农历新年 gala ['gɑːlə] *n.* 盛会，庆典 (the Spring Festival Gala 春晚) traditional [trə'dɪʃənl] *adj.* 传统的 poetic [pəʊ'etɪk] *adj.* 诗的，诗意的 legend ['ledʒənd] *n.* 传说	celebrate ['selɪbreɪt] *v.* 庆祝，庆贺 lunar ['luːnə(r)] *adj.* 阴历的 calendar ['kælɪndə(r)] *n.* 日历，历法 relate [rɪ'leɪt] *v.* 使有联系，有关联 riddle ['rɪdl] *n.* 谜，谜语

 Useful Expressions

A. Holiday greetings

- Wishing you all the best and Happy Holidays!
- Wishing yours is filled with fun and good cheer!

- Wish your home and heart is filled with the warmth of this holiday season.
- From the staff at ABC company, we wish you all the best for the festive season!
- Wish you a New Year that's sparkling with fun, bursting with joy, crackling with laughter.
- Hope you get all that you've been wishing for. Happy birthday!
- Though I am far away from you on this very special day of your life, my heartfelt wishes and thoughts make the distance insignificant. Happy Birthday dear!
- Hope you look back and feel proud of all you have achieved, look ahead at all that you are aiming for! Happy birthday!

B. Talking about holiday plan

- How are you going to spend the holiday?
- How do you celebrate the New Year's Day?
- What's special about this festival?
- I have some plans of travel for the coming holiday.
- We have 10 days off for our annual holiday.
- Where did you go for your holiday?
- Did you have a nice holiday?
- What do you usually have for Christmas dinner?

C. Holiday description

- Sunday is a holiday.
- The summer holidays begin.
- They had a five days' holiday.
- They had a five-day holiday.
- They had a holiday of five days.
- She is on holiday in France.
- I spent my holiday in the village.

 Exercises

I. Fill in the blanks according to the examples given below.

Examples:

When's Chinese New Year's Day? It's in January or February.

What do people usually do on Chinese New Year's Day?

They usually pay a new year call and eat dumplings.

1. When's Dragon Boat Festival? It's _____.
   What do people usually do during Dragon Boat Festival?
   They _____.
2. When's Mid-autumn Festival? It's _____.
   What do people usually do during Mid-autumn Festival?
   They _____.
3. When's Lantern Festival? It's _____.
   What do people usually do during Lantern Festival?
   They _____.
4. When's _____? It's in June.
   What do you usually do _____ summer holiday?
   We _____.

II. Describe the holidays you've filled in Exercise I to your partner based on the clues below.

— The holiday is in/on… (season/date). / The holiday falls on…

— The holiday originated from…

— People usually eat…

— People usually do…

— My favorite holiday is… and that's because…

III. Pair work: make dialogues based on the following situations.

1. Maggie is talking about the origin of Halloween with Li Ming.

2. Sherry is talking with her boyfriend Jeffrey about how to spend the coming Valentine's Day.

3. Tony asks Wang Ting about the traditional festivals in China.

IV. Topics for Discussion.

1. Talk about an unforgettable experience during a specific festival.

2. Talk about the difference(s) between a traditional Chinese festival and a western festival.

3. How do you think Chinese people spend the traditional western festivals?

Culture Tips

Labor Day is on May 1st. It is a national holiday in more than 80 countries in the world. It originated from a strike in Chicago in America. On May 1st, 1886, more than 200,000 workers in Chicago struck for the implementation of an eight-hour workday and finally won. In July 1889, the second International Congress, led by Engels, designated May 1st the "International Labor Day". In December 1949, China designated May 1st as a national holiday. Different countries celebrate May 1st in their own ways.

 Class Activities

Let's Guess

The class will be divided into 10 groups. Each group will be assigned a festival by the teacher and prepare five sentences to describe the festival. Then each group takes turns to present the five sentences to the whole class, and the other groups will guess the name of the festival.

 思 政

A Dip into Chinese Wisdom

1. 中华优秀传统文化是中华民族的根和魂。
China's excellent traditional culture is the root and soul of the Chinese nation.
2. 独在异乡为异客，每逢佳节倍思亲。
Alone, a lonely stranger in a foreign land,
I doubly pine for my kinsfolk on a holiday.
3. 爆竹声中一岁除，春风送暖入屠苏。
With crackers' cracking noise the old year passed away;
The vernal breeze brings us warm wine and a warm spring day.
4. 常常做，不怕千万事。
Make constant efforts and one will not be intimidated by a thousand tasks.

SECTION II

Parties
Unit 2

Lead-in

Below is a list of wine or alcohol that people usually drink at parties. How many of them do you know?

beer 啤酒	red wine/port 红葡萄酒 / 红酒
draft beer 生啤酒	sherry 雪利酒
stout beer 黑啤酒	champagne 香槟酒
canned beer 罐装啤酒	cocktail 鸡尾酒
gin 杜松子酒	martini 马提尼酒
brandy 白兰地酒	punch 潘趣酒
whisky 威士忌酒	vermouth 味美思酒 / 苦艾酒
vodka 伏特加酒	rose liquor 玫瑰酒
rum 朗姆酒	cider 苹果酒
light beer 淡啤酒	liquor/spirit 烈性酒
white wine 白葡萄酒	Scotch 苏格兰威士忌

Warm-up Activities

I. Read the following words and pay attention to the pronunciation of "are".

1. [eə] prepare   share   hare   stare   care

2. [ɑ:]   are

II. Read the story below and pay attention to your pronunciation and intonation.

Last week, we went to the countryside to have a picnic. We bought some sandwiches, fruit and water to take with us for lunch. We started out quite early before there was too much traffic. After 2 hours of driving, we came to a nice place, which is near a river with some large trees beside it. As it was a very hot day, we parked the car under a big tree, and went for a swim in the river, the water was refreshing. After having a swim, we had lunch in the cool shade under the trees. Then we went for a walk. We saw some beautiful birds and butterflies. After walking for about an hour, we returned to the car, however, we couldn't get the car started. Finally we had to push the car to the road and wait for help. Of course, the car breaking down ruined our picnic in the end.

 Dialogues

Dialogue 1

A: Hello. It's a pleasure to see you again.
B: Thank you. I've been looking forward to your party.
A: You'll have a drink, won't you?
B: I think I'll have a beer, if you have any.

Dialogue 2

Rose: You guys finally made it!
Mike: Thank you.
Billy: Yeah, Rose, thanks a lot.
Rose: My pleasure. What fun is a party if no guys show up?
John: True, but I really appreciate what you have done for us.
Rose: Don't mention it. Any friend of Mike's is a friend of mine. Hey, that's a nice tie, is it a clip-on?
John: No, I tied it myself. Do you really like it?
Rose: Yeah, and the stripes make you look taller.
John: Thanks.
Mike: Come on, John, Rose's my date. Let me talk to her a little. Why don't you and Billy go and meet some nice girls?
Billy: That's not what I want to do here.

Rose: You devil. I know what kind of girls you like.

Billy: Then introduce me a couple of them.

Rose: I'm sorry, Billy, but you'll just have to be content with one tonight.

Billy: Whatever you say, where is she?

Rose: Give me a second and I'll find someone.

Billy: OK, but only one second.

Dialogue 3

A: Mrs. Charles, I've been trying to figure out when to hold the New Year's party. Could you make a time schedule?

B: Sure. Either the twenty-eighth or the thirtieth of this month is fine.

A: Well, let's make it on the thirtieth. We can set it up from three to five. In that case, everybody can just go home afterwards.

B: Sounds good to me. You make up the invitations. I have to go. I will have a meeting in ten minutes.

Dialogue 4

(At a reception party)

A: Mr. Zhang, welcome to visit our company. Please allow me, on behalf of our company, to extend a warm welcome and sincere greetings to you all. Just feel at home and tell us if you have any trouble.

B: Thank you. I really appreciate what you have done for us.

A: It is our honor to have you here. It is a big event for us to sign the contract today.

B: Yes, exactly. I believe we two companies will have a deeper cooperative relationship in the future.

A: At this point, I propose a toast: to the cooperation between us, cheers!

B: Cheers!

Dialogue 5

(Today is Mary's birthday. She is going to hold a birthday party at home.)
(The doorbell rings)

Mary: (Opens the door) Ahh, Shelly, Mike, come in, please! Glad you can come!

Shelly, Mike: Happy birthday to you, Mary.

Mary: Come in, please.

Shelly: A music box for you.

Mary: Thank you. Wow, great! I love it.

Mike: Here is a present for you. I hope you like it.

Mary: (Opens the bag and sees the gift) Thank you, sweetie. Oh, it is a nail polish! It's lovely! You know I've been expecting this for a long time.

Mike: I'm very glad to hear that.

Nina: Hi, everybody, welcome to Mary's birthday party. We will sing Happy Birthday song first and then we share the birthday cake. Don't be shy and sing loud, and then we can play some games. Now Mary, come to the middle, everybody just make a circle, are you ready? Let's sing "Happy birthday to you..."

All: (Sing) "Happy birthday to you ..."

(Mary blows out all the candles on her birthday cake at one go.)

Shelly: Congratulations and warmest wishes for your birthday and every day.

Mike: Many happy returns of this special day. All our best wishes go to you on your birthday.

Nina: We all wish you a very happy birthday and many years of health and prosperity.

Dialogue 6

(At a wedding party)

Lucy: It is a grand wedding, isn't it?

Peter: Sure it is. I am happy to see Jack and Daisy get married.

Lucy: So am I. They've been in love for ten years.

Peter: That's not what I mean. I'm glad Daisy is the bride and you are the bridesmaid.

Lucy: Don't talk nonsense.

Peter: I'm serious. There were times when I thought you would marry Jack.

Lucy: This isn't the right time to discuss this. Here come the bride and the groom.

(Peter, the best man, stands up)

Peter: Hi, everybody! I am Peter, the best man. Today I am so excited to witness my two friends become a couple. I never knew two people better suited to each other. It's only once in a lifetime that a special dream comes true. And suddenly your entire world seems beautiful and new. Best wishes always! Jack, I have to say you're the luckiest guy in the world.

(All applaud)

Peter: Next the bridesmaid will offer her congratulations.

Lucy: Thank you, Peter. First, I'd like to give my sincere congratulations to the couple. I'm so happy for you both. The groom is truly lucky, because he is marrying such a lovely girl. I'd like to propose a toast to the happy couple. Congratulations!

(All stand up and drink)

(During the party)

Daisy: Lucy! So you're here with Peter. I've been looking all over for you.

Peter: Congratulations, Jack.

Jack: Thank you. Did you enjoy yourself?

Peter: Yes, a nice wedding party. Have you opened the gift I gave you?

Daisy: Yes, thank you very much. Las Vegas is a nice place for honeymoon.

Lucy: What did he give you as a wedding gift?

Daisy: Two plane tickets to Las Vegas. I want to thank you as well, Lucy. I love the watches. They are exactly what we wanted.

Lucy: I'm glad you like them.

Daisy: Lucy, I'm glad you've come. I'll call you when Jack and I come back from our honeymoon.

Jack: Thank you for coming.

Dialogue 7

(At a graduation party)

A: Dear graduates! Today is a big day to celebrate your graduation. After you leave here, you will be well-prepared for any endeavor you choose. Have faith in yourself, and a bright future is ahead of you. Just enjoy your big day and this grand party.

(All applaud)

B: Wow, time flies! We're graduating today!

C: Definitely. Four years!

B: Oh, would you like a drink?

C: No, thanks. I prefer a cup of coffee.

B: How about your job? I ran into Mr. Li the other day, and he told me you were having an interview from IBM. Is that true?

C: Yes. Yesterday I just got the offer, but it's just a low position.

B: Oh, I'm delighted to hear it. Please accept my congratulations. I knew it would be only a matter of time before your extraordinary abilities were recognized. IBM is a large company, so I think you will gain valuable experience from the job.

C: That's very nice of you to say. How about you?

B: I plan to go abroad to pursue my doctoral degree.

C: Really? Congratulations!

B: Thanks.

Vocabulary

be content with 满足于（以……为满足） figure out 想出 on behalf of 代表，为了 feel at home 畅快，自在 propose [prə'pəʊz] v. 提议 at one go 一次（一气，一举）	grand [grænd] adj. 壮丽的，重大的 bridesmaid ['braɪdzmeɪd] n. 伴娘 delighted [dɪ'laɪtɪd] adj. 高兴的，快乐的 pursue [pə'sju:] v. 追求；从事 prosperity [prɒ'sperəti] n. 繁荣，兴旺

Useful Expressions

A. Proposing a toast

- At this point, I propose a toast: to the cooperation between… and…, to the health of Senator…, cheers!
- Lastly, I propose a toast to…, bottoms up!
- I'd ask you to raise your glass and join me in a toast to the health of all our friends present here.
- Here's to you!
- Let's drink a toast to our friendship.
- Let's get our minds off work and have a good time.
- Let's forget about work and have some fun.
- Let's take our minds off work.
- Here's to the health of our friends!
- Here's to your health/success.
- Here's to our friendship!
- Here's to Tom for his new job!
- Friends, I'll give you a toast—to our president!
- I now propose a toast to the friendship between our two people—to our friendship.
- Cheers!
- Let's make a toast.
- Let's drink to your health.

B. Extending welcome

- I wish to extend my warm welcome to you.
- Allow me, first of all, to extend my warm welcome to the Chinese Delegation who

has been invited to this country by our company.

- On behalf of the Textiles Corporation, I wish to warmly welcome you, Mr. Smith, and all the members of the Canadian Mission Delegation.
- It is a great pleasure for me to preside at this dinner given by our trade mission in honor of the Chinese foreign trade officials.
- On behalf of the Beijing Municipal government, I wish to extend our warm welcome to the friends who have come to visit Beijing.
- I'll surely remember you and your invitation to him.
- American businessmen are welcome to make investment in Beijing.

 Exercises

I. Give possible answers for the requests.

1. Propose to a couple.

   a. _____

   b. _____

   c. _____

2. Wishes for a person in his birthday party.

   a. _____

   b. _____

   c. _____

3. Extend welcome to foreign guests.

   a. _____

   b. _____

   c. _____

4. Comments on a party.

   a. _____

   b. _____

   c. _____

5. Comments on different alcohol at a party.

   a. _____

   b. _____

   c. _____

II. Choose the appropriate expressions in the box to fill in the blanks.

A. Just blow out the candles and open the gifts.
B. But we have some traditional ways to celebrate it.
C. Why peach?
D. That's interesting!
E. Someone is celebrating his birthday.
F. 21 is the age when you're allowed to drink.
G. Longevity noodles will be prepared by parents.
H. No doubt about it.
I. It is said that Longevity Peaches express people's wish to live longer.
J. Your friends will take care of everything.

May: Look! What are they doing? __1__

Jimmy: This must be his 21st birthday. __2__

May: Why? Do you know that guy?

Jimmy: No. Well, in America, __3__ So, many guys celebrate it in the bars.

May: That's interesting. But it would be really expensive, I suppose. Just think about all the drinks.

Jimmy: No. If it's your birthday, then you don't need to pay a cent. __4__ That makes the birthday a special day. __5__

May: Wow. That's wonderful.

Jimmy: What about in China? What do you do to celebrate your birthday?

May: Nowadays, it's changing a lot. __6__

Jimmy: Oh, Anything special?

May: __7__ And Longevity Peaches will be made for old people.

Jimmy: Longevity Peaches?

May: Yes! But they are not real peaches. They are made of wheat flour, just like real peaches.

Jimmy: __8__

May: It's like this.

Jimmy: Oh. __10__

III. Complete the short dialogues by translating Chinese into English.

1	**Sam**: How are you doing, Van? _____ (感谢你的光临).	**Van**: I'm fine, Sam. _____ (谢谢您的邀请).

2	**Sam**: Dinner is ready, _____ _____ (请入席吧). Van, this is your seat. Sit down, please.	**Van**: Sam, _____ _____ (这是我第一次看到这么多的特色菜). Thank you.
3	**Sam**: What do you like to drink, Maotai or wine?	**Van**: _____ (茅台酒性太烈). Just a glass of wine, please.
4	**Sam**: I am glad we have signed the contract today.	**Van**: Now, _____ _____ (为我们的合作和友谊干杯).
5	**A**: Mr. William, _____ _____ (让我为您介绍我的太太，简).	**B**: Nice to meet you.
6	**A**: _____ _____ (这个聚会好极了).	**B**: _____ (很高兴您玩得开心).
7	**A**: Would you like something to drink?	**B**: Yes, _____ (给我来一杯白葡萄酒吧). Thank you.
8	**A**: Well, _____ _____ (您太太今晚不能来真是太遗憾了). I understand that she had to leave town for business.	**B**: Yes, unfortunately.
9	**A**: Well, _____ _____ (真是太巧了)! Our youngest goes to the same school as your daughter.	**B**: Really? We can introduce them to each other.
10	**A**: _____ (你有时间可以加入我们).	**B**: I'd love to.

IV. Pair work: make dialogues based on the following situations.

1. Zhang and Li used to be college classmates. Now they meet at an office party. Zhang introduces a job to Li.

2. At a cocktail party, Jack shows great interest in Nancy's friend Beth. He asks Nancy to introduce Beth to him. At last Jack gets Beth's phone number.

3. At Ming's birthday party, his girlfriend gives him a gift.

4. At a celebration party for a TV series, the director thanks all the actors and actresses.

V. Topics for discussion.

1. Do you like to celebrate your birthday with your family or your friends?

2. How do you like to celebrate your birthday?

Culture Tips

Party tricks are usually the key to amazing others at a party in a western country. Most party tricks are simple but fun, and people are proud of their unique tricks, which they'd love to show to others. Many people spend a lot of time learning new party tricks. Here is an example.

Press a coin into the middle of your forehead until it sticks to it. Then lean your head forward, and tap the back of your head until the coin falls into your hand. This trick is very easy to master with a little practice!

Now ask one of your friends if they would like to try it. Press the coin onto their forehead, but sneakily remove the coin so they will think it's still there.

Class Activities

Your Hero

Everyone names one hero, who can be anyone, dead or alive. Imagine these people are on a boat that is going to sink. Some of them have to be thrown overboard so that the boat can be safe. Provide reasons for not throwing your hero overboard.

A Dip into Chinese Wisdom

1. 做青年朋友的知心人、青年工作的热心人、青年群众的引路人。

Devote great energy to the work related to youths, and serve wholeheartedly as their confidant and their guide.

2. 正是江南好风景，落花时节又逢君。

Now the southern scenery is most sweet,

But I meet you again in parting spring.

3. 正有高堂宴，能忘迟暮心？

A banquet is held in the hall;

The guests forget their spring and fall.

4. 相见时难别亦难，东风无力百花残。

It is difficult for us to meet and hard to part;

The east wind is too weak to revive flowers dead.

Entertainment
Unit 3

Lead-in

What do you like better when you have spare time, watching TV or films? Discuss it with your partner. You may use the following examples for help.

A: I prefer TV to films, because it's more colorful and has more programs to choose.
B: I like films better. They're short and the film stars are very beautiful.

Warm-up Activities

I. Read the following words and pay attention to the pronunciation of "ere".

1. [eə] there   where
2. [ɪə] here   mere   sincere   sere   severe
3. [ə]   were

II. Read the story below and pay attention to your pronunciation and intonation.

    A great and venerable director unexpectedly dies when he is in his prime. He is called home to heaven. An angel meets him at the gate. "So sorry about your untimely death," he tells the director. "But God himself has called you home. You see, God wants you to direct a movie for Him." The great man is humbled.

"God wants ME to direct a film?" he asks. "Yes," the angel tells him, "and we've arranged to have the best of everything made available to you. For example, the script is by William Shakespeare." The director is stunned. "By William Shakespeare?" he asks. " Yes," the angel says, "and it's his greatest work ever. " "Wow!" says the director, and he is awestruck. "We've also got Leonardo da Vinci doing the sets. Your musical score will be an original work by Wolfgang Mozart, and your cast includes the greatest actors and actresses of all time." The director can't believe it. " This is incredible," he says. "This will be the greatest movie ever!"

"Well," the angel says, "we do have one tiny little problem." "Problem?" says the director. "What kind of problem?" The angel puts his arm around the director's shoulder, "You see," he whispers, "God's got this girlfriend…"

Dialogues

Dialogue 1

Thomas: I've heard *Avengers : Age of Ultron* would be on next Saturday. I want to see it.

Mary: Is it a horror movie?

Thomas: No, it isn't. But I love horror movies the most. Would you like to go with me next weekend?

Mary: OK, why not!

Thomas: Great. What kind of movies do you like?

Mary: Let me see. Romance, comedy, documentary, action, science fiction, cartoon and so on.

Thomas: How about horror movies?

Mary: Never!

Thomas: I also like romance and comedy movies very much.

Mary: We could find some other time to see a comedy.

Thomas: That's a wonderful idea!

Dialogue 2

Richard: Li Hua, could you come here for a second? Do you know what is on the TV?

Li Hua: It's called "Beijing Opera". It's basically a kind of Chinese opera, which is also called "National Opera" in China.

Richard: I can't understand it at all. What are they talking about?

Li Hua: I'm not sure. This program doesn't have closed captions. You know, the actors sing in a special way and use traditional Chinese music in the background.

Richard: They painted their faces. It looks interesting.

Li Hua: Yeah, in Beijing Opera, different roles call for different makeup, costumes, and voices. The different colors used in the painted faces indicate different characteristics of personality, and different colored clothes show different social ranks.

Richard: Oh, I see. It's quite different from western opera.

Dialogue 3

Ted: Would you like to try any extreme sports?

Sarah: What kind of extreme sports?

Ted: Bungee jumping, skydiving, and cliff diving are the most common, but there are other kinds of sports, such as motor racing and skateboarding.

Sarah: Bungee jumping looks like fun. It makes me nervous just to watch someone do it. It certainly takes a lot of guts to jump several hundred feet above the water with only a rope tied to your legs. It scares me just to think about it.

Ted: Bungee jumping might seem frightening, but it is a very safe activity if you go to a well-established bungee jump company. But people who have high blood pressure or a heart condition should not try bungee jumping.

Sarah: In bungee jumping, people of different weights should use different equipment, which is very important for their safety.

Ted: Yes, you're right. However, it is something I really want to do one day. It is said that when you bungee jump, you leave all the stress and negative thoughts behind, and you come back up with a new mind. But if you do not feel like experiencing it yourself, you can always watch other people jump.

Dialogue 4

Susan: David, I am so excited because we have finished our project! We should take our colleagues out to celebrate this Friday.

David: Yes, the project was a big success. How about holding a party?

Susan: I have a suggestion here. Why don't we go to a KTV and sing?

David: A KTV? Are you serious?

Susan: Yes, why not? Don't you like KTVs?

David: I don't know. I never went to one.

Susan: Never? Really? I'm surprised. Karaoke has become a major entertainment.

David: I don't know. How much fun is there in singing in front of other people, especially if you don't sing well?

Susan: Ah, that's the biggest fun of all. Singing songs loudly can make you feel relaxed and happy. You should try it.

Dialogue 5

Steven: So, you'll have seven days off. What are you going to do?

Lucy: I don't know. Probably I'm just going to hang around here and relax.

Steven: Watch TV, huh?

Lucy: Not just TV. I will probably watch some movies with Lisa. We can eat some snacks. Just relax.

Steven: You couch potatoes! That's pathetic.

Lucy: Huh? What do you mean "pathetic"? What's wrong with it?

Steven: Spending seven days like that! It's boring and meaningless!

Lucy: Hey, listen, I just want to relax.

Steven: Of course. But you should have better recreation than TV.

Lucy: Yeah? Like what?

Steven: You should get out of the house. Go out into nature. Or you should learn to play an instrument or something. Or learn to draw. Those things can be meaningful.

Lucy: OK, I'll think about it.

Dialogue 6

Linda: Do you buy that newspaper every day or just Sunday?

James: I have it delivered every day. I find it very informative.

Linda: How do you like this newspaper?

James: I should say it's quite a read! It always has plenty of articles from correspondents all over the world and the business section is very useful too.

Linda: What sections does it have?

James: Let me see. It has the news section, the entertainment section, sports, business, and world affairs. And I can find some local news ignored by the local TV news and barely covered on websites.

Linda: What's in that section?

James: World affairs. The most important stories are so widely covered and reported in such details. I find it fascinating. Do you buy a daily paper?

Linda: I don't like reading newspapers. I read most of the news online now. I still watch news program on TV at night time which is more timely than the newspaper.

Dialogue 7

Susan: I'm thinking about getting a pet. I want to keep a cat or a dog, but I'm really not sure which would be more suitable. Could you give me some advice?

Frank: Certainly! The first thing is how much time you can devote to your pet? You see, dogs are very demanding. You need to take them for walks and they love to play. Cats, on the other hand, are more independent.

Susan: I'm not very busy. I like having a pet in my home.

Frank: OK. Cats are better for cuddling, and I like the feeling when a cat sits on my lap.

Susan: But people often say that dogs have more of a personality and they're more attached to their owners.

Frank: Yes, sometimes they feel more like best friends. But dogs require a lot of training, exercise, and a lot of your time in general. They like being with people.

Susan: I see.

Frank: And cats enjoy lounging around the house and usually don't want to be around you. It matters if you like playing around or sleeping and resting.

Vocabulary

recreation [ˌriːkriˈeɪʃn] n. 消遣，娱乐
romance [rəʊˈmæns] n. 浪漫史，传奇文学
documentary [ˌdɒkjuˈmentri] adj. 文献的 n. 纪录片
closed caption （又称 CC）隐藏式字幕
costume [ˈkɒstjuːm] n. 服装，剧装
personality [ˌpɜːsəˈnæləti] n. 个性
gut [gʌt] n. 胆量，魄力
frightening [ˈfraɪtnɪŋ] adj. 令人恐惧的，引起突然惊恐的
couch potato n. 整天坐着看电视的人，电视迷

karaoke [ˌkæriˈəʊki] n. 卡拉 OK
pathetic [pəˈθetɪk] adj. 悲哀的，可怜的
correspondent [ˌkɒrəˈspɒndənt] n. 通讯记者，通信者
entertainment [ˌentəˈteɪnmənt] n. 娱乐
fascinating [ˈfæsɪneɪtɪŋ] adj. 迷人的
timely [ˈtaɪmli] adj. 及时的，适时的
cuddle [ˈkʌdl] v. 抚抱，拥抱
lap [læp] n. 大腿，膝盖
attach [əˈtætʃ] v. 附上，使依恋
lounge [laʊndʒ] v. 闲逛

Useful Expressions

A. Seeing a movie

- Would you like to see a movie?
- What do you say to going to a movie?
- What's on tonight?
- What movie do you want to see?
- What's your favorite kind of film?
- Who is in this movie?
- How long does it last?
- What time/When is the next showing?
- What time does it start/begin?
- What time will it end/be over?
- Do you like detective/romance/horror/documentary/action/science fiction/cartoon films?
- I bet the movie will soon become a box-office hit.
- That was boring/dull, wasn't it?
- I was moved.
- It touched me.
- It was a touching movie.
- I will be scared out of my wits.
- That film almost frightened me to death.
- I don't care for a detective film.
- I don't quite follow the plot.
- This movie was a box-office triumph.

B. Watching TV

- Please turn on the TV.
- What's on the TV?
- What's showing on Channel 5?
- How many channels can you get on that set?
- Which channel is that?
- How many hours do you watch TV each day?
- What's your favorite TV program?
- Do you know what is on the TV?

- What channel did you watch last night?
- What kind of TV programs do you like best?
- Please turn to Channel 4.
- Can we change the channel?
- Shall we switch to another channel?
- Some of the TV soap operas are boring, while others are very interesting.
- Which channel is this TV series on?
- The TV programs will be off the air in 20 minutes.
- The opening ceremony will be televised live through telstars.
- What's on the tube?
- Let's watch the movie on Channel 6.
- This is a repeat. I've seen it before.

C. Going to KTV

- Have you ever been to a karaoke bar?
- Have you ever sung with a karaoke?
- Let's go to karaoke.
- Here is the song list.
- You sing the bass so well.
- Your falsetto was so well controlled.
- Sorry, I'm tone-deaf.
- Are you good at singing?
- I'd like to request a song.
- Go ahead.
- What are you going to sing?
- Let's sing a duet.
- I don't have the nerve/guts to sing in front of people.
- I can't keep up with / keep track of the new songs.
- I can't learn the new songs fast enough.
- I have no ear for music.
- My singing is out of tune.
- What's your karaoke specialty?
- What's your best song?
- Which songs do you sing best?
- I've never heard of that song.

- You're a good singer!
- You sing very well!

D. Reading newspapers and magazines

- What's the most popular paper/magazine circulating in this community?
- Do you know the circulation of this paper/magazine?
- Who finances this newspaper/magazine?
- How would you comment on this paper?
- When was the newspaper/magazine first issued?
- Is the news in the paper reliable?
- Do you really believe what they say?
- Do you think it's a bit conservative?
- I find it very informative.
- What sections does it have?
- The news stories are usually truthful and accurate.
- It's all propaganda.
- The same old stories, nothing special.
- Do you prefer reading newspapers or reading news online?
- The news online attracts me more, because the pictures in it are colorful.
- An article in *China Daily* caught my attention.

Exercises

I. Match the English equivalents to the names of movies or programs in Chinese (there are three options that you don't need).

A — *The Dream Factory*
B — *Infernal Affairs*
C — *A World Without Thieves*
D — *American Beauty*
E — *Beyond the Sea*
F — *The God Must Be Crazy*
G — *Forrest Gump*
H — *The Mask*
I — *Brave Heart*
J — *Air Force One*
K — quiz show
L — variety show
M — sitcom
N — talk show
O — comic sketch

Examples: (N) 脱口秀　　　(J)《空军一号》

1	( ) 小品	6	( ) 《勇敢的心》
2	( ) 《上帝也疯狂》	7	( ) 《甲方乙方》
3	( ) 《变相怪杰》	8	( ) 情景喜剧
4	( ) 《天下无贼》	9	( ) 《无间道》
5	( ) 《海底总动员》	10	( ) 《美国丽人》

II. Complete the short dialogues by translating Chinese into English.

1	A：_____（你看哪个频道了）last night?	B：Channel 6. _____（一部电影）named *My People, My Country* was showing now.
2	A：What kinds of TV programs do you like best?	B：_____（综艺节目和访谈节目）, I think.
3	A：This dance music is too fast. We'd better dance later.	B：Alright... Listen, the music is changing. _____（节奏正适合我们）. May I, Miss?
4	A：I haven't seen _____（故事精彩、演技高超的好电影）for a long time.	B：I'm of the same opinion. It is said that _____（这部电影打破了以往的票房纪录）.
5	A：What kind of music do you like listening to?	B：I like _____（节奏轻快活泼的音乐）, like dance music.
6	A：Well, overall, I'm a little disappointed with the movie.	B：But you have to admit that _____（特技棒极了）, and the acting wasn't bad either.
7	A：I think Chinese characters look very artistic. It's said that _____（从写字的方式可以看出艺术家的性格）.	B：I think _____（任何优秀的艺术品都是如此）.
8	A：How about a lizard? I have some that are very brightly colored, not aggressive, and _____（容易喂养和照看）.	B：That sounds ideal. Could you show me some?
9	A: Nowadays, _____（蹦极运动已经成为全世界流行的一种极限运动方式）.	B：Some people think it's crazy. _____（过短暂而刺激的生活比过漫长却无聊的日子好得多）.

| 10 | A: It's difficult _____ _____ (找到四个人一起玩桥牌). | B: Do you know anyone who plays? If so, we could set up a game. |

III. Complete the dialogues with the expressions given in the box.

Dialogue 1

> You got it all right   Nearly everything
> Too easy questions   I can examine you by questions

A: How much do you know about Hollywood?

B: ___1___.

A: You are just boasting. ___2___. What is Hollywood? Where is it? What is the function of it?

B: ___3___. Listen carefully. Hollywood is the movie capital of the world. It's located in southern California. Many films have been made there.

A: Pretty good. ___4___.

Dialogue 2

> try something different   also makes me nervous
> are natural and cheerful   almost frightened me to death

A: Would you like to go to the cinema this evening?

B: Well, I saw a horror movie last night. It ___1___.

A: Maybe next time you should ___2___, like a detective film.

B: I don't care for a detective film. It ___3___.

A: How about a comedy?

B: No, I don't think comedies today ___4___.

A: How about a love story, then?

B: No, romance is boring. I like science-fiction films best.

Dialogue 3

> I'm pretty good at poker It looks complicated
> I'm terrible at cards The basic rule and moves are simple enough

A: Do you know how to play Chinese chess?

B: I've never played Chinese chess before, but I've seen old men playing it in the street. ___1___.

A: It's about as complicated as chess. ___2___, but there are many strategies that players need to learn.

B: I like playing cards. ___3___. Do you play cards?

A: ___4___ and I never play games which involve gambling, like poker. If I did, I'd lose all my money.

IV. Pair work: make dialogues based on the following situations.

1. Describe a recent movie you saw to your partner and tell your partner what you think of the movie.

2. Compose a dialogue talking about going to KTV to sing songs this weekend.

V. Topics for discussion.

1. How do you like to relax? What's your favorite way to relax?
2. Do you think it's important to have leisure time every day?
3. In your spare time, what do you usually do with your friends or family?

 Culture Tips

Hollywood

Hollywood is a neighborhood located in Los Angeles, California, surrounded by mountains. It is also synonymous with the American film industry. As a world-famous movie center, the Academy Awards (奥斯卡) ceremony held there every year is a grand gathering of world movies.

Hollywood is not only the birthplace of the film industry, but also home to many famous television and movie studios and record companies, such as DreamWorks, The Walt Disney Company, 20th Century Fox Film Corporation, Columbia Pictures, SONY Pictures Entertainment, Universal Pictures, Warner Bros., Paramount Pictures, etc.

Hollywood is home to many of the world's top directors, screenwriters, stars and stuntmen. People are deeply impressed by the stunning visuals, memorable characters, and compelling plots of the movies. As a paradise for filmmakers, Hollywood has also attracted a lot of Chinese stars and directors, such as Bruce Lee, Jackie Chan, Jet Li, Chow Yun-fat, Gong Li, Li Bingbing, Zhang Ziyi, etc.

One of the most important attractions in Hollywood is Grauman's Chinese Theater, which opened in May 1927. It was named for its distinctive Chinese-inspired architecture. The handprints and footprints of famous stars attract tourists from all over the world. Many famous Hollywood movie stars, such as Shirley Temple, Denzel Washington, Tom Hanks, Harrison Ford, Mel Gibson, Tom Cruise, Arnold Schwarzenegger, and Michael Jackson, have left their handprints and footprints here. Even Donald Duck has left his lovely footprints here.

 Class Activities

Karaoke

There are some English songs that are easy to understand and somewhat enjoyable.

1. You will be divided into groups of 4 or 5.

2. Every group will have a different song. Figure out all the words to the song. Make sure it is a group effort, not just one person doing the work.

3. You will have a certain amount of time to work on it. In the next class, you can return to the group to practice the song once. Then the whole group stands up and sings along with the recording.

 思 政

A Dip into Chinese Wisdom

1. 没有全民健康，就没有全面小康。

Prosperity for all is impossible without health for all.

2. 业精于勤，荒于嬉。

Excellence in work is possible only with diligence and wasted upon recklessness.

3. 一张一弛，文武之道也。

Labor and leisure should both be emphasized.

4. 儿童散学归来早，忙趁东风放纸鸢。

After-school kids come home early,

keen to fly kites while East Wind's spry.

SECTION II

On Campus
Unit 4

📖 Lead-in

Practice the following with your partner.

Q: Do you know the full name of your college?
A: The full name of our college is …
A: I come from Peking/Tsinghua University.

Q: What's your major?
A: My major is… / I'm majoring in…

📖 Warm-up Activities

I. Read the following words and pay attention to the pronunciation of "ire".

[aɪə]   fire   hire   expire   tire   require

II. Read the story below and pay attention to your pronunciation and intonation.

A professor was giving a big test one day to his students. He handed out all of the test papers and went back to his desk to wait. Once the test was over, the students all handed the test papers back. The professor noticed that one of the students had attached a $100 bill to his test paper with a note saying, "A dollar per point." In the next class, the professor handed the test papers back out. This student got back his test paper and $58 change!

 Dialogues

Dialogue 1

David: How do you spend your spare time?

Lily: I enjoy reading in the library. I also like to play table tennis and badminton with my friends. Sometimes I also surf the Internet. I think my college life is rather wonderful!

David: Are there any unions in your university?

Lily: Sure. There are many organizations in our university, such as the poetry, movie, music and dance clubs. I am a member of the Movie Club. I like watching movies and discussing ideas about movies with my friends in the club.

David: That's very good. I also want to join a club. I like dancing very much.

Dialogue 2

Jim: You are late again.

Louisa: I forgot to turn on the alarm clock last night.

Jim: It's just an excuse. It's not the first time you overslept.

Louisa: Yes, I know it's my mistake. I was busy finishing my paper, so I stayed up late.

Jim: Do you mean the paper for English short story?

Louisa: You are right. It is quite hard for me. I did a lot of research on it.

Jim: I quite agree with you. But you shouldn't leave work until the last minute.

Louisa: I'm not good at time management. I should make a schedule for my study.

Jim: Time management is very important in college life. By the way, early to bed and early to rise makes a man healthy.

Louisa: Thank you for your advice. I won't be late again.

Dialogue 3

Peter: Congratulations! I heard you got the full scholarship next semester.

Angela: Thank you very much.

Peter: You work very hard every day. You deserve it.

Angela: It's very kind of you. I think you can apply for the scholarship, too.

Peter: Really? Could you tell me how to apply for it?

Angela: Of course. First, you need to know what are the qualifications for the scholarship.

Peter: What are they?

Angela: It's a little complicated. You can check the school website. There are detailed instructions about it. If you have questions, you can always come to me.

Peter: OK. I'm going to the library. Do you want to go with me?

Angela: OK. I will check out some books, too.

Dialogue 4

Vivian: Do you want to join the Students' Union?

Nick: No. I have no time to do that kind of things. How about you?

Vivian: I'm very interested in it. Maybe it will be helpful to get a job after graduation.

Nick: You must have good academic records to win a position in the Students' Union.

Vivian: That's no big deal. Anyway, I can see I am a good student.

Nick: What on earth are you interested in joining the union?

Vivian: No other special reasons. I just want to make me more competitive in the future.

Nick: When is the Students' Union election?

Vivian: Next Friday.

Nick: Oh, I see. I can go there and vote for you.

Vivian: Thanks a lot.

Dialogue 5

Sarah: Do you know how many classmates can finally get their diploma?

Nathan: What do you mean?

Sarah: I heard that some of our classmates wouldn't be able to graduate.

Nathan: Oh, no. Is it because they haven't got enough credits?

Sarah: Yes. Daniel is one of them and he is ready to drop out.

Nathan: He shouldn't give up. How can he survive without a university diploma?

Sarah: Yes, I think so. I think he should take a make-up exam.

Nathan: Daniel should keep taking classes until he gets enough credits. I think he can make it.

Sarah: Yes, let's have a talk with him.

Nathan: OK, let's go together.

Dialogue 6

Karl: You wanted to see me, Mr. Wright?

Mr. Wright: That's right. We need to have a serious talk.

Karl: I'm sorry. Did I make some mistakes?

Mr. Wright: Your attendance—rather, lack of it.

Karl: OK, so I've missed classes for a few times.

Mr. Wright: A few times? I've been told you've missed five out of ten times in two different classes! That's really setting yourself up to fail.

Karl: I'm terribly sorry. I found a part-time job last month. I'm a little busy these days.

Mr. Wright: Doing a part-time job is not wrong. However, you should balance your study and job well. After all, study is your most important task now.

Karl: Thank you for your advice. I will talk with my boss and see if I can change the working time.

Mr. Wright: You'd better do that. Missing too many classes will get you into big trouble.

Karl: Well, I see. I will try my best to balance work and study. Thank you very much.

Mr. Wright: You are welcome. Please attend class on time next time.

Dialogue 7

Rachel: Jordan, how is your life in your college?

Jordan: Until now, pretty good.

Rachel: How do you think of the dining hall in your college?

Jordan: I have dinner in the dining room every day. We have different kinds of food to choose. I think the food there is delicious and nutritious.

Rachel: That's nice. I really hope the chef in our canteen can put more oil and seasoning in our food. That will make them taste much better.

Jordan: I heard that a new canteen has been open in your school.

Rachel: Yes. You see, the food there is really tasty. How about going there for lunch?

 Vocabulary

appreciate [ə'priːʃieɪt] v. 欣赏，感激 concentrate ['kɒnsntreɪt] v. 集中，专心 deserve [dɪ'zɜːv] v. 值得，应受 qualification [ˌkwɒlɪfɪ'keɪʃn] n. 获得资格 scholarship ['skɒləʃɪp] n. 奖学金 academic [ˌækə'demɪk] adj. 理论的，学术性的	competitive [kəm'petətɪv] adj. 竞争的，比赛的 diploma [dɪ'pləʊmə] n. 文凭 credit ['kredɪt] n. 学分 drop out 退出，退学 survive [sə'vaɪv] v. 生存，生还 make-up ['meɪk ʌp] n. 补考 attendance [ə'tendəns] n. 出席

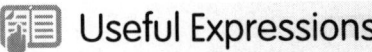 Useful Expressions

A. Talking about study

● Which is the most famous discipline in your college? / Which branch of learning is your college most famous for? / What is the most competitive major of your college?

● How many courses are you going to take this semester? / How many courses are you going to choose this semester?

● How many credits do we need to get the degree? / What are the required credits for the degree? / How many credits are needed for the degree?

● There are a variety of models of instructions at college.

● Students' grades are evaluated according to their regular performance and their performance in the tests.

● Taking notes won't work for me because I can't write very fast.

● I heard you would get full scholarship next semester.

● How did you do on your midterm/final exam?

● It's an open-book test.

● I think he should take a make-up exam.

B. Talking about extracurricular activities

● What do you do after class?

● What are your extracurricular activities? / Are you busy after class? / Do you join the clubs? / Do you take part in the after-class activities? / Do you participate in the volunteers' activities?

● There are many organizations in our university.

● I earned money to pay my tuition. / I work part-time to pay my tuition. / I take a part-time job to cover my expenses.

● — How do you like the college life?
　— It's rich and varied.

● Do you want to join the Students' Union?

C. Talking about facilities

● Can you tell me where the teaching building/listening lab/library/playground is?

● There are many football/basketball courts/gyms in our school.

● It's really a pretty campus with all these big trees and red brick buildings.

● It's an ideal place to study.

- What do you think of the dining hall in your college?
- Our new campus is well-equipped.
- We have different kinds of food to choose.
- How do you like your dormitory/roommates?

Exercises

I. Do you know the names of the facilities below? Write down the names on the line and then read them aloud.

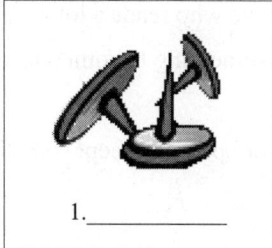
1._____

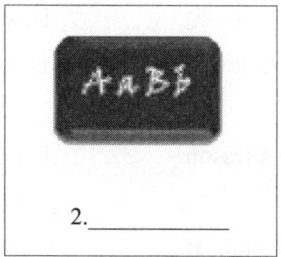
2._____

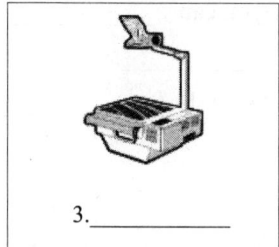
3._____

4._____

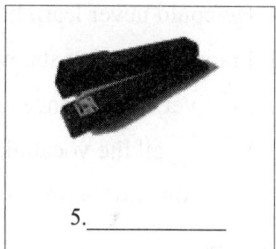
5._____

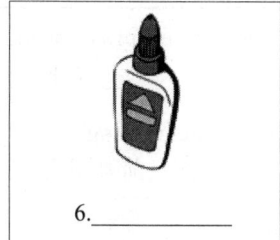
6._____

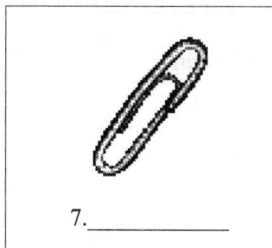
7._____

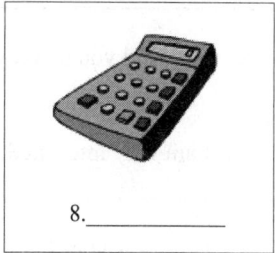
8._____

9._____

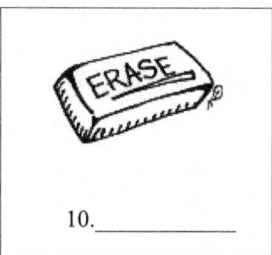
10._____

II. Do you know the following idioms? Match the meaning with them, and then fill in the blanks with the appropriate ones.

A.

1. bookworm
2. learn something off by heart
3. learn your lesson
4. live and learn
5. teach an old dog new tricks
6. teach someone a lesson

A. to suffer a bad experience and know not to do it again
B. no matter how old you are, you should learn all the time
C. to learn something in such a way that you can say it from memory
D. someone who reads a lot
E. to do something to someone, usually to punish him
F. make old people accept something new

B.

1. He's always reading. He's a real _____.
2. He could never learn how to use the Internet. Just show you can't _____.
3. I never knew that she was married. Oh well, you _____.
4. I got very drunk once and was really sick. I won't do it again, I _____.
5. I _____ all the vocabulary _____.
6. I hit him hard on the nose. That _____.

III. Complete the short dialogues by translating Chinese into English.

1	A：How did you do on your midterm?	B：Please don't tell anyone. I'm so embarrassed; _____ (不及格).
2	A：I am very interested in my major.	B：I know it's very demanding, _____ (而且前景相当不错).
3	A：How was your first class?	B：Pretty good. _____ (老师是我见过的最棒的一个).
4	A：_____ (玛丽作业得了全优).	B：She works very hard. Every time I see her, she's bending her head over books.
5	A：Excuse me. _____ (我能保留这些书多长时间)?	B：Our _____ (借书期限) is three weeks. If you cannot finish reading by then, you can _____ (续借) for another three weeks.

6	A: You'll pass the final exam.	B: _____ _____ (问题是我上个星期缺了两天的课).
7	A: _____ _____ (我要在三周内完成四篇研究报告). Help!	B: You're not alone.
8	A: I'm afraid the answer to your problem isn't in any of our textbooks, _____ _____ _____ (不过只要一点小小的常识，可能就可以协助你过关了).	B: I'm afraid I don't have much common sense, or I could figure out what to do on my own.
9	A: _____ _____ (你想看一下我的宿舍吗)?	B: Of course, I'd like to.
10	A: All right. It's _____ _____ (开卷考试).	B: I'm afraid I can't even answer these questions with the textbook.

IV. Pair work: make dialogues based on the following situations.

1. Charles and Laura are classmates. Charles doesn't know which selective course to choose and he needs Laura's advice.

2. Jane is a freshman. One day she met a sophomore, Bruce, on campus, and she asks Bruce about whether she should take part in the Student Union.

3. Cecilia wants to borrow books from the library. Make a dialogue between Cecilia and the librarian.

4. Tony and Danny are talking about their coming final exam.

V. Topics for discussion.

1. Do you have any suggestions for students who want to live a happy college life?

2. Nowadays, there usually exists a wide selection of electives for college students to choose from. What's your opinion about this?

3. What's your major? Why did you choose this major?

4. Do you think in college, study still plays an important role?

Culture Tips

Schools in the U.S.

In the United States, children start school when they are five years old. In some states, they must stay in school until they are sixteen. Most students are seventeen or eighteen years old when they graduate from secondary school (high school).

Most children go to public elementary and secondary schools. The parents of public school pupils do not have to pay for their children's education, because taxes support public schools. If a child goes to a private school, his or her parents have to pay for the child's education.

Today, about half of the high school graduates go on to colleges and universities. Some colleges and universities receive financial support from the government. A student at a state university does not have to pay very much if his or her parents live in that state. Private schools are expensive, however. Almost half of the college students in the US work while studying. If a student's family is not rich, he or she has to make money for part of the college expenses.

Most schools begin in early September and end around the middle or end of June. Classes are held Monday through Friday, with Saturday and Sunday free. However, some high schools and most universities have Saturday classes.

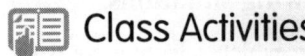 Class Activities

Lost on a Barren Island

A group of people were abandoned on a barren island. Then they made a small boat, with which they could escape from the island. But they were allowed to take only six items from the following list:

A bar of chocolate

50 meters of nylon rope

A knife

A torch

A tent

A cellular phone

9 gallons of water

Petrol

Alcohol

Blankets

Candles

Matches

A computer

Work in a group of six classmates. Have a discussion within the group and decide which six items you should take and give the reasons.

A Dip into Chinese Wisdom

1. 志存高远方能登高望远，胸怀天下才可大展宏图。

Only those aim high would scale the heights and look afar, and only those with a global vision would achieve great success.

2. 读书破万卷，下笔如有神。

Ample reading produces fluent writing.

3. 知之者不如好之者，好之者不如乐之者。

They who know the truth are not equal to those who love it, and they who love it are not equal to those who delight in it.

4. 百年大计，教育为本。

Education is the foundation of national development in the long run.

SECTION II

Renting an Apartment
Unit 5

📖 Lead-in

What factors influence you to choose a rental house? Discuss it with your partner. You may use the following examples for help.

I prefer to live in a quiet place where I can spend my time thinking and relaxing.

I think I'd like an apartment with a large balcony, because I like growing flowers.

I would like to live/an apartment in…

I like living/an apartment in… better than…

I don't think I like living/an apartment in…

I enjoy living…

I prefer to live… rather than live/an apartment in…

I think I'd like living/an apartment in… because…

📖 Warm-up Activities

I. Read the following words and pay attention to the pronunciation of "ore".

[ɔː]   score   more   before   tore   explore

II. Read the story below and pay attention to your pronunciation and intonation.

I carried all my stuff into the hall.

"What will you do?" my landlady peered at me over the top of her spectacles and asked.

"I'll leave, Mrs. White," I answered.

"Why?" she asked. "You have been here only a week."

"A week is too long, Mrs. White," I said. "There are too many rules in this house. My friends never dare to visit me. Dinner is always at 6 o'clock, so I frequently go to bed hungry. You hate noise, so I scarcely listen to the radio. The heating system often doesn't work, so I always feel cold. This is a terrible place for a man like me. Goodbye, Mrs. White!"

 Dialogues

Dialogue 1

Kate: What kind of place should we rent?

Mary: As long as it's close to the university, so we don't have to get up so early.

Kate: Absolutely. I don't really care about the size of the apartment.

Mary: Neither do I. So a small place is OK, but we'll get a bigger one if it's not too expensive.

Kate: Good. Let's go to the real estate agent and see what they can offer us.

Dialogue 2

Andy: I've been told you might have a vacant apartment.

Landlady: Yes, I have a spare apartment. Please come in.

Andy: The room here looks to the south, with a view of the garden. Not bad. But I'm afraid it's not big enough to be a sitting room. How much is the rent?

Landlady: No hurry. Let's talk about it later. Are you married?

Andy: Yes.

Landlady: How many children do you have?

Andy: Not a single one.

Landlady: Well, I would like someone like you to be our tenant. The moment I saw you, I knew you were a decent young man.

Andy: Did you? Then how about the rent, please?

Landlady: $200 a month. How about it?

Andy: You've got to come down a bit.

Landlady: I can't. Nowadays, the cost of everything is rising... All right, make it $190. You may move in any time. You haven't got bits of heavy furniture to move, have you?

Andy: No. Except a heavy piano.

Landlady: What? You have a piano!

Andy: You see, my wife is a pianist, while I am an amateur singer myself.

Landlady: Oh, young man. In that case, I'm afraid I can't let you have these rooms. We'd like to keep this house quiet. You see, I just can't stand noise of any kind.

Dialogue 3

Mark: I need to find a new place to live.

Jim: Yeah? Why? Don't you like living with me?

Mark: Oh, it's not you. I just want my own place.

Jim: Well, check the newspapers.

Mark: I didn't realize a one-bedroom apartment would cost so much these days.

Jim: Yeah, prices have really gone up in the past couple of years.

Mark: Oh, here's one. It looks like it's in this neighborhood, $360 a month. That's not too bad.

Jim: No, it's pretty good. Why not give the landlord a call?

Dialogue 4

Mark: Hello. May I speak to Mr. Sawyer?

Landlord: This is Tom Sawyer speaking.

Mark: I'm calling about the one bedroom in Brook Park. Is it still available?

Landlord: Yes, it's still for rent.

Mark: The rent is $360 a month?

Landlord: That's right.

Mark: Is the price negotiable?

Landlord: You may first come and have a look. How about discussing it face to face?

Mark: OK. Can I come tonight?

Landlord: Sure. Tonight at six is fine.

Mark: Thanks. See you then.

Landlord: See you.

Dialogue 5

Mark: Hi, I'm Mark Twain.

Tom: Hello, I'm the landlord, Tom Sawyer.

Mark: Nice to meet you, Mr. Sawyer.

Tom: Please, just call me Tom.

Mark: OK, Tom. Well, can I have a look at the place?

Tom: Of course. Come with me. As you can see, we've just finished rebuilding everything.

Mark: Oh, it hasn't been painted yet.

Tom: No, we're going to get that done this week.

Mark: It's very nice. You've really done a great job.

Tom: Thank you.

Mark: How about the rent? Can it be cheaper?

Tom: I'm afraid it can't. The market is rising. I think the price is quite reasonable.

Mark: Well, I think I'll take it.

Dialogue 6

Mrs. Brown: This apartment looks nice.

Landlady: Yes, it has two bedrooms.

Mr. Brown: That's convenient. And the living room is larger than I expected.

Mrs. Brown: The living room is really large, isn't it?

Landlady: Yes, about forty square meters.

Mr. Brown: The bathtub is large enough for two people.

Mrs. Brown: Great. We can give our two children a bath together.

Mr. Brown: Can I open the window and air out the room?

Landlady: Sure.

Mr. Brown: It's a nice apartment.

Landlady: As you can see, the apartment has been recently renovated and comes completely furnished.

Mr. Brown: How much is the rent?

Landlady: 2,500 yuan a month.

Mr. Brown: Are the utilities included in the rent?

Landlady: Only gas is included. You have to pay for the electricity and water.

Mrs. Brown: When can we move in?

Landlady: Next Wednesday, if you like.

Dialogue 7

Mark: Can I write you a check for the security deposit now? $500?

Tom: Yeah. How long do you want the place?

Mark: Six months.

Tom: Oh, well, that might be a problem. I usually only sign one-year leases.
Mark: Well, one year would be fine, too. I'm not planning on leaving the area any time soon.
Tom: Well, if it's not a problem. Then here you go.
Mark: Just let me look at it quickly.
Tom: Of course.
Mark: Looks like a standard lease.
Tom: Yeah, and don't worry about the security deposit. If everything's all right when you move out, you'll get it back.
Mark: OK. Great. Just sign and date it here?
Tom: Yes. Thanks. You can move your stuff in tomorrow.
Mark: Wonderful.

Vocabulary

rent [rent] n. 租金 vt. 出租，租用	stuff [stʌf] n. 东西
apartment [ə'pɑ:tmənt] n. (一户) 公寓房间 (AE)	available [ə'veɪləbl] adj. 可用的，有效的，空闲的
real estate agent n. (美) 房地产经纪人	negotiable [nɪ'gəʊʃiəbl] adj. 可磋商的，可转让的，可通行的
vacant ['veɪkənt] adj. 空的	landlady ['lændleɪdi] n. 女房东
spare [speə(r)] adj. 多余的，备用的，简陋的	renovate ['renəveɪt] v. 更新，革新，刷新
look to 面向	furnish ['fɜ:nɪʃ] vt. 供给，提供，装设
tenant ['tenənt] n. 房客，佃户	utility [ju:'tɪləti] n. 公共设施
decent ['di:snt] adj. 有分寸的，得体的，相当好的	security [sɪ'kjʊərəti] n. 安全
amateur ['æmətə(r)] adj. 业余的	deposit [dɪ'pɒzɪt] n. 存款；定金，堆积物
landlord ['lændlɔ:d] n. 地主，房东	lease [li:s] n. 租约，租期，租 v. 出租，租出，租得

Useful Expressions

A. Intending to rent a house

- I want to rent a furnished house.
- I'm interested in renting a one-bedroom apartment.
- We are looking for a house to rent for the summer.

- The lease on our flat runs out in a few months. I've got to rent a new house.

B. Making an appointment

- When could I see an apartment?
- Can we make a date for site visit?
- I'd like to see the apartment in person.
- Would it be possible for me to visit it tomorrow, say about 5 o'clock?

C. Introducing the facilities of the house

- The living room is large and full of sunshine.
- All the furniture has been arranged.
- The kitchen is small but fully equipped.
- There is a gas stove and a microwave oven. It's very convenient for cooking.
- That house is for rent. It has central heating.
- This is a rather old house. It needs painting.
- This apartment has two bedrooms and a kitchen.
- There's no gas range in the kitchen, but you can use the electric stove.
- There is a shower in the bathroom.
- The room has a big closet. You can put your baggage in it.
- It is not far from your school. It's only 15 minutes' walk.

D. Negotiating the rent

- How much is a 2-bedroom apartment for lease per month?
- How much is the rent for a month?
- What's the average cost of utilities?
- Does the rent include utilities?
- I need the price between $800 ~ $1,000.
- The rent is a bit high, but otherwise the house is satisfactory.
- The rent is reasonable.
- This split-level house is for rent. It's a bargain.
- The rent is 1,000 yuan a month.
- The first month's rent must be paid in advance.
- We rent that house according to month.
- He asked me 5 pounds a month as rent for that house.
- He has to lower the rent of his house.

 Exercises

I. Do you know the names of the facilities below? Write down their names and then practice asking and answering questions with your partner.

Examples:

A: Has your flat got a bathroom?　　B: Yes, it has. / No, it hasn't.

A: Have your rooms got a sofa and a wardrobe?　B: Yes, they have. / No, they haven't.

1. _____　2. _____　3. _____　4. _____

5. _____　6. _____　7. _____　8. _____

9. _____　10. _____　11. _____　12. _____

13. _____　14. _____　15. _____　16. _____

17. _____　18. _____　19. _____　20. _____

II. Complete the short dialogues by translating Chinese into English.

1	A: Does it include _____ (煤气费和电费)?	B: No, you have to pay for your own utilities.
2	A: Is it far from the subway station?	B: No, not at all. It's only _____ (走着去五分钟的路程).
3	A: May I come to your office tomorrow to _____ (签租房合同)?	B: Yeah, all right.

4	A：You can move your _____ (东西) in whenever you want.	B：Terrific.
5	A：Can you _____ (付定金) today?	B：Yes.
6	A：I like the living room. It's large and _____ (阳光充足).	B：That's right.
7	A：Where is your apartment?	B：It's in the suburb and _____ (周围环境很好).
8	A：Excuse me. Is this 21st Century _____ (房地产中介吗)?	B：Yes. What can I do for you?
9	A：How many bedrooms does it have?	B：Two. The _____ (主卧室) is quite spacious.
10	A：_____ (我想问一下) the apartment which was advertised in the local paper.	B：Oh, yes?

III. Replace the words or expressions underlined with their synonyms.

1. How much is the rent <u>for a month</u>?

   How much is the _____ rent?

2. Shall we sign the <u>lease</u> now?

   Shall we sign the _____ now?

3. We are expecting a <u>spare room</u> in about three weeks.

   We are expecting a _____ in about three weeks.

4. We've just finished <u>renovating</u> everything.

   We've just finished _____ everything.

5. The sitting room is <u>too small</u>.

   The sitting room is _____.

6. Does the apartment get much <u>natural light</u>?

   Does the apartment get much _____?

7. <u>May I</u> visit the apartment tomorrow?

   _____ to visit the apartment tomorrow?

8. I <u>want to</u> rent a single-bedroom apartment.

   I _____ renting a single-bedroom apartment.

IV. Pair work: make dialogues based on the following situations.

1. Mary is going to rent an apartment. She goes to a real estate agency and discusses it with the agent.

2. You have an apartment to let. A person telephones to inquire about the flat. You answer his/her questions and tell him/her that the flat will be available from next month.

3. You are going to rent an apartment. Negotiate the rent on-site with the landlord.

4. You have two children and want to rent a two-bedroom apartment. Unfortunately, the landlady doesn't want to rent the apartment to you because she likes to keep her house quiet.

V. Topics for discussion.

1. Nowadays many college students rent apartments outside school. What is your opinion?

2. Compared with buying a house, what are the advantages and disadvantages of renting a house?

# Culture Tips

Rental Tips: Ask All Your Questions

When you meet a potential landlord, it is a good time to ask questions and find out more about what is involved in renting the house. Prepare a list of questions that need answers in order to consider renting the house. Some sample questions are as follows:

- What is included in the rental?
- What utilities are you (the renter) responsible for?
- What is the length of the lease?
- Are pets allowed?
- What are the neighborhood and the neighbors like?
- Who will maintain the property?
- Where can you park?
- Is there additional storage included?
- Is there a security system?
- When is the current tenant leaving?

When looking for a rental house, a lot of things need to fall in line and be similar to what you want and need, so asking questions is the only way to determine if there is a fit.

 Class Activities

Bingo Game

Each group chooses a caller who will call words from the word list below randomly. The rest of the students draw a 5 × 5 grid and write down the words selected from the word list in each grid (they are not permitted to use the same words twice).

The words are announced quickly by the caller, so the rest of the students in the group must pay careful attention to the words that are called and mark them quickly and accurately on the card(s).

When one player completes a "Bingo" pattern, such as a line with five words in a vertical, horizontal or diagonal row on one of their cards, he/she wins the game. The caller keeps calling words until one or more players claim BINGO. Then the game stops, and the words are verified. If there is a winner, the prize is awarded, and a new bingo game begins with new cards. If there is more than one winner, the prize is split among all the winners.

Word List for Playing Bingo Game

landlord	landlady	tenant	bedroom	sitting room	living room
backyard	bathroom	study	basement	dining room	kitchen
balcony	attic	garden	garage	furniture	dresser
closet	wardrobe	armchair	cupboard	desk	sofa
stuff	bureau	cabinet	bookshelf	bed	bedside table
contract	lease	sign	window	shower	bathtub
computer	television	fridge	telephone	dishwasher	rent
microwave oven	washing machine	air conditioner	heating	vacuum cleaner	cooker
stove	security	deposit	include	utility	gas
electricity	water	garbage	vacant	spare	flat
apartment	house	single	double	furnish	renovate
remodel	rebuild	decorate	tidy	bright	clean
small	big	broken	view	real	estate
agent	expensive	come	down	bargain	available
move	check	anytime	whenever	leave	convenient
school	bank	supermarket	subway	shop	gym
inquire	ask	advertisement	bill	tea table	twin room

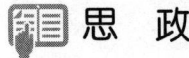 思 政

A Dip into Chinese Wisdom

1. 诚信是结交天下的根本。
Credibility is the foundation for interactions with the world.

2. 言必信，行必果。
Keep what you say and carry out what you do.

3. 渭城朝雨浥轻尘，客舍青青柳色新。
No dust is raised on the road wet with morning rain;
The willows by the hotel look so fresh and green.

4. 房子是用来住的，不是用来炒的。
Housing is for living in, not for speculation.

SECTION II

Making an Appointment
Unit 6

 Lead-in

Do you often give a phone call or send an email to someone in advance before you meet him/her? What do you often say if your answer is "yes"? You may use the following examples for help.

I'm calling for an appointment with… / Is it convenient for you if I drop by at…

 Warm-up Activities

I. Read the following words and pay attention to the pronunciation of "ure".

1. [jʊə]   cure   pure   bureau   endure   secure
2. [ə]   picture   pleasure   measure   furniture   texture

II. Read the passage below and pay attention to your pronunciation and intonation.

It's Monday morning. Benjamin made an appointment with Dr. Smith four days ago. He was supposed to see Dr. Smith on Wednesday. But now he has a severe toothache and has to reschedule his appointment. Benjamin calls Dr. Smith's office. He tells the receptionist that he wants to see the dentist earlier today. But the receptionist tells him that the dentist won't have any availability until 4 o'clock in the afternoon. Since Benjamin has a bad toothache, he wants to see Dr. Smith as early as possible. After the receptionist checks the schedule, she suggests 11:00 a.m. Benjamin agrees and thanks the receptionist for her sincere help.

Dialogues

Dialogue 1

A: Good morning. This is Doctor Johnson's office. What can I do for you?

B: Yes, this is Mrs. Reed. I'd like to make an appointment to see the doctor this week.

A: Well, let's see. I'm afraid he is fully booked on Monday and Tuesday.

B: How about Thursday?

A: Sorry, but I have to say he is also occupied on Thursday. So, will Wednesday be OK for you, Mrs. Reed?

B: I have to work on Wednesday. By the way, is Dr. Johnson available on Saturday?

A: I'm afraid the office is closed on weekends. Well, what about Friday? Let me have a check. Oh, great. Dr. Johnson will be available on Friday afternoon this week.

B: Friday afternoon is OK for me. I'll come then. Thank you.

Dialogue 2

A: Hello.

B: Hi, John. It's Amanda.

A: Hi, Amanda. What's up?

B: Well, I was wondering if you'd like to go for a bite this weekend.

A: Sure. What did you have in mind?

B: I'm in the mood for Italian food.

A: I know a really good place downtown.

B: What's the name of it?

A: Mario's. They have the best pasta in town.

B: Where is it located?

A: It's on Main Street next to the hospital.

B: Main Street next to the hospital? I think I can find it.

A: What time shall we meet?

B: Why don't we meet at 6 o'clock?

A: Sounds great. See you then.

B: See you!

Dialogue 3

A: Hello, Rose, there's something I want to ask you. Would you like to have a meal with us sometime next week?

B: Yes, I'd love to. When?

A: How about Thursday evening?

B: I'm afraid I can't make it on Thursday. I'll be busy preparing my lecture.

A: Are you free on Friday?

B: Friday? Let me see. Somehow I think I've already got something scheduled for Friday. Oh, yes! I've got an appointment with one of my friends, and it's essential that I keep it.

A: So that leaves Saturday. How about Saturday?

B: Saturday sounds good. What time?

A: Is 3 p.m. OK?

B: 3 p.m.? Fine, I'll be looking forward to it.

Dialogue 4

A: I'm sorry to tell you that I have to cancel our appointment.

B: What happened?

A: I must meet someone at the airport tomorrow afternoon.

B: I'm sorry to hear that. Shall we meet the day after tomorrow?

A: Let me see. Oh, I have another appointment that morning.

B: Then how about tomorrow morning?

A: OK. I'll be free from 9:00 to 10:30.

B: So I will see you in your office at 9:00 tomorrow morning.

A: No problem. I'll be there waiting for you.

B: We will discuss the contract in detail.

A: Sure. I'm really sorry for the trouble I've made.

B: Not at all. See you.

A: See you.

Dialogue 5

A: Hello.

B: Good morning, Prof. Wang. This is Ellen speaking.

A: Good morning, Ellen.

B: Prof. Wang, I'd like to discuss the assignment you gave last week with you. I was wondering if you could spare one or two hours tomorrow.

A: Let me have a look at my schedule. I'm afraid I can't make it. I'll be at a conference tomorrow morning. I'll have courses in the afternoon.

B: When will it be convenient for you?

A: I prefer the day after tomorrow.

B: Okay. Could you please fix a definite time for me?

A: I suppose you could come at eight o'clock in the morning.

B: I'll be there on time. Sorry to trouble you with that.

A: No trouble at all. See you then.

B: See you then.

Dialogue 6

A: Can I speak to Dr. Smith, please?

B: Yes. This is Dr. Smith speaking. What can I do for you?

A: Oh. This is Mrs. Lee. Please help me, Dr. Smith.

B: What's the matter with you, Mrs. Lee?

A: Oh, no, it's not me. My son Tony is sick.

B: What's wrong with Tony?

A: He has red spots on his arms and shoulders…

B: Does he have red spots all over his body?

A: Yes, he does.

B: Does he have a fever?

A: Yes, he does. This morning his body temperature was 39 degrees Celsius.

B: Well, that's too bad.

A: He cried all day long. I just couldn't stop him.

B: He has the measles.

A: Measles? Oh, dear. Can you come and see him now?

B: I'm going to be busy with an operation this morning. But I can come this afternoon.

A: Thank you, Dr. Smith.

B: Remember you must keep him from scratching the spots.

A: No, no. I won't let him do that. See you then, doctor.

B: Goodbye.

Dialogue 7

A: Excuse me, can you tell me where Richard Rice's office is?

B: Sure. It's the third office down this hall. Are you looking for Mr. Rice?

A: Yes. He told me to come by this morning.

B: I'm sorry, but he's not in the office now. Do you have an appointment?

A: An appointment?

B: Yes. What time did he expect you?

A: He said I should come by this morning. He didn't give me the time. He said I could come any time before noon.

B: I see. He's usually here on Tuesday mornings.

A: Today is Tuesday.

B: I know. He's usually here, but he's gone out to a site on the east side today.

A: That's too bad. I need to discuss these plans with him.

B: Why don't you make an appointment for later this week?

A: All right.

B: He's here on Tuesdays, Wednesdays and Fridays. What day do you want to see him?

A: Friday is good.

B: Morning or afternoon?

A: Morning.

B: I can put you down for ten o'clock. Is that all right?

A: Yes. My name is Jenny Wills.

B: All right. I have you down for 10 a.m. this Friday.

A: Thank you.

B: You are welcome.

Vocabulary

fully ['fʊli] *adv.* 完全地，充分地	schedule ['ʃedju:l] *n.* 计划
occupy ['ɒkjupaɪ] *vt.* 占据	cancel ['kænsl] *v.* 取消
occupied ['ɒkjupaɪd] *adj.* 已被占的，已居住的	contract ['kɒntrækt] *n.* 合同
available [ə'veɪləbl] *adj.* 可以见到的，有空的	in detail 详细地
	definite ['defɪnət] *adj.* 明确的
be available 有空，可以见到	suppose [sə'pəʊz] *v.* 推想，假设
What's up? 什么事？	spot [spɒt] *n.* 斑点，地点
go for a bite 出去吃东西	measles ['mi:zlz] *n.* 麻疹
downtown [ˌdaʊn'taʊn] *adv.* 在市区	scratch [skrætʃ] *v.* 搔痒
pasta ['pæstə] *n.* 意大利通心粉	expect [ɪk'spekt] *v.* 盼望，期待
	site [saɪt] *n.* 位置，场所

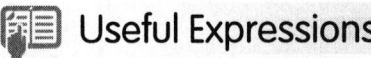 **Useful Expressions**

A. Making an appointment in a formal occasion

- I'm calling for an appointment with…
- Can you fix me an appointment with…, please?
- I'd like to make an appointment with…
- Could you please arrange me an appointment with…?
- Would 8 o'clock tomorrow suit you?
- Would 8 o'clock tomorrow be all right?
- Will… be able to see me sometime tomorrow?
- I'm wondering whether I could see… today.
- Will… be convenient to see me?
- I'm calling to ask if… could see me at 9 tomorrow.
- I wonder if… could see me at about 9 tomorrow.
- I have made an appointment with… I'm ringing you up to confirm it.

B. Making an appointment in an informal occasion

- When are you free?
- When can we meet?
- What time is good for you?
- How does this afternoon sound to you?
- May I see you again this afternoon?
- Why don't you come this Sunday?
- Say, shall we meet on Saturday afternoon at 3 o'clock?

C. Changing or canceling an appointment

- Can we make it a little later?
- Could you make it some other time?
- Could we meet at three instead of eight tomorrow afternoon?
- Do you think you could make it sometime next Monday?
- I'm afraid our appointment would have to be changed.
- I'm terribly sorry, but something unexpected comes up. Can we make it a little later?
- Is it convenient to change our appointment from Thursday to Friday at the same time?
- Something's coming up. We'll have to make our appointment a little later.
- We'll have to make it some other time.

 **Exercises**

I. Complete the short dialogues by translating Chinese into English.

1	A：Will Dr. Smith be able to see me at about 10 a.m. tomorrow morning?	B：I'm afraid _____ _____ (他直到下午三点才会有空).
2	A：_____ _____ (我想和李先生约个时间见面). Would 10 a.m. tomorrow be OK?	B：Do you think you could make it 10:30?
3	A：Our manager would like to see you on Wednesday morning. _____ _____ (方便在 10 点钟和您见面吗)?	B：Yes, that would be all right.
4	A：Mr. Smith, I'm sorry, _____ (这周五我不能赴约了). I have an urgent business trip this afternoon, and I'll be away for several days.	B：That's all right. We may make another time after you come back.
5	A：Hello, Mr. Wang. I'm calling to ask _____ (我们能把周五的见面推迟到下周吗)? I have an unexpected conference to attend.	B：Let me see. Monday and Tuesday are both booked up. What about Wednesday?
6	A：I'm sorry, but _____ _____ (我不得不取消我们的午餐约会).	B：I'm sorry to hear that.
7	A：I'm calling to make sure that I have an appointment with Mr. Smith. Maybe this morning at 11 o'clock?	B：Please wait a minute. _____ _____ (我查一下他的时间安排).
8	A：I can come to your house and pick you up. Is that all right?	B：Good. _____ (你的意思是说你会在 8 点到这儿吗)?
9	A：I have an appointment with you at 9 this morning, but _____ _____ (恐怕我会晚20分钟到).	B：That's all right.
10	A：_____ ___ (我能不能约个时间再和你见一面)?	B：OK. You might call me on Thursday morning.

II. Complete the dialogues with the words and expressions given in the box.

Dialogue 1

> find out if Mr. Smith could see me   what can I do for you   he is free then

A：Good morning. Is Mr. Smith in?

B: No, I'm afraid not. But _____1_____? I'm Mrs. Smith.

A: I'm calling to _____2_____ at 3 tomorrow afternoon? I have some problems to discuss with him.

B: Yes, _____3_____. I'll tell him you'll be coming.

Dialogue 2

> I'm quite desperate   cancellation   make an appointment to see Dr. Harbor
> is engaged for the entire week   waiting list

A: Good afternoon, Dr. Harbor's dental office.

B: Good afternoon. I'm calling to __1__. I've got a bad toothache.

A: I see, but I'm afraid Dr. Harbor __2__.

B: Is there any chance to squeeze me in? __3__. My tooth is giving me a lot of pain.

A: Well, I'll have to put you on the __4__. I'll call you as soon as there is a __5__.

B: That's great. I'm Sara. My number is 1234-5678. Thanks a lot.

III. Pair work: make dialogues based on the following situations.

1. Miss Li wants to make an appointment with her doctor, Dr. Williams. She speaks with the receptionist.

2. John asks Elaine if she would like to set a dinner date with him.

3. Li Ming would like a meeting with Mary, and now they're discussing a proper time.

IV. Topics for discussion.

1. Imagine that you want to hold a birthday party. Will you tell your friends on the very day or several days in advance? Why?

2. How long in advance do you think is polite to make an appointment with your doctor or clients? Why?

 Culture Tips

Appointment

In social life, time plays an important role. In the U.S., guests may feel that they are not highly regarded if the invitation to a dinner party is extended only two or three days before the party date. But it is not the case in all countries. In some other areas of the world, it may be seen as foolish to make an appointment too far in advance because plans made more than a week in advance tend to be forgotten.

The meaning of time differs in different parts of the world. Promptness is valued highly in American life. If you make an appointment with a business associate, you should arrive on time; otherwise, you may be considered impolite or not fully responsible. A person who is five minutes late is expected to make a short apology. If he/she is less than five minutes late, he/she will have to say a few words of explanation.

 Class Activities

Make an Appointment

Work in pairs. Now you are talking with your partner about appointments. You act as a company manager. Your partner acts as a customer who wants to make an appointment with you. You are very busy tomorrow and have no time available. When you give your answer, check the following timetable.

8:30 Meet Mr. Green	14:00 Write reports
9:00 Phone Mr. Smith	15:30 See the chairman
9:30 Meet department managers	16:30 Arrange a meeting
11:30 Lunch with a friend	17:30 Shop for daughter's birthday present

 思 政

A Dip into Chinese Wisdom

1. 国与国交往既要讲利，更要重义。赠人玫瑰，手有余香。

Countries must value friendship and righteousness above shared interests in their exchanges. The rose's in her hand, the flavor in mine.

2. 君子一言，驷马难追。

A word spoken is a word that must be honored.

3. 一万年太久，只争朝夕。

Ten thousand years are too long. Seize the day, seize the hour.

4. 时间就像海绵里的水一样，只要你愿意挤，总还是有的。

Time is like water in a sponge. As long as you are willing to squeeze, there will always be some.

SECTION II

Making a Reservation
Unit 7

Lead-in

How many ways do you know about reserving a table for four? You may use the following examples for help.

A: I'd like to reserve a table for four persons.

B: I want to reserve a table for four for tomorrow evening.

C: I'd like to make a reservation for four, for dinner tomorrow.

D: I'd like to have a table for four reserved please, for tomorrow evening.

Warm-up Activities

I. Read the following words and pay attention to the pronunciation of "air", "eir" and "oir".

1. [eə]　　　hair　　　chair　　　pair　　　stair　　　fair
2. [eə]　　　their　　　heir
3. [aɪə]　　　choir

II. Read the story below and pay attention to your pronunciation and intonation.

A man called to make a reservation, "I want to go from LA to Hippopotamus, New York". The agent was at a loss for words. Finally, the agent said, "Are you sure that's the name of the place?" "Yes, what flights do you have?" the customer replied. After some searching, the agent came back and said, "I'm sorry, sir, I've looked up every airport code in the country and can't find a Hippopotamus anywhere." The customer retorted, "Oh, don't be silly. Everyone knows where it is. It's in New York. Check your map!" The agent scoured a map of the state of New York and finally offered, "You don't mean Buffalo, do you?" "That's it! I knew it was a big animal!"

 Dialogues

Dialogue 1

Waiter: Good afternoon. Wenhua Restaurant. May I help you?

Mr. Bush: Yes, I'd like to reserve a table for 8.

Waiter: Certainly, sir. What time do you like your table?

Mr. Bush: At 8 p.m. on Tuesday evening.

Waiter: Would you like Chinese, Western, or Korean cuisine?

Mr. Bush: Chinese food, please.

Waiter: May I have your name, sir?

Mr. Bush: Yes, Bush.

Waiter: Thank you, Mr. Bush.

Mr. Bush: Oh, any chance of a window table? My friends love the bird's eye view.

Waiter: I see. We have already received many reservations but we'll try our best, Mr. Bush.

Mr. Bush: Thanks, I would appreciate it if it could be arranged.

Waiter: I'll try my best. We look forward to your visit, Mr. Bush. Thanks for calling.

Dialogue 2

James: Hi, I have a table reserved for 6, under the name James King.

Waiter: Sorry, but we don't have any reservation under that name.

James: Are you kidding me? Please check again.

Waiter: Sure... sorry, sir, but nothing shows up under that name. I'm afraid you'll have to wait until a table is available.

James: No, I don't think it's a good idea. I would like to speak to your manager, please.

(Later, the manager comes)

Manager: Hello, how can I help you?

James: Hello, I was just told that my reservation was not taken and now I am here with no table. Is there anything you can do to fix this?

Manager: OK, how about this then? We will take you to the reception room of the restaurant. You can wait there until a table that fits your requirements is available.

James: I guess there's no other choice. Well, thank you!

Dialogue 3

Man: Hello, is that Holiday Hotel? I'd like to book a single room.

Receptionist: Certainly. When?

Man: October 1st. Five nights.

Receptionist: OK. That would be 2,000 yuan. Would you like to make the reservation?

Man: Yes, please.

Receptionist: Thank you. And I need some more information. May I have your name and phone number?

Man: Tom Chang. My phone number is 13622145098.

Receptionist: Thank you.

Dialogue 4

Clerk: Room Reservations. May I help you?

Mr. Knight: Yes. I'd like to cancel a reservation, because the travel schedule has been changed.

Clerk: That's OK. Could you tell me in whose name was the reservation made?

Mr. Knight: Knight. K-n-i-g-h-t.

Clerk: And what was the date?

Mr. Knight: From August 24th for two nights.

Clerk: Excuse me, but is the reservation for yourself?

Mr. Knight: It's for myself.

Clerk: Well, may I have your name and phone number, please?

Mr. Knight: Yes, it's Will Knight, and my number is 13625830112.

Clerk: Thank you, sir. I will cancel your reservation from August 24th. We look forward to another chance to serve you.

Dialogue 5

Agent: Hello, Sir! May I help you?

Brant: I'd like to reserve a flight to Washington for the 30th of September.

Agent: Just a moment, please.

Brant: OK. I don't mind.

Agent: How do you want to fly, coach or first class?

Brant: I fly coach.

Agent: We have several flights from Beijing to Washington on September 30th. Which one will you take?

Brant: Anyone will do. How much is the fare?

Agent: $2,500.

Brant: OK. Here you are. By the way, what time does the flight get into Washington?

Agent: It'll arrive in Washington at 11:35. Any other questions?

Brant: Do I have to confirm my plane reservation?

Agent: Sure. You do have to. Remember the flight number is AA 202 at Gate 6, Beijing International Airport. You'd better arrive at the airport 2 to 3 hours before the departure time.

Brant: Thank you for your nice service, ma'am.

Agent: Thank you for flying with us. Hope you have a nice trip.

Brant: Have a nice day!

Dialogue 6

Mr. Wilson: Hi, Eastern Airlines? This is Benjamin Wilson calling. I have a reservation on the 10:25 a.m. flight to Shanghai tomorrow morning.

Agent: Yes, Mr. Wilson. How can I help you?

Mr. Wilson: Well, I'd like to reschedule my flight for the tomorrow afternoon one at 15:40. Is that possible?

Agent: I'm very sorry, Mr. Wilson, but the 15:40 flight is completely booked. I can put you on a waiting list if you would like.

Mr. Wilson: OK, I see. Thank you anyway.

Dialogue 7

Woman: Can I book tickets for the concert tomorrow evening?

Clerk: Yes, no problem. How many tickets?

Woman: Two please. How much are they?

Clerk: We've got tickets at 50 yuan, 80 yuan, 100 yuan and 160 yuan. What kind of ticket would you like?

Woman: The 100 yuan tickets will be fine, thanks.

Clerk: OK. That's two tickets at 100 yuan each—a total of 200 yuan, please.

Woman: The concert begins at 7:30 o'clock, right?

Clerk: Yes, please be on time.

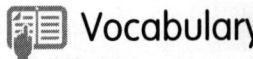 Vocabulary

cuisine [kwɪ'ziːn] *n.* 烹饪 bird's eye view 鸟瞰图 single ['sɪŋgl] *adj.* 单身的，单一的 shower ['ʃaʊə(r)] *n.* 淋浴 cancel ['kænsl] *v.* 取消，删去	coach [kəʊtʃ] *n.* 二等舱 fare [feə(r)] *n.* 费用，食物 confirm [kən'fɜːm] *vt.* 确定，证实 departure [dɪ'pɑːtʃə(r)] *n.* 离开，出发 reschedule [ˌriː'ʃedjuːl] *vt.* 重新安排时间，调整时间表

Useful Expressions

A. Making reservations at a restaurant

- When would you like your table?
- Do I need a reservation?
- Nine o'clock should be OK.
- I'd like to reserve a table for three.
- We'd like a table with a view of garden.
- I'd like a window table.
- We'll come around eight o'clock.
- I'd like to reserve/book a table for six at 7 p.m. please.
- I'd like to book a table for two at 9 a.m. in the name of Hilton, please.
- Could we have a table by the window, please?
- Could we have a non-smoking table, please?
- Could we have a table away from the kitchen/toilets, please?
- Could we have a booth, please?
- Could you make sure it's a quiet table, please?
- I'm sorry. We have so many guests this evening.
- I'm sorry. The restaurant is full.
- I'm sorry, sir. I'm afraid we're fully booked for that time.
- I'm sorry, there aren't any tables left now.
- Would you like to sit near the window?
- Where would you like to sit?
- Would you mind sitting here in the corner?

- Would you like smoking or non-smoking?

B. Making reservations in a hotel

- I'd like to book a single/double room for Thursday.
- What's the price difference?
- A double room with a front view is $120 per night, and one with a rear view is $96 per night.
- How long will you be staying?
- We'll be leaving on Friday morning.
- I'd like to book a single room with bath from September 6 to September 9.
- I'd like to cancel a reservation, because the travel schedule has been changed.
- We do have a single room available for those dates.
- What is the rate, please?
- The current rate is $210 per night.
- What services come with that?
- That sounds not bad. I'll take it.
- By the way, I'd like a quiet room away from the street if it is possible.

C. Booking a flight

- Happiness Travel Agency. May I help you?
- I'd like to make a plane reservation to Beijing, China.
- Let me see what's available. Yes, Air China has a flight on May 6th at 8:25 in the evening.
- I'll need a first-class/business class/an economy ticket.
- One way trip or round trip?
- What's the fare please?
- Economy fare for one-way trip from Beijing to New York is $600.
- Is my ticket confirmed then?
- Please arrive at the airport one hour before departure.
- May I have your flight number, please?
- You're flying economy class. Is that correct?
- Enjoy your flight.
- I'd like to reserve a flight to New York for the first of May.
- How do you want to fly, coach or first class?
- We have several flights from Los Angeles to Washington on June 1st.
- When do I have to check in?
- You have to be there forty-five minutes or an hour before the departure.

- Do I have to confirm my plane reservation?

D. Reserving seats for a(n) film/opera/concert

- I'm sorry, all the orchestra/balcony seats are gone.
- We've got tickets at…
- I'd like to reserve two tickets at…
- I wonder if there are some balcony seats still available.
- Do you have any seats for…?
- Please hold two orchestra seats for us.
- I have tickets reserved for tomorrow's matinee.
- Shall we go to the matinee or the evening performance?
- We have nothing at all left for today's matinee.

Exercises

I. Replace the words or expressions underlined with their synonyms.

1. I want to <u>reserve</u> a train ticket from Beijing to Shanghai.

   I want to _____ a train ticket from Beijing to Shanghai.

2. I'm sorry we are <u>fully booked</u>.

   I'm sorry we are _____.

3. Do you have a <u>vacant</u> single room?

   Do you have a single room _____?

4. She said she wanted to book <u>a table by the window</u>.

   She said she wanted to book a _____.

5. <u>What</u> is the fare?

   _____ is the fare?

II. Complete the short dialogues by translating Chinese into English.

1	A: I want to reserve _____ _____ (两张经济舱机票) to New York on Saturday, September 1st.	B: Let me see what's available.
2	A: Would you like _____ _____ (吸烟室还是非吸烟室)?	B: Non-smoking please.
3	A: I want to _____ _____ (搭经济舱).	B: _____ (单程票还是来回票)?

4	A: Have you got a big conference room for 300 people?	B: Yes, sir. Our multi-function hall can _____ (可以容纳600人). And it is available on the 8th.
5	A: Just a second and I'll _____ _____ (查对一下行程表).	B: I'll need _____ _____ (一张头等舱、不定期返程票).
6	A: Would you like _____ _____ (贵宾座还是包厢)?	B: Is there any difference?
7	A: Isn't there anything less expensive?	B: Not _____ _____ (除非你想要白天场的).
8	A: _____ _____ (餐厅是否有任何服装上的规定)?	B: No jeans, please.
9	A: It is a little high. I'm told that _____ _____ (你们酒店正在打折).	B: Yes, but the offer ended yesterday. I'm sorry.
10	A: I want to reserve a room from the 16th to the 22nd of this month.	B: Sorry, _____ _____ (16号的标准间已经没有了).

III. Fill in the blanks with expressions given in the box.

```
are fully booked              have a cancellation          be full up
to change your reservation date   the rate per night       reserve a double room
```

Clerk: Good evening. May I help you?

Man: Yes, I'd like to ___1___ for three nights.

Clerk: For what date?

Man: From Dec. 6 to Dec. 8.

Clerk: Just a moment, please. Let me check our computer here. I'm sorry, sir. We ___2___ on that date.

Man: Oh, that's too bad.

Clerk: Is it possible for you ___3___?

Man: No, that's not possible.

Clerk: Would you like us to put you on our waiting list and call you in case we ___4___?

Man: Thank you. That's very kind of you. But could you recommend me another hotel which won't ___5___?

Clerk: OK, I suggest that you try Garden Hotel.

Man: Do you know ___6___ for a twin room there?

Clerk: Well, a twin room at the moment would run you between 600 yuan and 750 yuan.

Man: I see. Do you know the telephone number?

Clerk: Yes, it's 6180-3102.

Man: Thank you very much. I really appreciate your help.

IV. Pair work: make dialogues based on the following situations.

1. Mr. Wright calls an agency and would like to book two economy tickets from Beijing to Paris on Jan. 6th.
2. Peter Wang wants to reserve a ticket for the performance tomorrow, but only the front balcony seats are still available.
3. Miss Jackson reserves a multimedia conference room for her company, for a lecture at 2 p.m. on Tuesday afternoon.

V. Topics for discussion.

1. Do you often make reservations before you go to a restaurant? Why or why not?
2. When traveling, do you prefer to make reservations in advance, or just take things as they come? Why?

Culture Tips

Tips about Booking a Table in a Restaurant

Eating out is quite popular in the U.S., and it is often necessary to make a reservation. Once you have decided on a place, it's better to book a table in advance to avoid unnecessary waiting during peak hours. If you forget to make a reservation, you'll have to wait in line for a table. Remember to arrive at the restaurant on time to avoid missing your chance. Restaurants usually give a 15~20-minute grace period before they give your table to the next person in line.

The table should be booked under one person's name—usually the family name—for a specific number of people at a specific time. Due to the high demand at restaurants, some people double-book tables at two different restaurants to ensure they have at least one reservation. For their own convenience, people sometimes book tables at multiple restaurants and decide at the last minute which one they prefer. However, this can be very unfair to restaurateurs, as they lose potential customers if you do not show up. As a courtesy, you should at least cancel the reservation at the restaurants you decide not to visit.

 Class Activities

Whispering Game

You will be in a team of 10 students. Some of you can serve as the teacher's helpers. The teacher and his/her helper will whisper a message to the first person of each team, such as Team A, Team B, Team C, etc. The game only starts when the first person of each team has received the message. Then, each player whispers the message to the next player in his/her group successively until the last player receives the message. The team that can repeat the message first and correctly will earn a point. Finally, one student from each team will be asked to repeat both the original and the final sentence.

 思 政

A Dip into Chinese Wisdom

1. 当今世界正经历百年未有之大变局，但时与势在我们一边。

The world is undergoing profound changes unseen in a century, but time and situation are in our favor.

2. 人无远虑，必有近忧。

If a man takes no thought about what is distant, he will find sorrow near at hand.

3. 君子欲讷于言，而敏于行。

The gentleman wishes to be cautious in his words and earnest in his conduct.

4. 来而不可失者，时也；蹈而不可失者，机也。

Opportunity may knock just once; grab it before it slips away.

SECTION II

Making an Apology
Unit 8

Lead-in

Have you ever done something wrong to your friends? How do you apologize? Discuss it with your partner. You may use the following example for help.

Alice: I must apologize for that. I do beg your pardon.
Louise: It's nothing serious. You don't have to upset yourself.

Warm-up Activities

I. Read the following words and pay attention to the pronunciation of "ear", "eer" and "eur".

1. [eə]	pear	bear	forebear	swear	wear
2. [ɪə]	hear	near	tear	ear	beard
3. [ɜː]	search	heard			
4. [ɪə]	beer	steer	sheer	deer	pioneer
5. [ɜː]	entrepreneur	farceur	saboteur		
6. [ə]	amateur	chauffeur			

II. Read the story below and pay attention to your pronunciation and intonation.

For two solid hours, the lady sitting next to a man on an airplane talked about her grandchildren. She even showed him a plastic foldout photo album of all nine of the children.

Finally, she realized that she had dominated the entire conversation about her grandchildren.

"Oh, I've done all the talking, and I'm so sorry. I know you must have something to say. Please, tell me... what do you think of my grandchildren?"

Dialogues

Dialogue 1

(Two men are chasing a boy on the street).

A: I'm terribly sorry for breaking into your room, but it's really an emergency.

B: That's okay. Don't let it bother you. So what's your problem?

A: Someone's chasing me and I need your help. Please don't tell them I'm here.

B: Just relax, everything will be all right.

Dialogue 2

Jack: Hey, Tom, did you remember to bring me the book?

Tom: What book?

Jack: You remember. The one is called Conan.

Tom: I'm terribly sorry. How could I be so thoughtless? I'm afraid I seem to have left it on the bus. I'll buy you another one when I go to the bookshop this weekend.

Jack: Don't worry about it. It's no big deal. I won't need it until Friday anyway.

Tom: Oh, I promise you can get the book before you use it.

Jack: Thanks.

Dialogue 3

A: I have to apologize.

B: May I ask why?

A: I broke your pen.

B: It doesn't matter.

A: You are kind. I will buy one for you in time.

B: I have another one. Just forget it!

Dialogue 4

(A=Mrs. Smith B=Clerk)

A: Hello. This is Mrs. Smith. I'd like to buy a new car. Could you offer me a new type of the car, please?

B: Oh, Madam, buy what?

A: A new car. And I've got a small family, two children, and I haven't got a lot of money and…

B: Oh, oh, madam, madam. I'm afraid you have the wrong number.

A: Isn't this the car store?

B: No. It's John's Sporting Goods Store.

A: Oh, sorry. Do you know the number for a car store, then?

B: No, I don't. I suggest you check the phone book.

A: I'm sorry to have bothered you.

B: No problem.

Dialogue 5

A: I'm sorry for being late last time.

B: Oh, that's okay. No problem for that.

A: But I'm feeling so bad for it, you need to accept my apology.

B: Don't keep it in mind, I have already forgiven you.

A: Thanks for your forgiveness. You're a really good friend. How about having dinner together this Friday evening? I just want to make up for you.

B: That's really great! I'll be there.

A: OK, see you on Friday.

Dialogue 6

W: May I come in?

M: Come in, please. Do you know what time it is?

W: It's 8:20. I am very sorry to be late again. And I am also sorry to disturb you and others.

M: All right, what's your excuse this time? Don't tell me your alarm didn't go off or your watch stopped. I don't want to hear it!

W: Excuse me, sir. I hit the rush hour. You just cannot imagine how terrible the traffic jam was.

M: Why didn't you get up earlier to avoid this time?

W: I'm sorry, sir. I indeed got up early, but my watch was 20 minutes slow.

M: I have never been late for work, you see. I always set my watch 15 minutes fast every day.

W: Oh, that's a good idea! I'll set my watch… 30 minutes fast… to avoid hitting the rush hour. I promise I won't be late in the future. And I hope you could forgive me once more.

M: That's right! You have already been late for work three times, if this happens again, you will be fired.

Dialogue 7

A: Adam, I am sorry!

B: But where have you been, Alice? You're over an hour late.

A: Yes, but I couldn't help it. I was late getting off work for a start, and then I missed the bus. The bus I did catch got caught in a traffic jam. It was one thing after another.

B: But why were you so late getting off work? The office closes at six, doesn't it?

A: Yes, but there's a rush on at the moment, and my boss asked me to write some urgent letters.

B: But didn't you tell him you had an appointment?

A: Well, no. I thought I'd finish it in about five minutes and I didn't expect it to be so difficult. If it hadn't been for missing the bus and the traffic jam, I wouldn't have been so late. I am sorry.

B: Well, you're here. And that's more important.

A: Thank you. I'll try not to be late again.

Vocabulary

careless ['keələs] *adj.* 粗心的，疏忽的 pardon ['pɑːdn] *n. & v.* 原谅 bother ['bɒðə(r)] *v.* 烦扰 harm [hɑːm] *v.* 伤害，损害，危害 terrible ['terəbl] *adj.* 可怕的 chase [tʃeɪs] *v.* 追逐 several ['sevrəl] *adj.* 几个，若干 apologize [ə'pɒlədʒaɪz] *v.* 道歉 thoughtless ['θɔːtləs] *adj.* 无深虑的， 　　　　　　　　　　　　轻率的	deal [diːl] *v.* 处理，应付 relax [rɪ'læks] *v.* 放松，松懈，松弛 disturb [dɪ'stɜːb] *v.* 扰乱，妨碍，使…… 　　　　　　　　　　　　不安 hit [hɪt] *v.* 撞见 excuse [ɪk'skjuːz; ɪk'skjuːs] *v. & n.* 原谅， 借口 fault [fɔːlt] *n.* 过失，缺点 kid [kɪd] *v.* 开玩笑 arrange to do 安排干某事

Useful Expressions

A. Making informal apologies

- I'm sorry for/about…
- I'm extremely/really/terribly/awfully/very sorry about it, but I am afraid…
- I'm sorry for giving you so much trouble.
- I'm sorry to have bothered you/kept you waiting.
- Please forgive me, I really didn't mean that.
- Oh, I'm sorry. That was really clumsy of me.
- Excuse me for not phoning you.
- Please excuse my coming late.
- Pardon my interrupting you.
- I do apologize for the inconvenience I brought to you last night.
- It was me to blame.
- I'm afraid I've taken up too much of your time.
- It was all my fault to have done…
- We really didn't mean that at all.
- It was most careless of me.
- I was really quite unintentional.
- A thousand pardons for doing…

B. Making formal apologies

- I must apologize for what I said rudely just now.
- Please excuse me for doing…
- Please forgive me for…
- I must ask for your pardon for…
- I would like to give you my apology for…
- May I offer my sincere apologies for…
- Please forgive me for a stupid choice of words.
- Please accept my apologies for my oversight.
- Please allow me to say sorry again.
- Once again, I'm sorry for any inconvenience caused.
- I hope you'll excuse/forgive me for doing…
- I can't say how sorry I am. I can't apologize enough.

C. Making replies to apologies

- It's/That's all right.
- It doesn't matter.
- Don't worry. It's all right.
- Oh, well, never mind.
- Oh, it can't be helped.
- How on earth did that happen?
- What? You should be careful!
- Oh, just forget it!
- Oh, well, not to worry.
- It's nothing.
- Think nothing of it.
- It's of no importance.
- Don't make such mistakes again.
- It was really not worth mentioning.
- Don't let it worry you.
- No harm.
- It's nothing serious. You don't have to upset yourself.
- It's not as bad as that. There is no point in getting upset.
- That's okay. Don't let it bother you.
- There's no need/reason to apologize for…

 Exercises

I. Finish the sentences with possible situations.

1. I'm sorry

a. _____.

b. _____.

c. _____.

2. I hope I didn't

a. _____.

b. _____.

c. _____.

3. I'm sorry but

a. _____.

b. _____?

c. _____.

4. Please accept my apologies for

a. _____.

b. _____.

c. _____.

5. I apologize that

a. _____.

b. _____.

c. _____.

II. Think of good excuses or reasons for having done the followings.

Examples:

Make apologies for being late for school/work.

I'm sorry I'm late. My alarm didn't go off and I overslept.

I apologize for being late again. I missed the coach.

I'm extremely sorry for being late again. There was a big traffic jam.

1. You haven't done your homework.
2. You stepped on someone's foot.
3. You borrowed a friend's camera and have damaged it.
4. You forget to send the email that your friend asked you to.
5. You knocked over a cup of coffee at a party.
6. You are having a meal with a friend at his house. You drop a plate.
7. You told Jane you would come over to study with her last night, but you forgot it.
8. The wife misunderstands her husband for not buying a gift for her birthday.
9. You didn't do your homework.
10. You forgot to lock the door.

III. Complete the short dialogues by translating Chinese into English.

1	**A**: Tim, I'm sorry!	**B**: But where have you been, Lucy? _____ (你迟到将近2个小时).
2	**A**: I have been waiting for Mr. T. Carpenter for thirty minutes.	**B**: I'm sorry, _____ (但他还在开会).

3	A: I'm sorry _____ _____ (在晚会上对你发火).	B: Don't worry. It was really not worth mentioning.
4	A: _____ (很抱歉打断你, 不过, 我们最好快一点).	B: That's right.
5	A: Well, how much longer do you think he will be?	B: _____ (他很快就会完成了).
6	A: _____ _____ (很抱歉打搅你, 我能和你私下谈一谈吗)?	B: Sure. What's up?
7	A: I wasn't sure which one was Mary. _____ (真对不起, 我真的喝醉了).	B: How could you do this?
8	A: _____ (你能再核对一下电话号码吗)?	B: OK, maybe it's my fault.
9	A: _____ (我不是故意伤害你的感情), I am sorry.	B: OK, it's not your fault.
10	A: _____ (到香港的传真发了吗)?	B: I lost it. I do apologize.

IV. Pair work: make dialogues based on the following situations.

1. You borrowed 500 yuan from your friend last month, promising to pay it back today. But you haven't got the money.

2. Your secretary made a mistake yesterday and you lost your temper. Today you apologize to her.

3. Luke forgot his girlfriend's birthday. He apologized to her.

V. Topics for discussion.

1. A line from the movie *Love Story* says, "Love means never having to say sorry." What do you think?

2. Some people think that when you do something wrong, saying sorry is unnecessary because sometimes you cannot make up for it. What's your opinion?

Culture Tips

When you do something wrong or fail to do something, you can save yourself a lot of trouble if you apologize first.

Usually, you make an apology, and the other person accepts your apology and reassures you. For example,

A: I'm sorry I'm late.

B: That's all right.

However, sometimes the situation is not so simple, and you have to make a longer conversation and put in more effort. In more serious situations, such as damaging someone's property or hurting someone's feelings, a more extensive apology is required. Generally, such an apology consists of the following three parts:

(1) A simple, apologetic statement of what has happened;

(2) An explanation;

(3) An offer to make amends, depending on the situation.

When you apologize, you may wish to provide an explanation or reason. Generally speaking, the closer your relationship with the person, the more detailed the explanation should be.

After someone apologizes to us, we need to respond or react to it. So how should we respond? Of course, it depends on the nature of what she or he apologizes for and the mood we are in when we receive the apology.

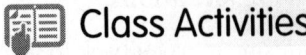 Class Activities

Word Association

Procedures:

At the beginning, you will be given a word, such as "Hotel", by the teacher or other students. Then, you should speak out any words related to this word. For example:

1. Teacher: Hotel
2. Student A: Bed
3. Student B: Room
4. Student C: Service
5. Student D: Food

As you can see, any association is acceptable. If a student cannot answer within 5 seconds, he or she must stand up. The last student remaining seated is the winner. If the association is not obvious, you will be asked to explain it.

A Dip into Chinese Wisdom

1. 我们要做的是，以对话代替冲突，以协商代替胁迫，以共赢代替零和。

What we need to do is to replace conflict with dialogue, coercion with consultation and zero-sum with win-win.

2. 有则改之，无则加勉。

Correct our mistakes when we have made any and guard against them when we have not.

3. 过而不改，是谓过矣。

Not to mend the fault one has made is to err indeed.

4. 忍一时之气，免百日之忧。

If you are patient in one moment of anger, you will escape a hundred days of sorrow.

SECTION II

Opinions
Unit 9

 **Lead-in**

What kind of films do you like? And why do you like them? You may use the following words and phrases for help.

    action film   affection film   comedy/comic film   tragedy/tragic film
    documentary film cartoon   thriller/thrill film   science fiction/sci-fi film
    horror film   war film

 Warm-up Activities

I. Read the following words and pay attention to the stress.

    absolutely ['æbsəlu:tli]   influence ['ɪnfluəns]   luxury ['lʌkʃəri]
    abstract ['æbstrækt]   institute ['ɪnstɪtju:t]   luxurious [lʌg'ʒʊəriəs]
    academic [ˌækə'demɪk]   interesting ['ɪntrəstɪŋ]   process ['prəʊses]
    academy [ə'kædəmi]   interview ['ɪntəvju:]   product ['prɒdʌkt]
    complicated ['kɒmplɪkeɪtɪd] invoice ['ɪnvɔɪs]   receipt [rɪ'si:t]
    income ['ɪnkʌm]   Italian [ɪ'tæliən]   television ['telɪvɪʒn]
    indicate ['ɪndɪkeɪt]   Italy ['ɪtəli]   written ['rɪtn]

II. Read the passage below and pay attention to your pronunciation and intonation.

    The United States has succeeded in building a supercomputer that can solve complex strategic or tactical problems. Military leaders are assembled in front of the new machine and instructed to feed a difficult tactical problem into it.

They describe a hypothetical situation to the computer and then ask the pivotal question: attack or retreat?

The computer hums and buzzes away for a few minutes and then provides the answer: "YES."

The generals look at each other, somewhat bewildered. Finally, one of them submits a second request to the computer: "YES, WHAT?"

Instantly the computer responds: "YES, SIR!"

 Dialogues

Dialogue 1

A: What do you think of driving a car after drinking alcohol?

B: Well, in my opinion, people who drive shouldn't drink.

A: Yes, that's my opinion, too.

C: I'm not so sure about that. I think they should be allowed to drink a little.

B: Well, I don't think they should. Once people start drinking, they never know when to stop.

C: Yes, but don't you think it's asking too much to ban it altogether? And what about all the pubs in the country? You can't get to them without a car!

B: As I see it, the obvious answer is to close them all down.

C: I'm afraid I don't think that's a practical idea. There are thousands of country pubs in Britain. And people can not live without pubs.

A: Anyway, I think it's time for us to take drinking and driving a little more seriously.

C: Yes, that's exactly my opinion.

Dialogue 2

(W=Woman M=Man)

W: What do you think about the Women's Liberation Movement?

M: I'm not in favor of it. I think women should accept their traditional role as housewives.

W: I really disagree with you. Women should enjoy the same rights as men. Why can't a woman have her own career?

M: Women and men have their respective strengths and weaknesses. Women are generally tender and considerate, so they are more suitable for caring for kids and doing housework. But because they're oftentimes too emotional, they're less likely to be as successful as men in the professional world.

W: Those are stereotypes. There are many cases that prove women are just as competent as men in fields such as law and management.

M: There are some, but not many.

W: That's because there are still too many prejudiced men. And too few women have realized their rights. That's where the Women's Liberation Movement comes into play in this context.

Dialogue 3

A: I don't think it's a good thing for children to play computer games all the time. They're in a world of their own. They don't go outside, and they don't know how to relate to other people.

B: It sounds like they're having a good time and learning a lot at the same time. A child can learn so much by playing, solving puzzles and getting better at something. And computer games can hold children's attention for such long periods. It must help their ability to concentrate and keep working at things.

A: Children need to run around and play with each other. They shouldn't just sit in front of their computer screens. It must be bad for their eyesight, too. I hate to think what all these children will be like when they grow up. They'll be so unsociable!

B: I expect they'll be pretty good at handling all the new technology that is being developed. They'll be more curious about things as well. Anyway, how much time did we use to spend watching TV? Our parents thought we'd all become dull and passive. Perhaps they were right, and interactive computer games could be the way of making sure it doesn't happen to the next generation.

Dialogue 4

A: I don't understand why so many people get upset if we eat some animals but not others. I realize that local customs and ways of looking at certain animals vary a lot, but it's not reasonable. We should either become vegetarians or accept that there is no difference between eating cows and eating whales.

B: I'm a vegetarian, and I think it's morally wrong to eat any kind of meat, but it's particularly wrong to eat more intelligent species like whales. I think they must feel pain more acutely than less intelligent species do. Moreover, surely it's wrong to eat any animal that's in danger of becoming extinct.

A: Yes, I agree with you on this point. I accept that we shouldn't eat endangered species, but not all types of whales are endangered. I'm also not sure whether intelligence should be the deciding factor.

B: There are experiments that show that plants have feelings, but most people accept that it's all right to eat plants. On the other hand, most of us would be horrified if somebody suggested eating a dog or a human. Perhaps it does come down to the intelligence level of the animals we eat, or at least their capacity to feel pain.

Dialogue 5

A: Do you mean to tell me you don't care for modern art? Not any of it?

B: That's right. I don't understand it and I don't like it.

A: That's a very narrow-minded viewpoint. If you don't understand it, how can you say that you don't like it?

B: Perhaps I am a little conservative. I just can't see how modern artists are really serious.

A: I won't argue with you, but I think you are unfair. Compared to traditional artists, modern artists have a different approach to their work.

B: Are you trying to tell me that these peculiar paintings mean anything? A child could paint better than that.

A: I guess there's no point in discussing this any further. You have your opinion, and I have mine.

B: I agree there are two sides to every issue, but this time I see only one of them.

A: Well, I am trying to explain that modern artists are trying to get across their personal feelings about the world around them.

B: Then they should keep those feelings to themselves.

Dialogue 6

Nina: I think we can tell a lot about a person's character from their blood type. I've no idea how it works, but it seems to be pretty accurate. My blood type is O, and people who have type O blood are supposed to be impulsive and ambitious. I think it's true. I'm considered very impulsive by my friends and associates, and I'm more ambitious than most people.

Mark: I don't believe a word of it! It's just superstition! Somebody probably made it up, and made a lot of money out of it at the same time. My blood type is A. What am I supposed to be like?

Nina: You needn't be so cynical! Type A people are good at teamwork and usually cooperate with others. Type B people are unconventional and stand back from the world around them. Type AB people are creative and good cooperators, but often selfish at home.

Mark: I am not good at teamwork, even when I play ball games. My cousin is Type B and she's the most conventional person I have ever known, and one of my friends is AB and he's very unsociable and has never created a thing in his life. I really don't know why so many people are fooled by this kind of nonsense.

Dialogue 7

A: I'm thinking of getting rid of my TV set.

B: Whatever for?

A: Don't you think that TV has a thoroughly bad effect on family life? We don't have any proper conversation anymore. My son makes mistakes in his homework because he has one eye on the clock in case he misses his favorite program.

B: But some of the programs are really interesting.

A: Occasionally, yes, but most of the time they're rubbish. They're either idiotic comedies or the sort of films that I don't want my child to watch.

B: I'm afraid I don't altogether agree with you. Too much television is bad, I grant you. But I think it teaches children a great many things they'd never have the chance to learn in any other way—what's going on in the world and how people live in other countries, and some of the popular science programs are fascinating. Then, too, they see things happening as they happen—like space launches, for instance.

A: Hmm—well, that was exceptional.

B: True, but it was TV that made it possible for the world to see it happening. And then, some of the serials are very good, especially those based on the classics.

A: They'd do far better to read them in the original.

B: Well, they very often do. And then, the news and documentaries are first-rate. It's all very well reading about an earthquake in the newspaper, but when you actually see the destruction on TV, well—it makes you more concerned about other people and their problems.

A: That's true, I suppose, but you can't deny that some programs are full of silly ideas and corrupting values.

B: But you can select, after all. You can always turn the program off, if you think it's unsuitable.

Vocabulary

pub [pʌb] n. 酒吧，酒馆
liberation [ˌlɪbə'reɪʃn] n. 解放
movement ['muːvmənt] n. 活动，运动
strengths and weaknesses 优缺点
tender ['tendə(r)] adj. 温和的，亲切的
considerate [kən'sɪdərət] adj. 考虑周到的，体谅的
oftentimes ['ɒfntaɪmz] adv. [古] 屡次，常常
emotional [ɪ'məʊʃənl] adj. 感情的，情绪的
stereotype ['steriətaɪp] n. 陈词滥调，刻板印象
in fields of... 在……领域
prejudice ['predʒədɪs] v. 使……存偏见，使……有成见
come into play 开始兴起
puzzle ['pʌzl] n. 谜
concentrate ['kɒnsntreɪt] v. 集中，专心
screen [skriːn] n. 屏，幕
unsociable [ʌn'səʊʃəbl] adj. 不爱交际的，不与人亲近的，不和气的
interactive [ˌɪntər'æktɪv] adj. [计算机] 交互的
generation [ˌdʒenə'reɪʃn] n. 代，一代
corrupt [kə'rʌpt] adj. 腐败的，败德的

species ['spiːʃiːz] n. 物种，种类
whale [weɪl] n. 鲸
acutely [ə'kjuːtli] adv. 剧烈地
extinct [ɪk'stɪŋkt] adj. 灭绝的
endanger [ɪn'deɪndʒə(r)] vt. 危及
condemn [kən'dem] vt. 判刑，责备，谴责
come down to 归结为，涉及
legal ['liːgl] adj. 法律的，合法的，法定的
narrow-minded [ˌnærəʊ 'maɪndɪd] adj. 狭隘的；心胸狭窄的；有偏见的
conservative [kən'sɜːvətɪv] adj. 保守的；保守派的，保守主义的
approach [ə'prəʊtʃ] n. 方法，态度
peculiar [pɪ'kjuːliə(r)] adj. 奇怪的，不寻常的；特别的，独特的
impulsive [ɪm'pʌlsɪv] adj. 冲动的
ambitious [æm'bɪʃəs] adj. 有雄心的，有抱负的
associate [ə'səʊsieɪt] n. 同伴，伙伴
superstition [ˌsuːpə'stɪʃn] n. 迷信
cynical ['sɪnɪkl] adj. 愤世嫉俗的
serial ['sɪəriəl] n. 系列片

Useful Expressions

A. Asking for opinions

- What do you think of your new job?
- How do you feel about studying here?
- How do you find our restaurant?
- Have you got any comments on this program?
- How do you like the book you bought last week?
- What is your opinion about the suggestion put forward last night?

- Do you have any idea/comment on the plan?
- What's your point of view on this issue?
- Could I know your reaction to this plan?
- What would you say about UFO?
- What kind of movies do you like?

B. Giving opinions

- In my opinion, their concerns are fully justified.
- In my view, the court made the right decision.
- I think that hunting should be banned.
- Personally, I believe poverty is still a great problem.
- In this writer's view/opinion, the present system is in need of reform.
- It seems to me that there is some truth in her argument.
- I believe that the death penalty is morally wrong.
- The general opinion is that the combined vaccine works better.
- Everybody has a different opinion of what America represents.
- They held the same opinions on many issues.
- For Chomsky, language is an abstract system of rules which is used by human minds for transmitting and receiving ideas.
- As far as he was concerned, the failure showed the limits of military intervention.
- From their point of view, the system worked quite well.

C. Refusing to give opinions

- If you ask me, I think it's difficult.
- I really don't have any opinion about that.
- I'd prefer not to say anything about his trouble.
- I'd rather not to say anything about that.

D. Expressing agreement

- I entirely agree.
- I totally agree with you.
- I agree with your point.
- I'm with you on that.
- I couldn't agree more!
- Exactly!
- That's absolutely true!

- That's (exactly) the way I feel.
- I have to agree with you.
- I'm in complete agreement with you.
- That's just how I see it.

E. Expressing disagreement

- Well, it depends.
- I am against your idea.
- I agree in principle, but...
- By and large I accept what you say, but...
- I would tend to agree with you on that.
- I agree up to a point, but...
- Unfortunately, I see it differently.
- Up to a point I agree with you, but...
- I'm afraid I can't agree.
- I can see your point of view, but surely...
- I take your point, but have you considered...?
- I'm afraid I can't really go along with you on that.
- You could be right, but I think...
- I respect your opinion, but I can't help feeling that...
- Frankly, I don't agree at all.
- To put it bluntly, you're completely mistaken.
- I totally disagree with you.
- I don't agree with what you said just now.

Exercises

I. Use what you have learnt in this unit to express agreement or disagreement to the following statements.

1. Women are as intelligent as men.
2. English is easier than Chinese.
3. Chinese food is the most delicious food in the world.
4. The CCTV Spring Festival Gala is undoubtedly a wonderful program.
5. Space travel to Mars is impossible.
6. Computers are more intelligent than human beings.

II. Complete the short dialogues by translating Chinese into English.

1	A: China is developing so quickly.	B: _____ (千真万确).
2	A: Do you agree with me?	B: _____ (当然，我同意).
3	A: Chinese is so difficult.	B: _____ (的确是这样).
4	A: Chinese culture is very different from western culture.	B: _____ (你说得太对了).
5	A: Chinese food is so good.	B: _____ (我有同感).
6	A: China has a lot of problems.	B: _____ (我不这样认为).
7	A: Blood type can decide a person's character.	B: _____ (我恐怕不赞同).
8	A: Playing computer games is a waste of time.	B: _____ (抱歉，我不这么看).
9	A: Smoking can make people relaxed.	B: _____ (说实话，我完全不同意).
10	A: Eating vegetables is better than eating meat.	B: _____ (我反对你的看法).

III. Complete the dialogues with the expressions given in the box.

Dialogue 1

> Well, in my point of view, it was terrible   What do you think about   As I see it

A: _____1_____ the book?

B: _____2_____.

A: Why did you think that?

B: _____3_____, it was too violent.

Dialogue 2

> How do you feel about it   Maybe you have a point there
>
> Well, in my opinion, it's not as good as we expected

A: Here is one of our latest designs. _____1_____?

B: _____2_____. Maybe it'll have to be done again.

A: Oh, dear! We have racked our brains. _____3_____, but there isn't much room for improvement.

Dialogue 3

> I think   I don't see any point in   Why are you   Well, you have your opinion

A: ___1___ so crazy about Beijing Opera? It's so boring.

B: But ___2___ it's fantastic and charming. ___3___ and I have mine.

A: Maybe you're right. But I just still can't understand.

B: Come on. ___4___ arguing about this. Everyone has the right to express his/her own opinion.

IV. Pair work: make dialogues based on the following situations.

1. Ann and Sue are talking about beauty. They have different opinions on its definition.

2. David and Charlie are talking about presidential candidates. They have different viewpoints.

3. Fang Fang and Wen are talking about language study. Both of them think it is difficult.

4. Steven and David are talking about the lecture given by a famous professor. Steven enjoyed it but David didn't.

V. Topics for discussion.

1. Some people think that playing a game is fun only when you win. Do you agree or disagree with the statement? Give specific reasons to support your answer.

2. Traveling is more important than reading books in order to understand people and the world. Do you agree or disagree with the statement? Give specific reasons to support your answer.

3. People should never be satisfied with what they have, and they should always want something new or something different. Do you agree or disagree with the statement? Give reasons for your choice.

Culture Tips

How often have you been in a situation where someone asks, "What do you think of…"? The person expects you to express an opinion on something. In both our personal and professional lives, when discussing with friends, colleagues or classmates, we often need to find out what others think about a variety of everyday topics, such as the weather, world events, a recent film or TV program, a new fashion in clothes or hairstyles, a new product and so on. The most common expressions we use are "What do you think of…?" or "How do you feel about…?"

When it comes to giving opinions, we often say, "I think…" or "I don't think…". However, the British like to use "It seems to me…" as an indirect way of offering an opinion. This is personal and can be adjusted as the conversation or discussion progresses. If the British feel strongly about a subject, they will often begin to give their opinion by apologizing for the strength of their feelings. For example:

A: "Don't you think that the new policy is an improvement on the old one?"

B: "Well, I'm sorry, but I feel that it's absolutely terrible in every way."

The British tend not to disagree too abruptly with others' opinions, as it can cause offence. For this reason, if you don't agree, you might say, "Well, it's not that bad," or "Well, I'm afraid I don't know."

Class Activities

Headmaster

Take out a piece of paper and imagine the following scenario.

Suppose you are the new headmaster of this school. You have two years to make this school a perfect one. You can have as much money as you want, but you must spend it all within two years.

What changes would you make immediately?

What would you do to make it a better school?

What kind of school do you want to change it into?

Be specific. For example, instead of saying "Hire better teachers," explain how you would find better teachers or what kind of teachers you would hire. And remember to think like a headmaster, not like a student! Making school easier and letting the students take no exams or homework will not make parents happy!

You have 15 minutes to work alone.

Then, form a group of 3~5 members and choose a group leader to summarize your ideas. Each group leader will present their group's ideas to the class in the following period.

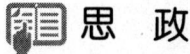

A Dip into Chinese Wisdom

1. 求同存异，聚同化异。

To seek common ground while shelving and narrowing differences.

2. 横看成岭侧成峰，远近高低各不同。

It's a range viewed in face and peaks viewed from the side,

Assuming different shapes viewed from far and wide.

3. 一花独放不是春，百花齐放春满园。

A single flower does not make spring while one hundred flowers in full blossom bring spring to the garden.

4. 仁者见仁，智者见智。

The benevolent see benevolence and the wise see wisdom.

SECTION II

Advice and Suggestions
Unit 10

Lead-in

Answer the following questions, starting with "If I were you, I'd..."

1. What can I do? I've got a bad cold.
2. What shall I do if I want to improve my English?
3. I'm putting on weight. What shall I do?
4. I can't sleep well. What do you suggest?
5. I feel tired and stressed out. What can I do?
6. I feel depressed. What can I do?

Warm-up Activities

I. Read the following expressions and find the pronunciation rule of linking.

1. an egg	a fried egg	a box of eggs
2. two eggs	three eggs	see it
3. for us	far away	Here are four eggs.

II. Read the story below and pay attention to your pronunciation and intonation.

After being away on business, Tim thought it would be nice to bring his wife a little gift.

"I want to buy a gift for my wife. What do you suggest?" he asked the cosmetics clerk.

"How about some perfume?" the cosmetics clerk showed him a bottle that cost $50.

"That's a bit expensive," said Tim.

"How about this one? It's just $30." she returned with a smaller bottle priced at $30.

"That's still quite expensive," Tim complained.

Growing annoyed, the clerk brought out a tiny bottle.

"What I mean is," said Tim, "I'd like to see something really cheap."

The clerk handed him a mirror.

Dialogues

Dialogue 1

Li Ming: Professor Liu, could you give me some advice on my English studies?

Prof. Liu: Sure, with pleasure. What's your trouble?

Li Ming: How can I improve my spoken English?

Prof. Liu: I think it might be a good idea if you seize every opportunity to practice spoken English.

Li Ming: But I don't think my pronunciation is good enough.

Prof. Liu: Have you ever tried to listen to the tape and imitate the native speakers?

Li Ming: Should I imitate American accent or British accent?

Prof. Liu: It's up to you, but I prefer the latter.

Li Ming: Thank you very much. Your advice is a great help to me.

Dialogue 2

Joe: Good afternoon, Dr. Smith. My name is Joe. I am a freshman in your department. There are a few things that I am not quite sure of and I do need your advice.

Dr. Smith: Thank you very much for your trust, Joe. As your academic advisor, I will try my best. Just tell me how I can help you, Joe.

Joe: I used to major in English, but now I have made up my mind to switch to English literature. I have been wondering if it is possible.

Dr. Smith: Well, we usually allow it, as long as you have enough credits.

Joe: That's good news for me but I'm worried about the make-up credits. Would you please let me know how many credits are required?

Dr. Smith: Usually 36 credits are needed. Are you OK on credits?

Joe: Not too many. I'll have to add about 12 credits as far as I can figure from my transcript.

Dr. Smith: That will be fine. What else can I do to help?

Joe: Nothing else. Thank you very much for your help, Dr. Smith.

Dr. Smith: Glad I can help.

Dialogue 3

Mike: Nancy, you'll graduate from the college in half a year. Have you found any jobs?

Nancy: I've been thinking about that company's job.

Mike: Have you decided yet?

Nancy: It's hard to make a decision. Give me some advice.

Mike: What are you most dissatisfied with that job?

Nancy: Work time. I think I'd like to take it, if they wouldn't ask me to work extra hours on weekends.

Mike: If I were you, I'd take the job anyway.

Nancy: Maybe you're right.

Dialogue 4

Maggie: Do you have some good suggestions on how to keep fit? I feel I have put on several pounds recently.

Rebecca: You are just a little chubby, not paunchy. The weight looks good on you.

Maggie: You see, I'm getting a thick waist. I need to find a quick fix to it.

Rebecca: Maybe jogging can promote weight loss.

Maggie: Yeah, but it takes time. Are there any shortcuts?

Rebecca: Dieting pills can help you lose weight, but they may have side effects and do harm to your body. As you can see, everyone wants immediate results. This is not going to happen.

Maggie: You said it.

Dialogue 5

Maggie: I heard you've just come back from England, and I'm going to attend a fortnight's conference there. Can you give me some suggestions about it?

Shelly: Sure. What do you want to know?

Maggie: First, what do you think I should take with me?

Shelly: When will you leave?

Maggie: Next month.

Shelly: Oh, in that case, you needn't take too much clothes with you. The climate in

England at this time of year is quite mild. But you must remember to take an umbrella with you, in case it rains a lot.

Maggie: What kind of gifts should I bring along?

Shelly: Anything Chinese. But since your luggage allowance is only 25 kilos, you'd better buy things that don't weigh too much. Things like scarves and paper-cuts are light, and they make lovely presents.

Maggie: Thank you. These have really been very useful.

Dialogue 6

Adam: I'm never going to finish my assignment in time! There is just no way. I have to finish writing this paper for tomorrow's seminar, but I've just started and I can't maintain focus.

Nelly: Can I make a suggestion? How about removing those distractions from your room?

Adam: What do you mean by that?

Nelly: Have you thought about turning off the TV and disconnecting from the Internet? They are the world's biggest distractions. If you want to be much more productive, you need to reduce noise and other distractions, such as entertaining items.

Adam: Yes. You are right.

Dialogue 7

Jessie: Do you feel like doing anything tomorrow, Sam?

Sam: Yes, all right. What do you suggest?

Jessie: How about going to see the Peking Opera, *Farewell My Concubine*?

Sam: Well, we could, I suppose. But I don't really like Peking Opera very much. Of course, if you'd like to see it…

Jessie: No, no… I don't mind. It was just a suggestion, that's all.

Sam: We could always go to Bill's party, I suppose.

Jessie: Bill?

Sam: Yes, Bill Cage. You know he works in Human Resources. He's celebrating his promotion as a vice president. Everyone's invited. So if you fancy going, we can tell him.

Jessie: No, I don't think so! There will be too many people drinking too much alcohol. It really isn't my idea of fun.

Sam: Well, it was only an idea.

Jessie: No, I'd prefer to go somewhere else, if you don't mind. Just the two of us.

Sam: Would you like to go for a walk along the river?

Jessie: Yes, that would be nice. Let's do that. And why not call in on Sandy and Julia while we're passing by? We've been promising to go and see them for ages.

Sam: Yes, good idea. We could even go on to Bill's party afterwards.

Jessie: Sam! If you think I'm going.

Sam: It's all right. I'm only joking!

Vocabulary

with pleasure adv. 愉快地（高兴地，十分愿意）	paunchy ['pɔ:ntʃi] adj. 大肚子的
pronunciation [prə,nʌnsi'eɪʃn] n. 发音	do harm to 对……有害
imitate ['ɪmɪteɪt] vt. 模仿	You said it. 你算说对了／你说得对。
accent ['æksent] n. 口音	fortnight ['fɔ:tnaɪt] n. 两星期
academic [ˌækə'demɪk] adj. 学院的，理论的，学术性的	luggage ['lʌɡɪdʒ] n. 行李
advisor [əd'vaɪzə(r)] n. 顾问	allowance [ə'laʊəns] n. 限额，定量
switch [swɪtʃ] v. 转变，切换	scarf [skɑ:f] n. 围巾
literature ['lɪtrətʃə(r)] n. 文学，文献	paper-cutting 剪纸
credit ['kredɪt] n. 学分	assignment [ə'saɪnmənt] n. 被指定的（课外）作业
transcript ['trænskrɪpt] n. 成绩单	seminar ['semɪnɑ:(r)] n.（大学的）研究班，研讨会
make a decision 作出决定	distraction [dɪ'strækʃn] n. 娱乐，分心的事物，分心
be dissatisfied with 对……不满	productive [prə'dʌktɪv] adj. 能生产的，多产的
work extra hours 加班	Farewell My Concubine 霸王别姬
keep fit 保持健康	alcohol ['ælkəhɒl] n. 含酒精饮品
chubby ['tʃʌbi] adj. 圆胖的	

Useful Expressions

A. Asking for advice or suggestions

- Could you give me some advice on how to improve English listening comprehension?
- What do you suggest us to do?
- What do you think I should do?
- What would you do if you were in my shoes?

- What would you do if you were in my position/situation?
- I'd like to have your advice about my research.
- I would appreciate your advice about buying a house.
- Maybe you can give me some feedback.

B. Giving advice

- Take my advice and leave it as it is.
- Why not talk to her about it?
- Believe me and don't put any salt in it.
- It's up to you but I wouldn't do that.
- You would be wise enough not to cheat in the exam.
- I think you should take advantage of this opportunity.
- I'd do the same thing, if I were you.
- If I were you, I'd work less.
- If I were in your position, I'd work less.
- If I were in your shoes, I'd work less.
- You had better work less.
- You shouldn't work so hard.
- Whatever you do, don't work so hard.
- I don't think you should work so hard.
- You ought to work less.
- You ought not to work so hard.

C. Making suggestions

- How about giving him a free hand and see how it will turn out?
- Why don't you take a few days off?
- Why don't you give this idea a chance?
- Shall we go for a walk?
- Would you like to play cards?
- Let's go and take a look.
- Do you fancy going out?
- Do you feel like eating something sweet?
- May I suggest that you put the money in a safe?
- Do you think it would be a good idea to buy a laptop?
- Have you ever thought of going to Disneyland during the golden week?
- Have you ever thought about using flowers to apologize?

- I think it'd be a great idea to have a talk with him.
- Would it be better to tell her the truth?
- You might as well see a doctor.
- I suggest you/we take all the factors into consideration before you/we decide.

D. Accepting advice or suggestions

- I'd love to.
- I don't mind.
- I'll do that. Thanks.
- I'll think it over.
- That will probably help. Thanks.
- That's certainly a possibility.
- That's not a bad idea.
- That sounds like a good idea.
- Good idea/OK.
- Yes, I'll try it.
- Yes, why not?
- Yes, great!
- Yes, fine!
- Thanks for your advice.

E. Making negative responses

- I regret to say I can't accept your suggestion.
- I'm afraid your proposal is not acceptable.
- I'd like that, but I can't afford the time.
- I'd rather not, if you don't mind.
- It's nice of you to tell me about that, but I don't think so.
- I don't think I'll do that, but thank you all the same.
- It's an idea, I suppose, but it may cost a lot of time, money and effort.
- That would be very nice, but I may not have enough time.
- That's not (such) a good idea (for me), because (there isn't much time left).
- Thanks, but I've already tried that.
- Isn't there anything else I can/could do?
- No, don't bother.

 **Exercises**

I. Complete the dialogue with the words or expressions given in the box.

> A. Please tell me how I should make my schedule
> B. Thanks. I'll have a try
> C. Next
> D. What do you think I should do
> E. Have you ever thought of making a study schedule
> F. Absolutely
> G. That's right

Li Yan: Hello, Miss Wang.

Miss Wang: Nice to see you, Li Yan. How are you doing?

Li Yan: Not too bad. But I've been wondering how to be an efficient student. ___1___?

Miss Wang: ___2___?

Li Yan: Do you mean I should have a definite plan for the day?

Miss Wang: ___3___. If you form the habit of studying a certain subject at a certain time each day, you'll need less energy to focus your attention upon it.

Li Yan: ___4___. I can avoid those last-minute cram-sessions before a quiz or an examination.

Miss Wang: If you follow a definite pattern, you can certainly make better use of your time.

Li Yan: ___5___.

Miss Wang: First, write down all the things you must do at a fixed time. That will include your class and time for eating and sleeping.

Li Yan: ___6___?

Miss Wang: Write down the exact time of day you will study each subject and also the time for reviewing each subject each week.

Li Yan: I see. Is there any time for recreation?

Miss Wang: Sure. You should also put it in your schedule. All work and no play makes Jack a dull boy, you know.

Li Yan: I don't want to be a dull boy.

Miss Wang: It's important to count the hours of study to see if you've provided for at least two hours of study for each class period of the course.

Li Yan: _____7_____.

II. Match the request in Column A with an appropriate suggestion in Column B.

A	B
1. What do you fancy eating tonight?	A. Let's go and stay with my aunt.
2. Do you fancy going to a Cantonese restaurant tonight?	B. Mmmm, but wouldn't you prefer to go to Hainan again?
3. Where do you want to go tonight?	C. How about a Korean barbecue?
4. What about going for a walk?	D. Why not go to a karaoke bar?
5. Shall we go to the concert tonight?	E. What about going to Yunnan?
6. Who do you suggest we invite to the New Year party?	F. I'm not sure. I don't really like Cantonese food very much.
7. What can we do at the weekend?	G. Why don't we ask our head teacher?
8. Where shall we go for our holidays?	H. Well, I'd rather not, if you don't mind.
9. How about having a party on Friday?	I. Well, I think I'd prefer to listen to a record if that's all right with you.
10. Why not go to Hawaii this summer?	J. Well, we could, I suppose, but remember we've got to get up early on Saturday morning.

III. Pair work: make dialogues based on the following situations.

1. Ask about or suggest a popular holiday resort.
2. Ask about or suggest how to grow flowers.
3. Ask about or suggest how to write a thesis.
4. Ask about or suggest how to memorize English words.

Culture Tips

When we face various problems, we often ask for advice from our friends or acquaintances, either directly or indirectly. We also give suggestions when other people have problems and ask for our advice. But we must remember that advice on personal matters is usually given only to close friends or when someone asks for it. People in the West like to "do their own things" and "mind their own business". Regardless of circumstances, being overly eager to offer advice or suggest a course of action might be seen as an intrusion upon privacy.

 Class Activities

Noughts and Crosses

The game Noughts and Crosses is also called Tic-tac-toe, hugs and kisses, and many other names. The aim of the game is to help students review the learned expressions and sentences.

Divide the class into two groups. Draw a 3 × 3 grid on the blackboard and write a number in each square (from 1 to 9). Prepare nine questions and assign one question to each number. Ask one group to call out a number, and the teacher (or a chosen student) reads the corresponding question. If the group answers the question correctly, they earn a point and draw an "O" in the respective square. Then ask the other group to do the same but draw an "×" instead in the corresponding square. The group that succeeds in placing three of their own marks in a horizontal, vertical, or diagonal row wins the game.

 思 政

A Dip into Chinese Wisdom

1. 新时代中国青年要听党话、跟党走，胸怀忧国忧民之心、爱国爱民之情。

Young Chinese of the new era should follow the instructions and guidance of the Party, and remain dedicated to the country and the people.

2. 劝君更尽一杯酒，西出阳关无故人。

I invite you to drink a cup of wine again;

West of the sunny pass no more friends will be seen.

3. 劝君莫惜金缕衣，劝君惜取少年时。

Love not your golden dress, I pray,

More than your youthful golden hours!

4. 莫等闲，白了少年头，空悲切。

Should youthful heads in vain turn grey,

We would regret for aye.

SECTION II

Instructions
Unit 11

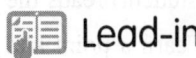 **Lead-in**

List some words or expressions you may use when you give someone instructions, and then describe how to make dumplings by using some of them.

You may use:

First of all… Then… After that… And finally…

chop up meat（剁 肉）/ meat filling（肉 馅）/ leek（韭 菜）/ soy sauce（酱 油）/ vinegar（醋）/ spices（调料）/ roll out dumpling wrappers（擀饺子皮）/ knead something with fingers（捏）/ ladle something out of…（舀出）

 Warm-up Activities

I. Read the following expressions and find the pronunciation rule.

doctor	blackboard	eighth	box	object
upset	grandfather	goodbye	lamppost	absent
outcome	kindness	want to	a big rabbit	a red shirt
a good time	good night	make sure	good morning	at that time
don't know	sit down	glad to	pop music	top student
a good time	a red tie	a red shirt	a black jacket	

II. Read the joke below and pay attention to your pronunciation and intonation.

Instructions to Husbands

An American woman, a British woman, and an Italian woman were having lunch. The American woman said, "I told my husband that I wasn't going to clean the house anymore. If he wanted it clean, he would have to do it himself. After the first day, I didn't see anything. The second day, I didn't see anything. Then, on the third day, voila! My husband had cleaned the whole house!" The British woman agreed, "I told my husband that I wasn't going to do the laundry anymore. If he wanted it done, he would have to do it himself. After the first day, I didn't see anything. The second day, I didn't see anything. Then, on the third day, voila! My husband had done both his and my laundry!" The Italian woman chimed in, "I told my husband that I wasn't going to cook anymore. If he wanted home cooking, he would have to either go to his mother or cook for himself. After the first day, I didn't see anything. The second day, I didn't see anything. Then, on the third day, I began to see a little out of my left eye."

 Dialogues

Dialogue 1

A: Excuse me, miss. Is this ATM working?

B: Yes, it is. Why?

A: I can't get money out of it.

B: Did you follow the instructions?

A: I think I did. Let me try again. I first insert my bank card here. I then type my personal ID number and then select the function to get cash. Now I enter the amount of money I need, and that's it. But no money comes out.

B: I think you did nothing wrong. Maybe there's something wrong with this cash machine. Let me contact the bank manager.

Dialogue 2

A: No, Wang Ling, it's not / e / as in "bed", but / æ / as in "bad".

B: I know I'm wrong. But I really have trouble getting the sound correct. There is no similar sound in my mother tongue.

A: Maybe not. Look, do it like this. Open your mouth wide with the front part of your tongue raised a little.

B: Do I have to push my tongue forward?

A: Yes, make sure that your tongue touches the back of the lower teeth, and your muscles in the throat are tense. Now try it.

Dialogue 3

A: Excuse me, I notice that there are two kinds of medicine here. Are there any instructions on how to take them?

B: The pills are to be taken before meals, one pill each time and three times a day. The cough syrup is to be taken once every four hours and one teaspoonful every time.

A: Sorry, I didn't quite catch you. Did you say I should take the pills before or after meals?

B: Before meals. By the way, the instructions are printed on the labels.

A: Thanks a lot.

Dialogue 4

A: Can you tell me how to make tea with dried tea leaves in a teapot, please?

B: Yes, with pleasure. First, get the boiling water ready. Before you put some dried tea leaves in a teapot, warm the pot with hot water and empty it out. Put tea leaves into the pot, add fresh boiling water and then leave them to steep for three minutes before serving.

A: Could I add flavors to it by putting some chrysanthemum flowers or ginseng?

B: Sure. You can also add milk or lemon juice into it. Some people even serve tea with sugar. I, however, prefer to have pure clear tea.

A: But I like it mixed with milk. It is both nutritious and refreshing.

B: You said it. Each person has his own preference.

A: Do you drink tea very often?

B: Sure. I drink several cups of tea a day and I enjoy the mild soothing aroma rising from the tea cup to my nostrils.

Dialogue 5

A: I want to make chicken and rice for dinner. Do you know a recipe?

B: Of course.

A: What do I need then?

B: Chicken and rice, of course. You also need onions, tomatoes, mushroom, and green peppers.

A: Anything else?

B: Yes. You also need garlic. Not too much, though.

A: Then what do I do next?

B: You cut all the vegetables into slices. Boil the chicken and cut it into pieces. Mix the chicken and vegetables with rice, and cook the mixture for about 20 minutes. Add spices as you like and it's done.

A: Are you sure that's the way to cook chicken and rice?

B: To be honest with you, I'm not quite sure. My mother cooks that way. I observed and tasted it, but never cooked it myself.

Dialogue 6

A: Mum, have you tried the washing machine we bought last week?

B: Not yet. I'm still not quite sure how to use it.

A: Let me check the instructions and show you.

B: That's good.

A: First, open the door, put the clothes in and then close the door.

B: Next?

A: Put the washing powder in the tray and select the program. After that, you should check the water supply and make sure the drain pipe is in the right place.

B: Is it ready to go now?

A: No, you have to plug in the machine and then switch it on.

B: Can I do something else while it's working?

A: Yes.

Dialogue 7

A: Hi, Bob. You have a mobile phone, right?

B: Yep, what's up, buddy?

A: I just bought one yesterday. And I still don't know how to use it. It's hard for me to use such small stuff.

B: It is not difficult. Hand your cell phone to me, and let me see.

A: You know, I know how to answer a phone call and call others. I just don't know how to send a text message. Can you help me out?

B: Don't worry, I'll show you. Enter the menu, and here you go, choose this option. See the message box, and then open it. There are lots of options inside. For example, you can read and write messages here. Next step, click the "Write Message" option, right, that's it. Use the keyboard and type what you want to say, and it will show on the screen. When you finish, press the "Send" button, and a message will pop up asking you to enter the phone number. Try my number, 123456789.

A: OK. Slow down 1…2…3…, done!

B: See, I got your message. You made it! Isn't it easy?

A: Awesome. Thank you, man!

B: Any time!

A: I am starving to death now. Do you know any place where we can eat?

B: Oh yeah, I know a fantastic restaurant.

A: Great. Let's go, man, my treat!

B: Thanks, next is on me.

 Vocabulary

ATM n. 自动取款机	aroma [ə'rəʊmə] n. 香气
insert [ɪn'sɜːt] v. 插入	nostril ['nɒstrəl] n. 鼻孔
function ['fʌŋkʃn] n. 功能，作用	washing powder 洗衣粉
amount [ə'maʊnt] n. 数量，总额	tray [treɪ] n. 盘，碟
alert [ə'lɜːt] adj. 警觉的	program ['prəʊɡræm] n. 节目，程序，计划
tense [tens] adj. 紧张的，拉紧的	pipe [paɪp] n. 管
syrup ['sɪrəp] n. 糖浆	plug in 插入
teaspoonful ['tiːspuːnfʊl] n. 一茶匙容量	switch on（用开关）开启
label ['leɪbl] n. 标签，商标	buddy ['bʌdi] n. 伙伴，好朋友
tea leaves 茶叶	stuff [stʌf] n. 材料，东西
teapot ['tiːpɒt] n. 茶壶	text message 短信
steep [stiːp] v. 浸泡，浸透	help sb. out 帮助某人解决难题
ginseng ['dʒɪnseŋ] n. 人参，高丽参	option ['ɒpʃn] n. 选择
squeeze [skwiːz] n. 压榨，挤	keyboard ['kiːbɔːd] n. 键盘
nutritious [njuː'trɪʃəs] adj. 有营养的	pop up 弹出
refreshing [rɪ'freʃɪŋ] adj. 提神的，使人有精神 / 恢复活力的	awesome ['ɔːsəm] adj. 引起敬畏的，可怕的
preference ['prefrəns] n. 偏爱，喜爱物	my treat 我请客
soothing ['suːðɪŋ] adj. 安慰性的	fantastic [fæn'tæstɪk] adj. 极好的，难以相信的

Useful Expressions

A. Asking for instructions

● What should I do if I want to…?

● What's the procedure for…?

- Could you tell me the best way to…?
- Excuse me, but can you tell me how to…?
- What's the first thing we should do?
- Could you show me how to…?
- Anything else I should pay attention to?

B. Giving instructions

- The job should be done according to the following procedure: …
- This is how you do it: First of all… Then… After that… And finally…
- It's really not very hard. All you do is…
- You may do it like this: …
- Look, the first thing you have to do is…
- The next thing you do is…
- Be careful not to…
- Remember to…
- Be sure to…
- Bear in mind that…
- First of all, you should…
- Let me show you. First…
- Look, all you need to do is…
- The first thing you have to do is…
- Now you do like this. First… Then… After that…

Exercises

I. Complete the short dialogues by translating Chinese into English.

1	A：Can you show me how to use a hammer?	B：Look, _____ (真的没那么困难). You need to be more patient.
2	A：_____ (你能告诉我在学生食堂怎么买饭吗)？	B：Certainly. This is a self-service cafeteria. You pay at the cashier's at the exit.
3	A：I have a sore throat and headache.	B：I'll prescribe some medicine for you. _____ (一天三次,一次三粒,饭后吃).
4	A：So what should I do?	B：_____ (首先你需要报警) and file a report.

5	A: I would like to get some information on what I need to do to apply to your school.	B: _____ (你需要填写一份申请表) and have your official copy of school transcripts sent to us.
6	A: I really love babysitting your son. _____ (告诉我应该做什么).	B: Well, you need to prepare dinner for him. And then he has to read for about an hour before going to bed.
7	A: I don't know how to insert the battery. Can you show me?	B: Sure. _____ (我给你演示一下). First you remove the battery holder. Then you insert the battery. And finally, you refit the holder.
8	A: Could you give me some tips about how to take the listening tests?	B: Well, _____ (这需要特殊的技巧).
9	A: It sounds easy for me.	B: Well, _____ (说说容易, 做起来难).
10	A: I suffer from a lot of stress at work.	B: Drink plenty of water and stay in bed to catch up on sleep. _____ (你需要放轻松).

II. Complete the dialogues with the expressions given in the box.

Dialogue 1

> Wait for a few minutes and the tea is ready   Do it like this   What should I do next

A: Could you tell me how to make Chinese tea?

B: ____1____. First, boil the water and put some tea leaves in the cup.

A: ____2____?

B: When the water boils, pour it over the tea leaves in the cup and put on the lid. ____3____.

A: Thank you very much. That doesn't sound very difficult, does it?

Dialogue 2

> how to use the pay phone please   What if I can't get through?
> then deposit the coin as required

A: Excuse me, but could you tell me ____1____?

B: Yes, of course. Pick up the phone first, ____2____ and listen for the dial tone. Once you hear the dial tone, dial the number you want.

A: ____3____?

B: Hang up and press the "Coin Release" button. You will get your money back.

Dialogue 3

First, don't forget to feed the cat   I do need to tell you a few things

if an emergency occurs

A: Do you have any special instructions for me to look after your house?

B: ____1____.

A: Okay, let me take notes of them.

B: ____2____. Second, please leave the light on at night. Call me at this number ____3____.

III. Put the following instructions in the right order, and then make a dialogue with your partner.

1. On how to cook fried rice with eggs

    A. Put some cooked rice into it and then mix them up.

    B. Heat the pan, then put oil into it and wait until the oil gets hot.

    C. Break the eggs, beat them, and then put the beaten eggs into the pan.

2. On how to shop online

    A. Wait for the seller to dispatch the goods.

    B. Log in to the website and search for your favorite goods online. If you want to buy the goods, click the "Purchase" button on the website.

    C. After the deal is made, you can give the seller a rating: good, average, or bad.

    D. Open an account with an online banking service and register on the website.

    E. Select "Pay by Online Banking" when choosing the payment method.

    F. Check the goods sent by the seller after you receive them.

IV. Pair work: make dialogues based on the following situations.

1. You have agreed to look after your neighbors' dog while they are away on vacation. They are giving you some instructions about how to care for the dog before they leave.

2. David is showing Harry how to operate a computer.

3. Joan wants to buy a birthday gift for her mom online. She asks her friend Mary to give the instructions on online shopping.

V. Topics for discussion.

1. Give instructions about how to use a washing machine.

2. Give instructions about how to cook "scrambled eggs with tomatoes".

3. Give instructions about how to protect our eyesight.

Culture Tips

How can you ask someone to do something for you in English without sounding rude? Here are some tips:

1. It's important to make instructions clear and concise.

2. Before giving instructions, make sure everyone is listening to you. Don't give instructions until everyone is ready and paying attention.

3. When giving instructions, ask the listener to repeat what you said to make sure he/she knows what to do.

4. Take time to repeat the instructions if necessary.

Besides, when giving instructions, pay attention to the sentence structures you use to avoid sounding rude or impolite.

5. Use the imperative form.

The imperative form is used to give orders, warnings, and advice.

Examples: Be quiet! / Take care! / Listen to me carefully!

Since direct orders can sound rude (especially when speaking to adults), we often "soften" the imperative form with "let's" or "please".

Examples: Let's go now. /Please listen to what I'm saying.

6. Use modal verbs to turn orders into requests. Modal verbs can make sentences sound more polite.

For example, "You should help her" is more polite than "Help her!".

Other modal verbs for making requests include:

Could: Could you make me some tea?

Can: Can you come here, please?

Will: Will you shut the door, please?

Would: Would you wait here until the doctor is ready for you?

 Class Activities

Simon Says

The student who is chosen as "Simon" stands at the front of the classroom and issues commands. The rest of the class should only follow these commands if they are prefixed with the words "Simon says". If someone follows a command without "Simon says", he/she is out of the game. The last remaining student becomes the next "Simon". Some examples of commands include: stand up, sit down, touch your left ear, say "yes", etc.

 思 政

A Dip into Chinese Wisdom

1. 听党话、跟党走始终是共青团坚守的政治生命，党有号召、团有行动始终是一代代共青团员的政治信念。

Following the instructions and guidance of the Party remains the political career of the Communist Youth League, and that the League will act upon the Party's call is the political belief of League members from generation to generation.

2. 明月松间照，清泉石上流。

Among pine trees bright moonbeams peer,

Over crystal stones flows water clear.

3. 父母教，须敬听；父母责，须顺承。

When your parents need to instruct you, respectfully do as you're told.

Whenever your parents must scold you, acknowledge your errors and faults.

4. 己所不欲，勿施于人。

Do not do to others what you do not want others to do to you.

SECTION II

Comparing and Contrasting
Unit 12

 **Lead-in**

What are the similarities and differences between Chinese people and Westerners?

You may discuss it from the following aspects: festivals, food, family, attitude...

 Warm-up Activities

I. Read the following words and find the pronunciation rules.

scale	speak	skyscraper	street	stand	spare
scanner	skill	space	spoil	spirit	skip
school	skin	stream	spoon	space	storm
scream	skirt	stress	sponsor	special	stump
study	student	speech	Spain	stroll	strike

II. Read the story below and pay attention to your pronunciation and intonation.

　　Jimmy's family was very thrifty. Jimmy's father often told him, "A penny saved is a penny earned." Jimmy usually put half of his allowance in the bank. He was frugal and never spent money on foolish things. He thought carefully about every purchase, never used a credit card, and only bought with cash.

His wife, Gertie, had different spending habits. In Gertie's family, money was "easy come, easy go". Her mother took Gertie and her sisters to the department store and let them buy anything they wanted. Gertie always wore new clothes. She was extravagant, liked to give her family expensive gifts, and enjoyed going out to nightclubs and staying in the best hotels. She was often broke and needed to borrow money from Jimmy.

Jimmy and Gertie often fought about money. They were seeing a marriage counselor to work out their difficulties. Maybe Jimmy would have to spend more, and Gertie would have to save more.

Dialogues

Dialogue 1

M: I hear that you have just returned from Australia and New Zealand. Would you please tell me something about the two countries?

W: Well, Australia is much bigger than New Zealand. You can leave a town and drive for hours before coming to the next one. There is a greater diversity of nationalities there. But New Zealand has a much cooler climate.

M: Is there anything similar between them?

W: They both have beautiful beaches and great forest mountains. So traveling in both countries is a pleasant experience.

M: What about the cultures?

W: They have very similar cultures. Perhaps because they are such close neighbors, both cultures are very relaxed and friendly. You can go to a corner shop to buy a drink and end up talking to the shopkeeper for hours. What's more, people in both countries are crazy about sports.

Dialogue 2

A: Mary and Jerry are a perfect couple. They are exactly the same.

B: I don't think so. They are completely different! One is obese and the other is skinny.

A: But both of them have the same hobbies. They like the same music, read the same books and do the same sports.

B: I'm afraid you don't quite understand them. They have completely different tastes in clothing. The guy wears only black—black shoes, black socks, black pants, a black shirt, and probably even black underwear. And she wears every color in the rainbow. You name it—red, orange, yellow, green, blue, indigo and violet, and even hot pink! She wears them all at once.

A: So how do you explain that they get along so well?

B: You know the old saying, "Opposites attract."

A: So maybe you have a point.

Dialogue 3

A: How time flies! I feel that I just enrolled in the university last year.

B: But now you'll be graduating in two months.

A: Yes. By the way, are you going to look for a job or are you going to a graduate school?

B: I really like to go into a career. However, it's hard to get a satisfying job without holding a graduate degree. How about you?

A: Well, I've been thinking about it but I haven't made up my mind. I'd rather take a job if I get a good one.

B: What would you like to do after graduation?

A: I'd like to work in a big state-owned company where they offer a good salary and welfare benefits.

B: Oh, really? I'd prefer to work in a joint venture. I think maybe I'll be under great pressure with the fast-paced work, but I can get a sense of achievement after fulfilling difficult tasks.

A: To speak frankly, both have their own advantages.

B: Let's see if we can get our favorite jobs.

Dialogue 4

A: I predict that in a hundred years, hardly anybody will have to work because almost everything will be done by robots. We'll have much more leisure time. And scientists will have discovered how to extend people's lifespans significantly.

B: If people live much longer, there'll be a terrible population problem. And if hardly anybody works, don't you think people will get very bored? That might lead to a lot of materialism and other social problems. It could mean crime would increase, too.

A: It's true that materialism may increase, but there will also be more time to have a richer and more cultured life. I don't think crime will increase. We'll learn more about what causes crime and be able to prevent it more effectively. Everybody will be much happier than now, doing whatever they like. Of course, there'll have to be some rules.

B: I don't want to throw cold water on your ideas, but I think you are over-optimistic. I guess it will be the robots who will enforce the rules. There'll be very few human police because hardly anybody will be working. We might even be governed by robots, too. It sounds like we could lose control of our own lives.

Dialogue 5

Sam: Have you ever heard of the saying "East is East and West is West, and never the twain shall meet"?

Liu Fang: Yes. Are you implying that you and I are very different in our ideas and habits?

Sam: No. To my great surprise, I've discovered we have much in common.

Liu Fang: Speaking of similarities and differences, do you like the way we steam our bread instead of baking it? Most foreigners find it unique.

Sam: For me, either steamed or baked bread is OK, but neither of my American roommates likes it steamed.

Liu Fang: Some Chinese feel the same way, especially those from the South. They like rice, three times a day.

Sam: Oh, I can't stand having rice all the time for my meals.

Liu Fang: Neither do I. I hate having rice for every meal.

Sam: But sometimes I have to. So whenever I'm in Beijing, I have bread, steamed or baked, but in Shanghai, I mostly have rice.

Liu Fang: There are many other respects in which people from our two countries are different. For example, Chinese people like soccer. But none of us has ever seen an American football match.

Sam: Strange to say, I don't like either of those games. Basketball is my favorite game.

Liu Fang: It's my favorite too. Let's go and watch a game sometime.

Dialogue 6

Bill: Hey, Tom. You've been surfing the Internet for quite a while. What on earth are you searching for?

Tom: The media has always latched on to stories of so-called "hackers" breaking into computer systems and wreaking havoc. I'd like to know something about hackers.

Bill: Well, generally speaking, a hacker is a person who enjoys exploring the details of programmable systems and how to stretch their capabilities, as opposed to most users, who prefer to learn only the minimum necessary.

Tom: But why do people often have a very negative attitude toward them?

Bill: They must have mixed hackers with crackers.

Tom: What are crackers then?

Bill: There is another group of people who call themselves hackers, but they actually aren't. They can easily break into other people's systems and do what they want. Real hackers call these people "crackers" and want nothing to do with them.

Tom: So they are totally two different concepts.

Bill: Well, hackers mostly think crackers are irresponsible and malicious. Crackers destroy vital data, deny legal users' service, or basically cause problems for their targets.

Tom: I see. Then the basic difference is that hackers build things, while crackers break them.

Bill: You got it.

Dialogue 7

Liu Ying: Isn't it exciting to go abroad? Just imagine living where the sights, sounds and smells are different!

Zhang Li: Yes, in a way. But living abroad can also be very disturbing.

Liu Ying: How come?

Zhang Li: Uh, you can't communicate in a culture that is quite different from yours.

Liu Ying: But what if I speak a bit of the language?

Zhang Li: It helps. However, you'll find, sometimes, you still can't make yourself understood. The reason is that what you say may mean something different to your listener.

Liu Ying: You bet. I once said we Chinese people are descendants of the dragon. The foreign teacher looked puzzled when she heard it.

Zhang Li: And your behavior may seem very alien and even exotic. As a matter of fact, one's behavior is a product of one's culture. And when what you've learned in your culture doesn't function in another, you experience culture shock.

Liu Ying: What do you mean by "culture shock"?

Zhang Li: I mean, you'll experience a sense of loss and a sense of shock when you meet something new and unexpected.

Liu Ying: Well, possibly. But is there any way to avoid the shock?

Zhang Li: I'm afraid not. No matter how well you are prepared, there will always be many things in a culture that you won't find in books. It's common among immigrants and foreign students.

Liu Ying: Sounds terrible. What should we do then?

Zhang Li: Be a person who is adaptable to new environments.

 Vocabulary

obese [əʊ'biːs] *adj.* 极肥胖的	hacker ['hækə(r)] *n.* 电脑黑客（中性）
skinny ['skɪni] *adj.* 皮包骨的	wreak havoc 对……造成严重破坏
rainbow ['reɪnbəʊ] *n.* 彩虹	explore [ɪk'splɔː(r)] *v.* 探险，探测，探究[计算机]，探讨
opposites attract 异性相吸	
state-owned *adj.* 国有的	stretch [stretʃ] *v.* 伸展，张开，延伸
joint venture *n.* 合资企业	minimum ['mɪnɪməm] *adj.* 最低的，最小的
fulfill [fʊl'fɪl] *vt.* 履行，完成	cracker ['krækə(r)] *n.* 破解者（贬义）
predict [prɪ'dɪkt] *v.* 预知，预言，预报	want nothing to do with sb. 与……无关
leisure ['leʒə(r)] *adj.* 空闲的 *n.* 空闲，闲暇	malicious [mə'lɪʃəs] *adj.* 怀恶意的，恶毒的
lead to 导致	data ['deɪtə] *n.* 资料，数据
materialism [mə'tɪərɪəlɪzəm] *n.* 唯物主义	legal ['liːgl] *adj.* 法律的，合法的，法定的
crime [kraɪm] *n.* 犯罪	How come? 怎么会这样？
over-optimistic *adj.* 过于乐观的	descendant [dɪ'sendənt] *n.* 子孙，后代
enforce [ɪn'fɔːs] *vt.* 厉行，强迫，执行	you bet 的确，真的
govern ['gʌvn] *v.* 统治，支配	alien ['eɪliən] *adj.* 外国的，相异的
twain [tweɪn] *n.& adj.* 对，双	exotic [ɪg'zɒtɪk] *adj.* 异国的，外来的
to one's surprise 让人惊奇的是	culture shock 文化冲击
have sth. in common 有共同之处	adaptable [ə'dæptəbl] *adj.* 能适应的

Useful Expressions

A. Talking about similarities

- They have something in common.
- They have many things in common.
- They have very little in common.
- They are roughly similar in…
- They are exactly the same.
- They are more or less the same.

- They are identical.
- There is no difference between them.
- What a striking similarity/likeness!
- There is only a formal likeness between the two brothers, for their natures are very different.
- There was an uncommon likeness between the two boys.
- There is much likeness between the two cousins.

B. Talking about differences

- There's a large number of differences between A and B.
- We have very different ideas.
- They are completely different.
- He feels differently from me.
- She's very unlike her mother.
- They're completely unlike each other.
- The old and new conditions of travel are exactly opposite.

C. Comparing and contrasting

- A is as happy/excellent/beautiful as B.
- A is not as/so good/nice/healthy as B.
- A makes fewer mistakes than B.
- A is the taller of the two.
- It is one of the longest rivers.
- A is the biggest/thickest/oldest of all.
- It/This was the worst film that he had ever seen.
- If you compare A and B, you will see that A is better.
- A train is slow in comparison with a plane.
- Compared with B, A is more industrious/clever/useful.
- They contrast sharply in interests and abilities.
- The contrast is remarkable.
- The difference/contrast is notable.
- This is a strong contrast.
- By contrast with B's marks, A's marks were excellent.

 **Exercises**

I. Discuss with your partner the similarities and differences between the following objects.

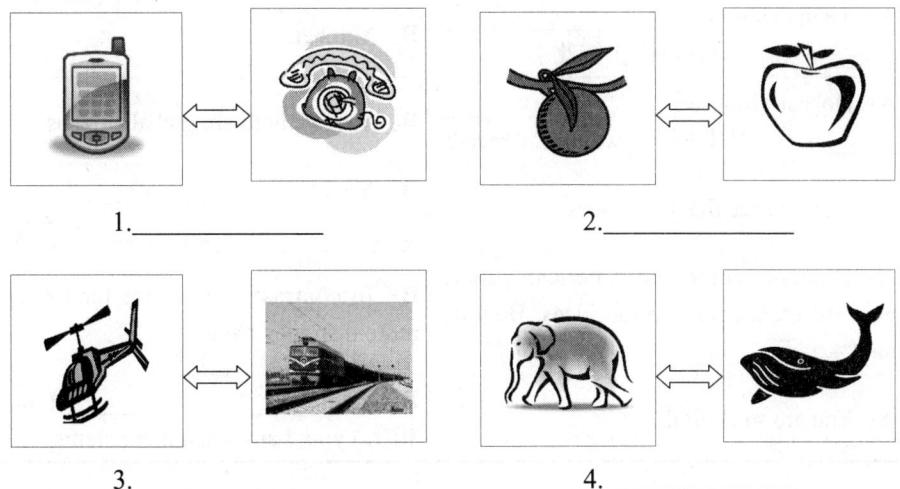

1._____ 2._____

3._____ 4._____

II. Find pairs of words in this list with similar or opposite meanings and make sentences.

dangerous	violent	stupid	gentle	industrious	merely	enough
against	safe	latter	attack	accidental	former	vacant
happiness	defend	sadness	abundant	intentional	nervous	depart
knowledge	scarce	only	wise	critical	intelligent	occupied
joy	greatly	adequate	fat	skinny	arrive	grief
extremely	for	calm	lazy	important	ignorance	foolish

III. Complete the short dialogues by translating Chinese into English.

1	A: It was such an interesting lecture. I hope you enjoy it _____ _____ (和……一样) I did.	B: I must admit that I almost fell asleep in the first 30 minutes.
2	A: Hamburgers and French fries are so good.	B: Maybe, but my spinach salad is _____ _____ _____ (比……更健康) a hamburger.
3	A: Is China the largest country in the world?	B: No, it's _____ Canada (它比加拿大小) and it's _____ _____ (第三大国) country.

4	A: Which sport is _____ (更受欢迎), swimming or jogging?	B: Jogging. It's easier to do.
5	A: Are there any animal performances in traditional Chinese acrobatics?	B: No, Chinese acrobatics is _____ _____ (与……不同) the Western circus.
6	A: Twins sometimes _____ _____ (非常不同于彼此).	B: You bet.
7	A: Do you think we _____ _____ (有一些共同点) with westerners?	B: Yes, we both are global citizens.
8	A: Can you see the differences?	B: Yes, _____ _____ (差别很大).
9	A: Chinese people and American people have different consumption ideas. How do they _____ (不同)?	B: In contrast, Americans tend to spend more than they have.
10	A: You are so skillful.	B: _____ (和……相比) you, I am much more clumsy.

IV. Pair work: make dialogues based on the following situations.

1. Compare a fever with a cold.
2. Compare middle school life with college life.
3. Share the similarities of ball games.
4. Tell the differences between modern buildings and ancient buildings.

V. Topics for discussion.

1. Some people become friends because they have similar personalities, while others prefer making friends with those who have quite opposite personalities. Compare the benefits of these two types of friendships. Which kind of friends do you prefer? Explain why.

2. Some people prefer buying books to read, while others prefer borrowing books from libraries or other people. Compare the advantages of these two ways of accessing books. Which way do you prefer? Why?

Culture Tips

Comparison and contrast are two different ways of looking at objects and thinking about how they are alike and different. To compare is to examine two or more objects, ideas, people, etc., in order to note similarities and differences. To contrast is to compare in order to show unlikeness or differences.

Take fruits, vegetables and meat for example, all of them are alike because they are kinds of food, but there are many ways in which they are different. For instance, they belong to different food groups. Some must be cooked before eating, while some can be eaten raw.

When you compare and contrast, you must pay attention to every detail. An effective way is to make a list of similarities and differences, and then decide which of them are interesting, important, and relevant enough to discuss. Sometimes a particular point of comparison or contrast might be relevant but not terribly revealing or interesting. So making your comparison or contrast unique is especially critical, and you should always keep it in mind.

 Class Activities

Find out the Differences

Divide the students into groups of four. Select a student who is good at drawing and ask him/her to draw two pictures with slight differences on the blackboard. Ask the other students to find out the differences and discuss the similarities and differences within their groups.

 思 政

A Dip into Chinese Wisdom

1. 各国体量有大小、国力有强弱、发展有先后，但都是国际社会平等一员，都有平等参与地区和国际事务的权利。

Countries may differ in size, strength or level of development, but they are all equal members of the international community with equal rights to participate in regional and international affairs.

2. 野径云俱黑，江船火独明。

O'er wild lanes dark cloud spreads;

In boat a lantern looms.

3. 少小离家老大回，乡音无改鬓毛衰。

Old, I return to the homeland while young,

Thinner has grown my hair, though I speak the same tongue.

4. 满招损，谦受益。

Haughtiness invites disaster, humility receives benefit.

SECTION II

Banking
Unit 13

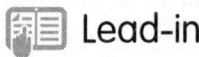 Lead-in

How many kinds of Chinese and foreign banks do you know? Can you name them in English?

Examples:
Bank of China
  Agricultural Bank of China
  Bank of Communications
  Barclays Bank
  Midland Bank…

 Warm-up Activities

I. Read the following sentences and pay attention to the stress and rhythm.

Hello!   Look out!
Have a **try**!   **Wait** until **six**.   **Throw** it into the **fire**.
Glad to **meet** you.   **Wait** a **moment**.
Who **did** it?   It's hard to say.
He **started** to **talk** to her.
She **bought** me an **English** book.

II. Read the passage below and pay attention to your pronunciation and intonation.

The Bank Robber

A bank was robbed by an armed robber. He walked into the bank, went up to the bank teller, pointed a gun at her and said, "Give me all the money or I'll shoot."

The bank teller was frightened and did as the robber demanded.

The police later asked the bank teller if she could tell them anything about the robber.

"He wore a stocking over his face," the bank teller said. "I'm afraid I can't tell you what he looked like."

A week later, the bank was robbed again.

"I'm sure it was the same man," the bank teller said. "I didn't see his face because he had a stocking over it again, but the voice was the same when he said, 'Give me all the money or I'll shoot.'"

A week later, the bank was robbed for the third time.

"Was it the same man?" the police asked the bank teller.

"Oh, yes, I'm sure it was," the bank teller said. "I didn't see his face because he wore a stocking over it again, but it was the same voice."

"Are you sure you didn't notice anything else about the man?" the police asked. "A little detail. Anything that might help us find him."

The bank teller thought for a minute, then she said, "There is one thing."

"And what is that?" the police asked hopefully.

"Every time he comes in and robs us," the teller said, "he's better dressed than before."

 Dialogues

Dialogue 1

Jimmy: I'd like to cash this check, please.

Clerk: Do you have an account with us?

Jimmy: No, I don't. Does that matter?

Clerk: Well, you cannot cash your check without an account.

Jimmy: How do I open a bank account?

Clerk: Have you got your passport?

Jimmy: Yes. Here it is.

Clerk: Please go to the fifth counter, and they'll attend to you.

Dialogue 2

Clerk: May I help you?

Nelly: I'd like to open an account, please.

Clerk: Fine. What kind of account do you want, checking account or savings account?

Nelly: What's the difference between them?

Clerk: A checking account will let you write as many checks as you want. With a savings account, you have to come into the bank to get your money.

Nelly: How much does each account cost?

Clerk: There's a service charge for a checking account but no charge for the savings account.

Nelly: I'll have a savings account then.

Clerk: OK. Please give me your ID card and fill out this form with the necessary information.

Nelly: All right. Is this OK?

Clerk: Yes. Please choose a password of six numbers and confirm it.

Nelly: I'll do that.

Clerk: Here is your card and passbook. Please bring either one when you deposit or withdraw money. Keep them safe and inform us if you lose them.

Nelly: Thanks a lot.

Dialogue 3

Marc: I would like to open a current account. What's the proper procedure?

Clerk: First, you fill out the application form and then we'll issue you a passbook.

Marc: Is there any minimum for the first deposit?

Clerk: The minimum deposit for a savings account is one yuan and you should always have at least one yuan in your account.

Marc: What is the annual interest rate?

Clerk: It varies from time to time. At present it is 3.36%.

Marc: I'll have a current account right now.

Clerk: You may apply for a magnetic card at the same time and the card makes it easier for you to withdraw money from an ATM or any branch of our bank.

Marc: Do I need to pay a fee when I withdraw money from other banks?

Clerk: Two yuan each time.

Marc: By the way, can I open a checking account too?

Clerk: By all means. But you have to deposit enough money before you can write out your checks.

Dialogue 4

Mr. Bell: Can you change some money for me, please?

Clerk: Certainly. What is it that you want to change?

Mr. Bell: Here it is. Some euros and pounds. You'd better count them.

Clerk: Wait a moment please. I'll find out the rates of exchange. Here we are. Let me see, that'll make RMB 688.75. How would you like it?

Mr. Bell: Would you please give me six 100-yuan notes, eight 10-yuan notes, eight 1-yuan notes and the rest in small change.

Clerk: OK. Will that do?

Mr. Bell: Er… Would you mind giving me 5 yuan in coins?

Clerk: Certainly. Here is your money and receipt.

Dialogue 5

Clerk: What can I do for you?

Woman: I'd like to know if my money has arrived from Australia.

Clerk: All right. Give me your account number, please. Your account doesn't show any deposits.

Woman: Oh, no! How long will it take to get here?

Clerk: Well, it takes a few days for the money to get here, even a week. You may come again tomorrow. Or here's a number that you can call.

Woman: Would you please give me your number?

Clerk: Sure. 8838-5678.

Dialogue 6

Clerk: May I help you?

Li: I'd like to withdraw all the money from my deposit account and close it.

Clerk: Your CD hasn't yet matured. Would you mind showing me your ID card?

Li: Of course not. Here you are.

Clerk: Please write your name and ID number on this form.

Li: Like this?

Clerk: All right, fine. Please sign your name on this receipt.

Li: OK. Oh… Excuse me. May I ask where I should sign?

Clerk: Right at the bottom right-hand corner.

Li: Thanks.

Clerk: Here is your money. The total are three thousand and fifteen yuan.

Li: Thank you very much. By the way, I'd like to know my balance in my current account. Can you help me? Here is the bankbook.

Clerk: Your balance at the bank is 300 yuan.

Li: Thanks a lot.

Dialogue 7

A: Excuse me, is this the Peony Credit Card Department of the ICBC?

B: Yes. Is there anything I could do for you?

A: Could you tell me something about your Peony Credit Card?

B: Yes, of course.

A: How can I get the benefits from a personal credit card?

B: First of all, it saves more money to use a credit card than to use cash. So it is very helpful for managing family finances. In addition, the card-issuing offices will calculate interest for the deposits linked to the credit card.

A: Is it convenient to use?

B: Of course. Our ATMs provide 24-hour self-service. It is very convenient to do cash withdrawal, accounts checking, password changing and funds allocating, etc.

A: Can I buy things with it?

B: Yes, you can. A quick swipe of your Peony Card on the POS terminal and a few keystrokes will complete your payment instantly.

A: What should I do if I am in bad need of funds?

B: You can immediately access funds by using the credit function of the Peony Card, which allows you to obtain overdrafts.

A: That sounds very nice.

B: Try a Peony Card.

Vocabulary

cash [kæʃ] *v.* 兑现，付现款	savings account 储蓄存款账户
check [tʃek] *n.* 支票	password ['pɑ:swɜ:d] *n.* 口令
account [ə'kaʊnt] *n.* 账户	passbook ['pɑ:sbʊk] *n.* 银行存折
attend to 注意（留意，专心于，照料）	current account 活期存款账户
open an account 开立账户，开户	interest rate 利率
checking account 支票账户	magnetic card 磁卡

withdraw [wɪð'drɔ:] *v.* 撤回，取回，撤退	balance ['bæləns] *n.* 结存，结余
by all means 好的，当然可以	Peony Credit Card 牡丹卡
deposit [dɪ'pɒzɪt] *n.* 存款，定金	ICBC 中国工商银行
vt. 储蓄	allocate ['æləkeɪt] *v.* 分配
deposit account 定期存款账户	complete one's payment 完成支付
CD = Certificate of Deposit 存款单	consumption [kən'sʌmpʃn] *n.* 消费
mature [mə'tʃʊə(r)] *adj.* 到期的	in bad need of 急需
v. 到期	overdraft ['əʊvədrɑːft] *v.& n.* 透支

 Useful Expressions

A. Opening an account

- What kind of account did you have in your mind?
- Do you like to open a current account?
- A deposit or current account?
- Please tell me how you would like to deposit your money.
- There's a service charge for the checking account but no charge for the savings.
- Is there any minimum for the first deposit?
- Our minimum deposit for a savings account is 100 dollars.
- Five yuan is the minimum original deposit.
- You can open a savings account at any time with an initial deposit of 50 dollars.
- Even one yuan is all right.
- Here is your passbook. Please bring it back when you deposit or withdraw money any time you like. Keep it well and inform us whenever you lose it.
- I need a checking account so that I can pay my bill.
- I think I'd like a deposit/current account.
- Please tell me the procedure for opening a savings account.
- Could you tell me how to operate this account?
- How much does each account cost?

B. Depositing or withdrawing money

- How much do you want to deposit with us?
- How much money do you plan to keep in your account on a regular basis?
- I want to deposit my salary and be able to get money whenever I need it.
- Would you please fill in the depositing form, giving the sum of money you're to

deposit as well as your name, address and professional unit?

- Please endorse the check.
- The traveler's checks cost 1.5% of the total amount of purchase.
- I want to withdraw all the money in cash.
- I'd like to know whether I can cash a check here.
- Will you please cash this traveler's check?
- I want to cash the balance of a traveler's letter of credit.
- Will you please tell me whether you charge for checks?
- Could you tell me how much the checks cost?
- What if I overdraw?
- Your balance at the bank is 300 yuan.
- Your deposit is exhausted.
- Please tell me how you wish to draw your money.
- I'd like to know if I can draw on my account for payment of things I buy in Tianjin.
- I want to withdraw 200 dollars from my deposit account.
- I want to close my account with you.
- I'd like to draw 100 yuan against this letter of credit.
- May I draw money against the letter of credit here?
- Could you tell me how much my balance is?

C. Changing money

- Please tell me how much you want to change.
- How much of the remittance do you want to convert into Japanese yen?
- What kind of currency do you want to change?
- In what denominations?
- Please tell me what note you want.
- How would you like it?
- Will seven tens be all right?
- Would you kindly sign the exchange form, giving your name and address?
- Would you please give me seven five-pound notes, four one-pound notes, and the rest in small change?
  - Would you mind giving me the six pence in coppers?
  - I'd like to know if you could change this money back into U.S. dollars for me.
  - Can you give me 100 dollars in Swiss francs?
  - I'd like to convert the full amount of the remittance into U.S. dollars.

- I'd like some coins for this note.
- I'd like to break this 50-dollar note.
- Five 20-dollar bills and ten 1-dollar bills, please.
- In 5-dollar bills, please.
- Could you give me some small notes?

D. Talking about interest rate

- What is the annual interest rate?
- What's the interest rate for the savings account?
- Do you pay interest on this account?
- It allows you to earn a little interest on your money.
- The account carries interest of 4%.
- The interest rate for the savings account is 4%.
- It varies from time to time. At present it is 6%.
- Tell me the current rate for RMB, please.
- What's your selling rate for RMB in cash today?
- Our buying rate for notes is 623 yuan for 100 dollars.
- I'd like to know the exchange rate for euros.
- What's the exchange rate today?
- Please wait a moment, and I'll check the exchange rates.
- Please wait a moment. I'll find out the exchange rate between U.S. dollars and RMB.
- The rate for traveler's checks is 300 yuan against 100 dollars.
- These dollars are worth 1,000 yuan.

Exercises

I. Replace each of the underlined sentences without changing its meaning.

1. A: Good morning. <u>May I help you</u>?
   B: I'd like to open an account.
2. A: I need to open a savings account. What's the procedure for it?
   B: First, <u>you need to complete a deposit slip.</u>
3. A: Is there any minimum for the first deposit?
   B: <u>Our minimum deposit for a savings account is 100 dollars.</u>
4. A: I'd like to change these pesos, please.

B: How do you want them?

   A: It doesn't make any difference.

5. A: How much does each account cost?

   B: Each account is free. There is no service charge.

6. A: What kind of account do you want?

   B: Well, I'd prefer to open a current account.

II. Complete the short dialogues by translating Chinese into English.

1	A: May I help you?	B: _____ (我可以把这些英镑兑换成美元吗)?
2	A: Do you want small bills or large?	B: _____ (什么都可以, 无所谓).
3	A: Do you want anything else?	B: Yes, _____ (我想知道日元的兑换率).
4	A: What can I do for you?	B: _____ (我想知道我还有多少余额)?
5	A: Good afternoon. What can I do for you?	B: _____ (我想取消这个账户).
6	A: Welcome to our bank, sir. Can I help you?	B: _____ (我想开一个活期存款账户).
7	A: How much money do you want to deposit?	B: _____ (最低起存额是多少)?
8	A: Good afternoon. Can I help you?	B: _____ (我想把钱都取出来).
9	A: Excuse me. _____ (我忘记磁卡的密码了). What can I do?	B: Don't worry. If you have brought your ID card, I can help you out right now.
10	A: I have brought my ID card with me. Here you are.	B: First, _____ (您需要挂失您丢失的卡). Please pay 15 yuan, including 5 yuan cost and 10 yuan handling charge. Then we'll issue you a new card.

III. Complete the dialogue with the expressions given in the box.

A. Please fill out this deposit slip

B. You may make three withdrawals each quarter without charge

C. How much would you like to deposit

D. It's profitable to save your money

> E. I'd like to open a savings account
>
> F. What is the interest rate

Clerk: Good morning. Can I help you?

Man: Yes, ____1____, please.

Clerk: I'll get you the application blank. ____2____?

Man: To start off, I'd like to deposit $50.

Clerk: ____3____.

Man: How often may I withdraw money?

Clerk: ____4____. If your balance is less than $500, each additional withdrawals costs 50 cents.

Man: ____5____?

Clerk: It's 5.25%.

Man: That is to say, if I had $1,000 in the bank, I would make over $50 in interest.

Clerk: That's right. ____6____.

IV. Pair work: make dialogues based on the following situations.

1. Opening an account.
2. Withdrawing money.
3. Asking about the interest rate.
4. Changing money.
5. Applying for a card.

V. Topics for discussion.

1. What are the advantages and disadvantages of using credit cards for purchases?
2. How do you wish to settle your account, in cash or by credit card?
3. What is a bank? What services do banks provide?

Culture Tips

A banker or bank is a financial institution whose primary activity is to act as a payment agent for customers and to borrow and lend money. It is an institution for receiving, keeping, and lending money.

The first modern bank was founded in Italy in Genoa (热那亚) in 1406, and its name was Banco di San Giorgio (Bank of St. George).

Over time, many other financial activities were introduced. For example, banks are important players in financial markets and offer financial services such as investment funds. In some countries such as Germany, banks are the primary owners of industrial corporations, while in other countries such as the United States, banks are prohibited from owning non-financial companies. In Japan, banks are usually the nexus of cross-shareholding entities known as zaibatsu (industrial and financial conglomerates). In France, "Bancassurance" (the sale of insurance products by banks) is highly prevalent, as most banks offer insurance and real estate services to their clients.

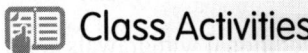
Class Activities

Guess the Words or Phrases from Actions

Ask one student to stand in front of the class. Give him/her a word or a phrase from this unit, which other students cannot see.

He/she will act out the meaning of the word.

The rest of the students have to guess what the word is.

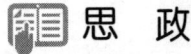
思 政

A Dip into Chinese Wisdom

1. 共同富裕是社会主义的本质要求，是人民群众的共同期盼。

Common prosperity is an essential requirement of socialism and a common expectation of the people.

2. 天生我材必有用，千金散尽还复来。

Heaven has made us talents, we're not made in vain.

A thousand gold coins spent, more will turn up again.

3. 君子爱财，取之有道。

A gentleman makes fortune in a proper way.

4. 不当家不知柴米贵。

Not in my shoes, don't know the pinch.

SECTION II

Advertisements
Unit 14

 Lead-in

Do TV commercials have any influence on you? Discuss it with your partner. You may use the following examples for help.

A: Yes. I think TV commercials can tell us some information about a new product.

B: I don't think so. Because I think TV commercials are misleading and deceptive.

 Warm-up Activities

I. Read the limerick below and pay attention to the rhythm.

There was a young lady from Niger,
Who smiled as she rode on a tiger;
They returned from the ride.
With the lady inside,
And the smile on the face of the tiger.

There once was a lady named Lynn,
Who was so uncommonly thin,
That when she essayed
To drink lemonade,
She slipped through the straw and fell in!

II. Read the story below and pay attention to your pronunciation and intonation.

Advertisers use many methods to get us to buy their products. One of their most successful methods is to make us feel dissatisfied with ourselves and our imperfect lives. Advertisements show us who we are not and what we do not have. Our teeth aren't white enough. Our hair isn't shiny enough. Our clothes aren't clean enough. Advertisements make us afraid that people won't like us if we don't use the advertised products. "Why don't I have any dates?" asks a good-looking girl sadly in a commercial. "Here," replies her roommate, "try Zest toothpaste!" Of course she tries it, and immediately the whole basketball team falls in love with her. "That's a stupid commercial," we might say. But we still buy Zest toothpaste out of fear of being unpopular and having no friends.

 Dialogues

Dialogue 1

A: We are considering advertising our product. What do you think of that?

B: I think ads are necessary and useful. They give publicity to your products and generate popularity among the public.

A: I agree. But I'm just wondering where to advertise.

B: You can consult advertising agencies. They will give you some suggestions.

A: OK. Thank you.

Dialogue 2

A: There are so many commercials on TV these days. They make me feel sick.

B: I enjoy commercials. I think they are interesting.

A: Commercials are simply misleading and deceptive.

B: Well, in a way, I suppose, but we don't have to believe them, do we?

A: Yeah, maybe you are right.

B: Besides, don't you think they have become more creative and visually appealing nowadays?

Dialogue 3

A: We intend to launch our new products soon. Do you have any suggestions?

B: Advertising is the key to the success of your products. You should invest in advertisements.

A: Yes. We are planning to advertise in several newspapers.

B: That's good. But I also recommend pursuing TV advertising.

A: It's costly.

B: Costly as it is, it's worth the price. TV, with its sound, movement, and color, is highly engaging, making the ads easy to remember.

A: I see. Thank you for the advice.

B: You're welcome.

Dialogue 4

Salesman: Good afternoon, sir. Can I help you?

Customer: Well, I'd like to buy a new cell phone. What do you have to suggest?

Salesman: We have cell phones in various designs and at different prices. How about this model? They are our latest products, just released.

Customer: They look very pretty. I like this one.

Salesman: This type of cell phone is reliable and durable. It has a three-year warranty. If you are not satisfied with our product, we have a 15-day unconditional money-back guarantee. We also have a 90-day return and exchange guarantee. Please be assured that the after-sales service is very reliable.

Customer: How much is it?

Salesman: 2,380 yuan.

Customer: Can it be any cheaper?

Salesman: I'm sorry, since this is a new product, the price cannot be lowered.

Dialogue 5

A: Hello, may I speak to the Personnel Manager, please?

B: Hello, this is Maggie Wang speaking.

A: Good morning, Ms. Wang. I saw your advertisement in the newspaper for a secretary, and I wonder if you could give me a few more details about the job. It's not very clear in the ad.

B: Yes, certainly. It's a part-time job. And we would need you from nine in the morning until three in the afternoon.

A: Well, I'm quite interested, but to some extent, it would depend on the salary.

B: Yes, we're offering about 1,000 yuan a week.

A: I think I'd like to give it a try. Do I need to come in for an interview?

B: Yes, could you come here at 10 o'clock tomorrow morning?

A: Sure, that works for me.

B: Well, see you then.

A: Bye.

Dialogue 6

A: Good morning, ladies and gentlemen. Welcome to our exhibition. This is the latest model of our company. All those bikes are improved models. They are all made of high quality materials…

B: Excuse me, may I ask a few questions?

A: Yes, of course. Go ahead, please.

B: I'm doubtful about the plastic cover.

A: Actually, they are very durable, because the frame and wheels are made of top quality stainless steel.

B: I see. Are they all suitable for riding in mountain areas?

A: Yes, this model can be used in many ways.

B: The design is beautiful. How fast can it run?

A: According to the test drive, about 40 km per hour.

Dialogue 7

A: There are advertisements everywhere in Beijing. The city is so bright at night, with all the neon signs.

B: I like it. It makes the city alive. I like all the different colors and the billboards with eye-catching pictures and slogans.

A: I think there are too many of them. I think that companies spend far too much money on advertising. They should lower their prices instead. Then they would sell more.

B: I see your point, but if the companies didn't spend money on advertising, no one would know about their products. I agree that some forms of advertising can be annoying.

A: I don't like it when people hand out leaflets for products I have no intention of buying. I also dislike having to listen to advertisements when they are broadcast in stores or on the subway.

B: Yes, I agree. Billboards can be ignored, but broadcasts are unavoidable.

Vocabulary

consider [kən'sɪdə(r)] v. 考虑，思考，认为	artistic [ɑː'tɪstɪk] adj. 艺术的
ad [æd] abbr. (advertisement 的缩写) 广告	launch [lɔːntʃ] n. & v. 发射，开始
publicity [pʌb'lɪsəti] n. 宣传，宣扬	pursue [pə'sjuː] v. 追求，继续从事
generate ['dʒenəreɪt] v. 产生，发生	invest [ɪn'vest] v. 投资
popularity [ˌpɒpju'lærəti] n. 普及，流行	engaging [ɪn'geɪdʒɪŋ] adj. 吸引人的
agency ['eɪdʒənsi] n. 办事处，代理商	plastic ['plæstɪk] adj. 塑料的
commercial [kə'mɜːʃl] adj. 商业的 n. 商业广告	billboard ['bɪlbɔːd] n. 布告板，广告牌
	eye-catching adj. 引人注目的，耀眼的
misleading [ˌmɪs'liːdɪŋ] adj. 使人误解的	slogan ['sləʊgən] n. 标语，口号
deceptive [dɪ'septɪv] adj. 欺骗性的	annoying [ə'nɔɪɪŋ] adj. 恼人的，讨厌的
intention [ɪn'tenʃn] n. 意图，目的	leaflet ['liːflət] n. 传单

Useful Expressions

A. Talking about advertising

- Are you going to cut down our advertising budget again?
- I have to design an advertising leaflet for the new products.
- What kind of image do you want to convey in the advertisement?
- Do you think we should include some performance data?
- We are sure the sales will start to recover with the successful advertisement.
- Even products of average quality can sell well if the ad is well done.

B. Talking about products

- It's durable/portable/reliable.
- It's of top quality.
- Quality and quantity are assured.
- This is excellent workmanship.
- This vase is a piece of exquisite workmanship.
- The set of furniture is of fine workmanship.
- We guarantee the best quality at affordable prices.
- This product is of very high quality.
- Our product is distinctive and novel, offering high quality at a low price.
- Our product is first-rate (or top-quality).

- We have all sizes available.
- It's wonderful both in appearance and performance.
- Our price is reasonable.
- We have fashionable styles, rich varieties / a wide selection of colors and designs.
- The quality of our product can catch up with and surpass the highest international standards.
- It is popular both at home and abroad.
- We have a long history in production and marketing.
- We have fashionable and attractive packaging.
- This is a product with a long-standing reputation.

 Exercises

I. Here are some classic advertising slogans. Can you identify the brands they belong to? Match the slogans with their respective brands.

1. Good to the last drop.	A. Nokia
2. Take time to indulge.	B. Maxwell coffee
3. Just do it.	C. Olympus
4. No business too small, no problem too big.	D. Nestle ice cream
5. Connecting People.	E. IBM
6. Make yourself heard.	F. Nike
7. Start ahead.	G. Ericsson
8. Good teeth, good health.	H. Rejoice
9. Time is what you make of it.	I. Colgate
10. Focus on life.	J. Swatch

II. Complete the short dialogues by translating Chinese into English.

1	A: I'd like to buy a washing machine, and I _____ _____ (喜欢小机型).	B: In that case, I recommend Little Swan brand, the Mini Type. It's _____ _____ (在家庭中很受欢迎).
2	A: I'm afraid the quality of this product _____ _____ (可能不如外国品牌质量好).	B: I can assure you that the quality is first-class. Their performance is superb. Our product has already _____ (建立了自己的品牌), and they _____ _____ (在国内外销量很好).

3	A：Is this machine _____ _____ (自动还是半自动)?	B：It's automatic.
4	A：What kind of TV do you like most?	B：Oh, let me think. I prefer _____ _____ (创维电视的外观), but my wife likes Samsung best.
5	A：I'd like to _____ _____ (支持国内品牌).	B：It seems that you're very patriotic.
6	A：What's the most obvious advantage of your product?	B：Its quality. The high quality of our product has _____ _____ (确保了它在市场上的主导位置).
7	A：Sounds like an ideal approach. ___ _____ (我们会有新的口号吗)?	B：Definitely. _____ _____ (广告代理商正在设计呢).
8	A：What's the status of our advertising campaign?	B：As I mentioned before, _____ _____ (我们下个月开始的宣传活动，是全国范围内的).
9	A：_____ (这款车很坚固，很可靠).	B：Yes, I know. I think Honda is the most reliable car on the road.
10	A：_____ (最简单的一种广告就是分类广告).	B：Yeah, every day the newspapers carry a few pages of these ads.

III. Fill in the blanks with the given expressions.

> unique design   outstanding performance   from our customers
> the best-selling products   manufacture warranty   on sale

The "Qingfeng" 326 vacuum cleaner is one of ___1___ of ABC Household Appliances Company. This type of vacuum cleaner has been ___2___ for over ten years. A dual airflow has been purposely designed to form along the front and back of the rotating floor brush. This unique design improves the dirt and dust collection into the floor head, thus reducing dust particles being dispersed back onto the floor surface. Because of its ___3___ and ___4___, we have received a lot of compliments ___5___. With a 2.5-litre capacity for its dust bag, a 12-metre cable length, a 3-year ___6___ and a 3-piece on-board tool storage, this vacuum cleaner will certainly have a bright future.

IV. Pair work: make dialogues based on the following situations.

1. Susan is discussing with her manager Mr. Thompson about the advertisement for their new models of PCs.

2. Mr. Smith is talking with Teresa, a clerk at an advertising company, about the outdoor advertisement for his company.

3. Mary wants to buy a new TV set. She is asking the salesman for information about various TV sets.

V. Topics for discussion.

1. As is known, tobacco is bad for health. Do you think tobacco advertising should be permitted or not?

2. Do you think the benefits of advertisements outweigh the costs?

3. Do you consider the brand when buying a product? Do you think famous brands are always the best choice?

 **Culture Tips**

The Development of Advertising in the U.S.

The function of advertising has remained constant since the advent of modern advertising, but its form has evolved as new forms of media have emerged. Radio broadcasting began in 1922, and with it came radio advertising. By 1930, 40 percent of households in the U.S. owned a radio; more than 80 percent owned one by 1940. Radio advertising expenditures doubled between 1935 and 1940, reaching $216 million in 1940.

Television emerged in the 1950s and quickly found its way into almost everyone's living room: 11 percent of households owned a television in 1950, but 88 percent owned one just a decade later. Television advertising expenditures increased nearly tenfold between 1950 and 1960, reaching $1.6 billion by 1960.

Outdoor advertising grew alongside the expansion of paved roads. In the decade after World War II (1939–1945), outdoor advertising expenditures, adjusted for inflation, increased by 5 percent annually, as paved mileage in the U.S. increased by 3 percent annually. One of the more famous billboard campaigns, which began in 1925, was for Burma-Shave, a brushless shaving cream manufactured by the American Safety Razor Company. Their jingles appeared one line per sign over the course of a mile or more, always ending with the name of the product.

The introduction of the videocassette recorder (VCR) led to further changes in advertising.

New in 1980, by 1990 over two-thirds of U.S. households owned a VCR. Viewers could fast-forward through commercials when watching taped shows, presenting a new challenge to advertisers. "Product placement" became the solution. Firms began paying to have their products featured in television shows and films. The practice was spurred by one phenomenal success: the use of Reese's Pieces candy in the 1982 film *E. T. The Extra-Terrestrial*, which increased candy sales by over 65 percent. By 2000, product placement had been pervasive.

Class Activities

Design an Advertisement

Divide the class into several groups of 6 students. The teacher assigns each group a product. Within twenty minutes, each group designs an advertisement for the product. The most imaginative and persuasive group will be the winner.

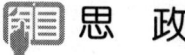
思 政

A Dip into Chinese Wisdom

1. 胸怀大局、自信开放、迎难而上、追求卓越、共创未来。

Bear in mind the big picture, be confident and open, rise to challenges, pursue excellence, and create a better future together.

2. 烟水茫茫，千里斜阳暮。

Misty waters outspread,

I found the slanting sun on turning my head.

3. 朝辞白帝彩云间，千里江陵一日还。

Leaving at dawn the White Emperor crowned with cloud;

I've sailed a thousand miles through canyons in a day.

4. 说起来容易做起来难。

Easier said than done.

SECTION II

Computers and the Internet
Unit 15

 **Lead-in**

Below are the things you can do with computers or the Internet. Which one is extremely important to you? Find out and explain why.

- Access information
- Shop
- Chat online
- Download your favorite movies or music
- Download software
- Access data easily and quickly
- Create, edit, send, and print documents
- Edit, send, and print images
- Send and check emails
- Check the weather
- Plan trips
- Play games
- Make free voice or video calls online
- Store data
- Study and teach online

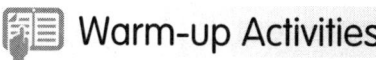 Warm-up Activities

I. Read the poem below and pay attention to the rhythm and rhymes.

Sonnet XVIII
by William Shakespeare

Shall I compare thee to a summer's day?
Thou art more lovely and more temperate.
Rough winds do shake the darling buds of May,
And summer's lease hath all too short a date.

Sometime too hot the eye of heaven shines,
And often is his gold complexion dimmed;
And every fair from fair sometime declines,
By chance or nature's changing course untrimmed.

But thy eternal summer shall not fade,
Nor lose possession of that fair thou ow'st;
Nor shall death brag thou wander'st in his shade,
When in eternal lines to time thou grow'st:

So long as men can breathe or eyes can see,
So long lives this, and this gives life to thee.

II. Read the passage below and pay attention to your pronunciation and intonation.

We are truly living in the "age of information". With computers and the Internet, the answer to almost any question is at your fingertips. You can buy a plane ticket or reserve a book at the library without leaving home. You can easily check the weather forecast, sports scores or bus schedules. You can find a company's email address or phone number in minutes. You can call a theater on your cell phone to check movie listings and then go online to read reviews.

In the past, families communicated by snail mail. Today, blogs allow you to share your latest news with everyone. Grandparents can watch their grandchildren grow up through blog photos and videos. You can email vacation photos to your friends via a smartphone while still on vacation. Emails and cell phones make it possible to stay in touch 24 hours a day.

Dialogues

Dialogue 1

Allen: Hey! Emily, we've learned so many words about computers. Now, let's play a word guessing game.

Emily: OK! No problem.

Allen: Please listen carefully! You play music through it. Do you know what it is?

Emily: Hmm… I got it! It's a CD-Rom.

Allen: No, no, no. It's a speaker.

Emily: Oh, sorry! I didn't get it.

Allen: That's OK! You have another chance.

Emily: Sure, I will do my best.

Allen: A computer displays information on it. Please guess it!

Emily: Easy! It's a monitor. Is it right?

Allen: Good job!

Emily: Yeah, I got it!

Dialogue 2

(S=Shop assistant J=John)

S: What can I do for you?

J: I'm looking for a computer.

S: What kind of computer would you like to buy?

J: Oh, I'm not sure. I don't know much about computers.

S: Do you want to play games or write documents on it?

J: What's the difference?

S: Well, for playing games, it's better if you have a larger memory and a better video card.

J: Do you mean CPU? I guess Core i3 would be good.

S: OK. What size hard drive do you want?

J: Just big enough to play games.

S: What about the rest?

J: I've no idea. What do you suggest?

S: If you're concerned about gaming performance, I suggest you buy one with a higher quality sound card and video card.

J: Effects? Yeah, that's important. And I'd like a big screen.

S: A big screen monitor will take up more space. What about a flat screen? They're more expensive, though.

Dialogue 3

Jane: You really go online a lot, don't you? Every time I see you, you're in the middle of browsing the Internet.

Mike: Yeah. I really enjoy it.

Jane: I am curious about this. What's so exciting about it?

Mike: What I love about it is that it's so relaxing. Without leaving your home, you can enter a completely different world. You can leave your own world behind, and go somewhere else.

Jane: But you must be careful.

Mike: What do you mean?

Jane: It's very easy to get infected with viruses and spyware these days, especially if you spend a lot of time online.

Mike: I know. I've already installed an anti-spyware program and a firewall to protect my computer.

Jane: How often do you run your antivirus program?

Mike: I run it every day. There are too many computer viruses these days. You can never be too careful.

Jane: Exactly.

Dialogue 4

A: With the development of technology, the Internet has become more and more popular.

B: Do you think students should surf the Internet after class?

A: Yes, I do. I see it as a great tool.

B: Why?

A: For example, you can quickly find the information you need online.

B: It sounds so convenient.

A: It is convenient to communicate with others using the Internet.

B: However, many people think that there are many disadvantages of the Internet, because there is also some information that is not good for students.

A: That is also true. Well, it will not only have a bad effect on your studies, but also do harm to your health, if you spend too much time playing games online.

B: What do you think we should do?

A: We should make proper use of the Internet. It is of great importance for us to distinguish useful information from harmful content.

Dialogue 5

Liu Wen: Hi, Wan Lin. What are you going to do this weekend?

Wan Lin: I'm not sure, any suggestions?

Liu Wen: Try the game Zuma. It's fascinating.

Wan Lin: I'm afraid I can't. My parents don't permit me to play computer games. They think it will take up too much time and has a bad effect on my study. Besides, it will do harm to my health. They say sitting before computers for a long time will cause eye fatigue, back pain and heart problems.

Liu Wen: I don't think so. In my opinion, playing games is another way of study. You know computers are important in the world. You learn better computer skills by playing video games. It's not a waste of time. At least it can help you relax.

Wan Lin: My parents are very assertive. They say teenagers should try something creative and something good for mental development. They buy me lots of model planes and ships to build. I think it's all right for me. I don't want to make them sad.

Liu Wen: Well, parents may have their own way to bring up their children. They may be right in their own perception of the good and bad. But I think values, morals and ethics are dependent on changing times and environment. Parents should move with the times and provide their children with a value system in order to enable them to be their own judge.

Wan Lin: That's exactly the way I feel, but as children, I think we'd better respect their opinions.

Dialogue 6

Peter: Hi, Jenny. Have you finished teaching for the day?

Jenny: Yes. I'm going home. See you tomorrow.

Peter: Why are you in such a hurry?

Jenny: I've got to browse some related information on the Internet for my lesson.

Peter: Really? You use the Internet to find teaching materials? That's a brilliant idea!

Jenny: Yes, but that's not the only reason I use the Internet.

Peter: So what's the other reason, to meet a guy?

Jenny: No, it's to understand my students. They all use the Internet.

Peter: So why don't you take full advantage of the Internet?

Jenny: What do you mean?

Peter: All you think about is your students and lesson!

Jenny: That's my job. I love my job!

Peter: But there's more to life than a job, Jenny.

Jenny: Yeah, you may have a point. But I think being a workaholic is much better than being love-obsessed.

Dialogue 7

Lily: People like using abbreviations while chatting online.

Nancy: Yes, that's what stumps me. I don't know what they mean.

Lily: I can tell you some. If someone writes "JK", it means "Just kidding", "BFN" means "Bye for now", "BBS" means "Be back soon", "DIKU" means "Do I know you?", and so on.

Nancy: Oh, I see. How interesting! Now I can guess what these abbreviations might mean.

Lily: Really? Please tell me what "TU" might mean.

Nancy: Mm, I've no idea. Does it mean "to you"?

Lily: No, it means "Thank you".

Nancy: Ah, I should have guessed the answer. Go on, please.

Lily: OK. Can you tell me what these numbers imply, "886" and "687"?

Nancy: The first one is easy. It means "Goodbye", because in the Chinese pronunciation, the sound of "886" is just like "bai bai le". But the second one is difficult. I don't know the meaning of it.

Lily: "687" means "I'm sorry." It's also widely used by Chinese people.

Nancy: Oh, I see. Different countries may have their own online abbreviations.

Vocabulary

CD-Rom [ˌsiːdiːˈrɒm] n. (只读) 光盘驱动器
monitor [ˈmɒnɪtə(r)] n. [计算机] 显示器，监视
video card 显卡
Core i3 酷睿 i3
hard drive 硬盘驱动器
sound card 声卡
browse [braʊz] v. 浏览
infect [ɪnˈfekt] v. 传染，感染

fatigue [fəˈtiːg] n. 疲乏，疲劳
assertive [əˈsɜːtɪv] adj. 独断的，武断的
perception [pəˈsepʃn] n. 认识，观念
ethic [ˈeθɪk] n. 道德规范
virus [ˈvaɪrəs] n. 病毒
spyware [ˈspaɪweə(r)] n. 安装在电脑上用于监视用户活动的间谍软件
install [ɪnˈstɔːl] v. 安装

take advantage of 利用 workaholic [ˌwɜːkəˈhɒlɪk] n. 工作第一的人，专心工作的人	abbreviation [əˌbriːviˈeɪʃn] n. 缩写 stump [stʌmp] vt. 难住

Useful Expressions

A. Talking about software

- Do you use an antivirus program to protect your computer?
- How often do you run your antivirus program?
- How often do you upgrade your antivirus program?
- Using computer software, you can edit and resize photographs.
- It's incompatible with the older version of the operating system.
- How will I install everything?
- You must uninstall Windows XP.
- The professional version of Microsoft Office includes Microsoft Word, Microsoft Excel, Microsoft PowerPoint, Microsoft Outlook, Microsoft Access, and Microsoft Publisher.

B. Talking about hardware

- Is that the new laptop you bought last week?
- The hard drive has almost 160 gigabytes of storage.
- A desktop computer tends to be cheaper than a laptop computer of similar specifications.
- It comes with a hard drive and a 17-inch monitor.
- The sound card and an Asus video card are built-in.
- Can you tell me how to install a DSL Modem?
- When you want to highlight a word, just double-click your mouse on that word.

C. Talking about the Internet

- I'm just surfing the Internet.
- You can attach picture files to emails and send them to anyone, anywhere, at any time.
- The hotel offers Wi-Fi.
- Which website should I visit to download it?
- I met Sally through an online forum.
- In chat rooms, you can talk with people one-on-one.
- I pretended to be a 17-year-old girl.
- I'm going to meet my new Internet friend on Friday night.

- If you want, we can shop online together.
- I've never shopped online before. How do you do it?
- How long does it take for delivery?
- I was playing a network game on the LAN.
- You may come across many abbreviations while chatting online.

Exercises

I. Find the English equivalents of the given Chinese expressions and fill them in the brackets.

A — standalone sound card	B — homepage
C — integrated video card	D — laser printer
E — website	F — zip file
G — Microsoft Edge	H — laptop
I — CD-Rom player	J — function key
K — scanner	L — moderator
M — sticky	N — hard drive
O — World Wide Web	P — desktop computer
Q — monitor	

Examples：(F) 压缩文件　　　(H) 手提电脑

1	( ) 台式电脑	6	( ) 主页
2	( ) 激光打印机	7	( ) 帖子置顶
3	( ) 万维网	8	( ) 斑竹 (版主)
4	( ) 微软 Edge 浏览器	9	( ) 独立声卡
5	( ) 硬盘	10	( ) 显示器

II. Create sentences using the groups of words in the box, paying attention to the differences between them.

Internet　　　　online

Examples:

1. I am greatly interested in chatting on the Internet, especially in English.
2. I am greatly interested in chatting online, especially in English.
3. I am greatly interested in online chatting, especially in English.

> browse   surf   visit   log on to

Examples:

1. I like browsing the Internet very much.
2. I like surfing the Internet very much.
3. I like visiting websites very much.
4. I like logging on to the Internet very much.

> update   upgrade

Examples:

1. Can you tell me how to update yahoo messenger?
2. Can you tell me how to upgrade yahoo messenger?

III. Complete the short dialogues by translating Chinese into English.

1	A: _____ (你喜欢在网上购物吗)?	B: Yeah. It's really convenient to shop online from home. It also saves time.
2	A: _____ (你多长时间上一次网)?	B: Very often. Because it's very convenient to search for information via the Internet.
3	A: How do you like this game?	B: _____ (我对它很上瘾). The various pictures and sounds made me frightened, but it's also like watching a movie.
4	A: I'm going to miss you when you go abroad.	B: Don't worry. _____ (我们可以互发邮件). It's very quick and cheap. The Internet can shorten the distance between us.
5	A: Your computer is a dinosaur.	B: Yes, my computer is really old. _____ (大多数软件都不能和它兼容).
6	A: What's going on in your room? Where did all that sound of gun shots come from?	B: Relax. _____ (你没见过别人玩网络游戏吗)?
7	A: What have you been doing recently?	B: _____ (我一直在网上同朋友聊天).

8	A: Do you think you could download some mp3 for me?	B: Sure, just let me know what you want. _____ (我可以帮你拷贝成光盘).
9	A: Where do you go to chat?	B: _____ (我喜欢使用 QQ).
10	A: Do you use the Internet a lot?	B: Yes, I do. _____ (我尽可能经常上网). I use the Internet a lot to study English.

IV. Pair work: make dialogues based on the following situations.

1. Victor spends most of his time chatting online. Lily warns him about its disadvantages.

2. Marco likes playing computer games. His father doesn't want to stop him but asks him to play in moderation.

3. Mary wants to buy a pair of jeans. Jessie suggests shopping online and helps her complete the transaction.

4. Susan wants to download some popular songs. Helen teaches Susan step by step.

V. Topics for discussion.

1. What are the advantages and disadvantages of computers and the Internet?

2. What do you usually use your computer for?

3. Which communication method do you prefer, the Internet or telephone? Why?

 Culture Tips

Virtual Worlds

Virtual worlds provide insights into how users are adapting natural language for communication within these new mediums. The Internet language that has emerged through user interactions in text-based chatrooms and computer-simulated worlds has led to the development of slang within digital communities. Examples of these include *pwn* and *noob*. Emoticons are further examples of how users have adapted expressions to suit the limitations of cyberspace communication, particularly the "loss of emotional clues".

Communication in niches such as role-playing games (RPGs) and Multi-User Domains (MUDs) is highly interactive, emphasizing and speed, brevity and spontaneity. As a result, Computer-Mediated Communication (CMC) is generally more vibrant, volatile, unstructured and open. There is often a complex organization of sequences and exchange structures evident in the connection of conversational strands and short turns. Some CMC strategies include capitalization for EMPHASIS, the use of symbols such as asterisks to enclose words (e.g., *stress*), and the creative use of punctuation like "???!?!?!?". In addition to contributing to these new forms of language, virtual worlds are also being used to teach languages. Virtual world language learning provides students with simulations of real-life environments, allowing them to find creative ways to improve their language skills. Virtual worlds are effective tools for language learning, especially among younger learners, as they already perceive such environments as "natural places to learn and play".

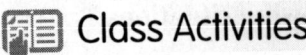 Class Activities

Chain Spelling

The teacher gives a word and asks a student to spell it. Then, the second student must say a word beginning with the last letter of the previous word. The game continues until someone makes a mistake—whether by pronouncing the word incorrectly, misspelling it or repeating a word that has already been said. That student is then out. The last remaining player is the winner.

To review the words learned in the lesson, the teacher may limit the words to the category of computers and the Internet.

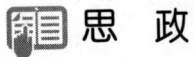 思 政

A Dip into Chinese Wisdom

1. 信息技术为超大规模国家治理提供新路径。

Information technology provides new ways for the governance of a super large-scale country.

2. 工欲善其事，必先利其器。

A workman must sharpen his tools if he wants to do his work well.

3. 活到老，学到老。

It is never too old to learn.

4. 安危不贰其志，险易不革其心。

One must not change his commitment or give up his pursuit even in the face of danger and risk.

SECTION II

Job Interviews
Unit 16

 Lead-in

1. Name three occupations you would like to pursue when you graduate.
(For example: to be a secretary)

2. Name three occupations that you will never pursue.

 Warm-up Activities

I. Read the tongue twisters below and pay attention to your pronunciation.

1. A proper copper coffee pot.
2. Around the rugged rocks the ragged rascals ran.
3. Long legged ladies last longer.
4. Mixed biscuits, mixed biscuits.
5. A box of biscuits, a box of mixed biscuits and a biscuit mixer!
6. Three grey geese in green fields grazing.
7. Pink lorry, yellow lorry.
8. Red leather, yellow leather; red leather, yellow leather.
9. She sells seashells by the seashore.

10. The sixth sick sheik's sixth sheep is sick.

11. Swan swam over the pond,

    Swim, swan, swim!

    Swan swam back again—

    Well swum, swan!

12. Peter Piper picked a peck of pickled peppers.

    Did Peter Piper pick a peck of pickled peppers?

    If Peter Piper picked a peck of pickled peppers,

    Where's the peck of pickled peppers Peter Piper picked?

II. Read the passage below and pay attention to your pronunciation and intonation.

What Does Two Plus Two Equal?

A mathematician, an accountant and an economist apply for the same job. The interviewer calls in the mathematician and asks, "What does two plus two equal?"

The mathematician replies, "Four."

The interviewer asks, "Four, exactly?" The mathematician looks at the interviewer incredulously and says, "Yes, four, exactly."

Then the interviewer calls in the accountant and asks the same question, "What does two plus two equal?" The accountant says, "On average, four—give or take ten percent—but on average, four."

Finally, the interviewer calls in the economist and poses (提出) the same question, "What does two plus two equal?"

The economist gets up, locks the door, closes the blinds (窗帘), sits down next to the interviewer, and says, "What do you want it to equal?"

Dialogues

Dialogue 1

Lin Li: May I come in?

Robert: Yes, please.

Lin Li: How do you do, sir? I'm Lin Li. I've come for an interview as requested.

Robert: How do you do, Miss Lin? I'm Robert Jones, the personnel manager, take a seat, please.

Lin Li: Thank you.

Robert: First of all, would you please say something about yourself?

Lin Li: It's my pleasure to do so. I was born and raised in Tianjin. I'm 23 years old and now studying at Nankai University. I specialize in English Secretarial Studies.

Robert: What courses have you taken in English Secretarial Studies?

Lin Li: I've taken courses such as secretarial principles, office administration, business English, public relations, etiquette studies, psychology, computer programming, typing, stenography and file keeping.

Robert: Do you have any working experience?

Lin Li: No. But I did some practice work in class.

Robert: Do you have copies of your reference letters with you?

Lin Li: Yes. One is from Dr. Zhang and one from Mr. Wang.

Robert: OK. We'll be hiring two people. The president will make the final decision after reviewing the applications.

Lin Li: I hope I can work here.

Robert: You'll hear from us sometime next month. Good luck and thanks for coming today.

Dialogue 2

Brian: Do you have any working experience as a secretary?

Chen: Yes. I worked as a secretary for a small company for two months.

Brian: What did you do there, office work?

Chen: Yes, mostly office work and sometimes running errands.

Brian: Oh, very good. You've had some practical experience in office work. By the way, do you have any experience as a guide?

Chen: Well, not exactly. But I have shown some of my foreign friends around the city of Beijing and the Great Wall as well.

Brian: Once in a while, we organize tours for our visitors, and I would like my secretary to take them sightseeing when there is not much to do in the office.

Chen: I think I would like to do that.

Brian: Fine. You are the very person we want.

Chen: Thank you, Sir.

Brian: What date can you start work?

Chen: I won't be able to leave the university until I get my diploma at the end of this month. Would early next month work?

Brian: That works for us. I'll see you on August 1st then. Thank you very much for coming today. We're pleased to have you join us.

Chen: Thank you. I'm sure I'll enjoy working here, too.

Brian: I hope so. Goodbye.

Chen: Goodbye.

Dialogue 3

Interviewer: What kind of work are you doing now?

Lucy: I'm working as an accountant.

Interviewer: For how many years have you been working there?

Lucy: I have been working there for six years.

Interviewer: What are your responsibilities at your present work unit?

Lucy: My work involves various routine bookkeeping and basic accounting tasks, such as journal entries, preparing detailed reports from raw data, and checking accounting documents for completeness, mathematical accuracy and consistency.

Interviewer: Have you received any honors or rewards?

Lucy: Yes, I received the title of "Advanced Worker" for my work in 2025.

Interviewer: Does your present employer know that you are planning to leave the company?

Lucy: Yes, I talked about it with him.

Interviewer: If we hire you, how soon can you start?

Lucy: I would need two weeks after receiving your official offer.

Interviewer: Is there anything else you'd like to know?

Lucy: No, not at the moment.

Interviewer: Well, I enjoyed talking with you. We'll contact you with our decision within a week.

Lucy: Thank you. I appreciate the time you have given me.

Dialogue 4

Interviewer: What salary would you expect to get?

Applicant: I don't have a specific salary in mind. What is the usual salary for someone with my qualifications?

Interviewer: Here, you would start at 3,000 yuan for the first three months — a training period. After that, your raises would depend on how well you perform.

Applicant: That sounds fair enough.

Interviewer: Anything else?

Applicant: Yes, one last thing. How much holiday time do you give your employees every year?

Interviewer: Our employees receive fifteen days of paid vacation every year. Unused days can be carried over to the following year.

Applicant: How about sick days?

Interviewer: You get five paid sick days.

Applicant: Any other benefits?

Interviewer: Yes, we have an excellent retirement plan and medical insurance as well.

Applicant: Is there any opportunity for advancement?

Interviewer: Yes, there're good prospects for promotion.

Applicant: Great. Thanks so much for your time.

Interviewer: We'll contact you soon. Thanks for coming.

Dialogue 5

Mr. Levis: Hello, Miss Wang. I'm Blake Levis. Glad you could come.

Miss Wang: Thank you for inviting me.

Mr. Levis: May I ask why you are interested in the job?

Miss Wang: When I saw the position your company advertised in the paper, I decided to have a try. I've always enjoyed a challenging job.

Mr. Levis: I learned from your résumé that you have worked in your present company for 3 years. Can you tell me why you want to leave your present post and apply for the vacancy here?

Miss Wang: Well, for one thing, I'm eager to work in a large company like yours that offers more opportunities for growth. For another thing, my present post does not involve me much in speaking English. I think I will have more opportunities to use English in your company.

Mr. Levis: Why do you think you are qualified for this position?

Miss Wang: I have excellent communication skills and I am familiar with the procedures for the last company I worked for. Besides, I am a team player with strong interpersonal skills.

Dialogue 6

Interviewer: Were you in a leading position when you were a college student?

Applicant: Yes, I was the president of the Student Union at our institute, and served as the monitor for three years.

Interviewer: Did you get any honors or rewards at your institute?

Applicant: Yes, I received the university scholarship for the 2022 to 2023 academic year. I won first place in the National English Speech Competition in 2024.

Interviewer: Great. Were you involved in any club activities at your university?

Applicant: Yes, I was on the school badminton team.

Interviewer: What extracurricular activities did you usually take part in at your college?

Applicant: I was active in recreational activities. Sometimes I sang in the chorus and sometimes I performed crosstalk with my classmates.

Dialogue 7

Shelly: What are the chances of getting a raise this year?

Bessie: Chances are slim!

Shelly: Wow! How many years has it been since you last got a raise?

Bessie: It's been three years! The company keeps losing money and they can't afford to give anyone a raise.

Shelly: That's too bad. Did you ever think of working somewhere else?

Bessie: Yeah. In fact, I just had an interview yesterday.

Shelly: Oh. How did it go?

Bessie: I hope it was alright. It seemed to go well but it's hard to tell. They said they would make a decision by the end of the week.

Shelly: By the end of the week? It seems they want to hire the person as quickly as possible.

Bessie: Yeah! I think so, too.

Shelly: What are your chances of getting that job?

Bessie: I believe I have a very good chance. The director seems to like me.

Shelly: Well, good luck, then.

Bessie: Thanks. I hope it helps.

Vocabulary

request [rɪ'kwest] vt. 请求，要求
secretarial principle 秘书准则
etiquette study 礼仪学习
stenography [stə'nɒgrəfi] n. 速记，速记法
errand ['erənd] n. 差使，差事
accountant [ə'kaʊntənt] n. 会计
bookkeeping ['bʊkki:pɪŋ] n. 记账
journal entry 日记账分录，流水分录
raw data 原始数据
accuracy ['ækjərəsi] n. 准确，精确度
consistency [kən'sɪstənsi] n. 一致性
honor ['ɒnə(r)] n. 荣誉
reward [rɪ'wɔ:d] n. 报酬，酬谢，奖赏
retirement [rɪ'taɪəmənt] n. 退休
chorus ['kɔ:rəs] n. 合唱队

insurance [ɪn'ʃʊərəns] n. 保险
advancement [əd'vɑ:nsmənt] n. 晋升
promotion [prə'məʊʃn] n. 晋升
résumé ['rezju:meɪ] n. 简历，履历
vacancy ['veɪkənsi] n. 空缺，空职
procedure [prə'si:dʒə(r)] n. 程序，手续，步骤
team player n. 善于团队合作的人
interpersonal [ˌɪntə'pɜ:sənl] adj. 人与人之间的，人际关系的
monitor ['mɒnɪtə(r)] n. 班长
scholarship ['skɒləʃɪp] n. 奖学金
academic [ˌækə'demɪk] adj. 学院的，学术性的
crosstalk ['krɒstɔ:k] n. 相声

Useful Expressions

A. Asking interview questions

- Would you please say something about yourself?
- What can you tell me about yourself?
- Tell us a bit about yourself.
- What courses did you take in college?
- Do you have any working experience?
- Do you have any experience in this field?
- What date can you start work?
- What are your strengths and weaknesses?
- What are your responsibilities at your present work unit?
- Have you received any honors or rewards?
- Why do you want to work for this company?
- What do you see yourself doing in five years? Ten years?
- What are your salary expectations?

- What is your expected salary?
- Can you work overtime?
- If we need you to travel frequently on business, would that be okay with you?

B. Talking about educational experience

- I graduated from Peking University in 2023.
- I attend Renmin University of China.
- I am studying in the Department of Business Administration.
- I studied computer science at Peking University and earned an MS degree.
- I specialized in international banking.
- I majored in English at college.
- My major subject is economics and my minor subject is English.
- I completed courses in business administration and management, sales management, economics, accounting, statistics, business statistics, and business English.
- I received my MBA degree from Peking University in 2024.
- I was a member of the computer club for four years.

C. Talking about working experience

- I have five years of experience with a company as a salesman.
- I have been working as an accountant in a small company for two years since my graduation.
- Since graduating from university two years ago, I have been employed as a cashier at the Astor Hotel.
- I have eight years of experience working in the IT industry.
- For the past two years, I have been working as a project manager for a company.
- I worked in a fashion shop last summer as a part-time salesgirl.
- Although I have no experience in this field, I'm willing to learn.
- I am sorry to say that I have no experience in this field.

D. Talking about achievements and strengths

- I served as the monitor for two years.
- I was the class monitor in charge of activities.
- I won second place in the long jump at the university sports meeting in 2022.
- I received the second prize in the English Speech Competition of our province in 2022.

- I got the title of "Advanced Worker" in 2018 and 2020.
- I passed the Band Four and Band Six in the College English Test.
- I've received a Business English Certificate.
- With my strong academic background, I am highly competent.
- My graduate school training and internship experience qualify me for this job.
- Adaptability, cheerfulness and friendliness are among my strongest traits.
- My colleagues say that I'm friendly, caring, helpful, determined, and have a sense of humor.
- I can see what needs to be done and do it.
- My strength is in building relationships and solving problems.
- A key strength of mine is my passion for developing new ideas and innovations.
- I have very strong observational skills. I can generate interesting ideas from minor things and once the idea is formed, I have a strong urge to put it into action.
- I'm willing to make decisions.
- I work well with others.
- I can organize my time efficiently.

E. Giving reasons for switching jobs

- It's within the field of my study.
- I've set some goals for myself and my career, and unfortunately I'm at a standstill in my current situation.
- I have begun to explore options available before I spend too much time in a job where I can't advance.
- I feel there is no opportunity for advancement.
- I am hoping to get an offer of a better position. If opportunity knocks, I will take it.
- I am looking for a company that I really want to work for so that I could settle down and make long-term contributions.
- I'm leaving the present job due to the expiry of my employment contract.

 Exercises

I. Make a mind map.

Here is Nancy's mind map starting from "ideal job".

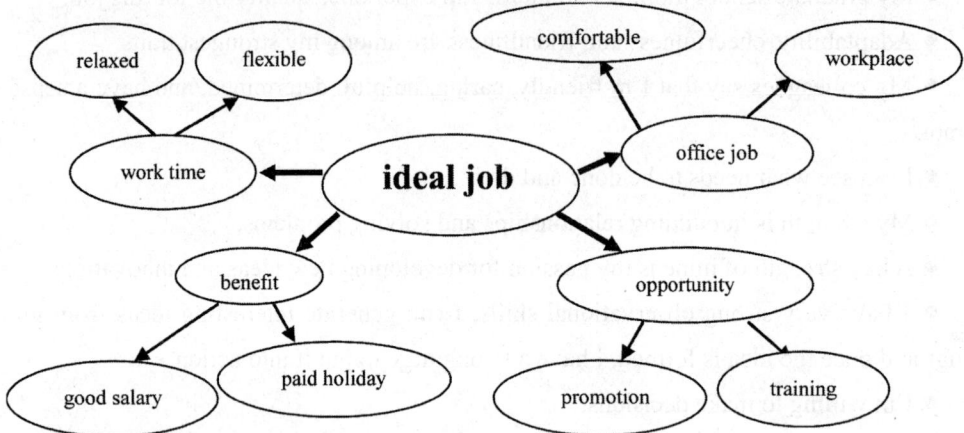

Now make your own mind map centered on one of the following: "ideal job", "ideal boss", "ideal profession", "ideal part-time job" or "ideal company". Discuss your mind map with your partner.

II. Match the type of job with what it involves.

Types of jobs	What it involves
1. photographer	A. interviews people or finds out about events from on-lookers
2. programmer supervisor	B. takes photographs of important people or events
3. salesman	C. makes sure the writing is clear, concise and accurate and checks facts
4. doctor	D. handles large volumes of cash, performs data entry, and deals with customers face to face
5. secretary	E. prescribes medication and provides healthier life-style recommendations
6. cashier	F. receives clients, answers telephones, types memo-randums and reports, arranges appointments and so on
7. aircrew	G. writes computer programs, advises and instructs less experienced programmers, and offers operating

8. waiter		instructions
	H.	ensures the safety of the passengers in case of an emergency, provides for the comfort of the passengers and serves meals
9. reporter	I.	evaluates the customers' requirements, creates new sales channels, and sells goods door to door
10. editor	J.	greets customers, explains the specials, takes the order, relays the order to the kitchen, brings food to the customer's table, and clears the table

III. Complete the short dialogues with the expressions given in the box.

> A. Thanks. I'll wait here.
> B. No, but I'm good at math and I'm a quick learner.
> C. Can I make an appointment, please?
> D. No problem.
> E. OK, can I submit an application for future opportunities, please?

1. **A**: Excuse me. I'm interested in a job. Do you have any openings?
   B: Not right now, but we can keep your name on file.
   A: _____

2. **A**: I want to make an appointment to see the manager.
   B: Just a moment, I'll see if she's free.
   A: _____

3. **A**: Are you interested in a job as a clerk?
   B: Yes, that's right.
   A: Do you have any experience?
   B: _____

4. **A**: Here is my application. Can I see the manager?
   B: Not just now, because he's busy.
   A: _____

5. **A**: I have an appointment with Mr. Levis. Will you please tell him I'm here?
   B: I'm sorry. He is on the phone at the moment. Will you please wait a minute?
   A: _____

IV. Pair work: make dialogues based on the following situations.

1. Student A interviews Student B, asking about the job duties of his/her previous job.
2. Student A interviews Student B, asking about his/her performance in the university.
3. Student A interviews Student B, asking about the reasons for changing his/her job.
4. Student A asks Student B about his/her performance in a recent interview.

V. Topics for discussion.

1. Is it better to be self-employed or to work for a large corporation? Why?
2. Which do you think is more important: to make a lot of money or to enjoy your job?
3. What do most people prefer, indoor or outdoor jobs?
4. Are there any jobs that can only be done by one gender? If so, what are they?

Culture Tips

Typical Questions at Traditional Interviews

Questions about yourself: your background and future ambitions:

Tell me about yourself.

Why did you choose the University of Kent / your degree subject?

Explain any gaps on your application form (e.g., a year out; unemployment; travel).

How would the experiences you describe be useful in this company?

What are your main strengths and weaknesses?

What other jobs / careers are you applying for?

Where do you see yourself in five years? (This is quite a common question. Read the employer's brochure to get an idea of the normal pace of graduate career development. Be ambitious but realistic.)

Tell me about your vacation work / involvement with student societies / sporting activities.

Questions about your knowledge of the employer or career area:

Why do you want to work for us?

Why have you chosen to apply for this job function?

Who do you think are, or will be, our main competitors?

What do you think makes you suitable for this job?

What do you see as the main threats or opportunities faced by the company?

What image do you have of this company?

 Class Activities

Who Is the Right Person?

Objectives: Review or learn personality adjectives.

1. Divide the students into groups of five.

2. Ask each group to choose one interviewer and four applicants.

3. Ask each applicant to think of two personality adjectives and write them down on a piece of paper.

4. The teacher shows the interviewers a chart and asks them to choose their roles from the first column and select the right person they need from the four applicants.

The chart may look like this:

Job recruiter	Vacancy
An owner of a café	A waiter or waitress
A manager of a small company	A typist
A president of a hospital	A nurse
A boss of a factory	A designer
A shopkeeper	A shop assistant
A housewife	A cleaner
A headmaster of a school	An English teacher

5. The teacher may also provide students with a list of personality adjectives to ensure the game runs smoothly.

6. Ask each interviewer to state the reason why he/she chooses his/her employee.

 思 政

A Dip into Chinese Wisdom

1. 中央政府已经加大措施来创造就业和稳定就业市场。

The central government has scaled up measures to create jobs and stabilize the job market.

2. 老骥伏枥，志在千里。

Though the old horse is in the stable,

It still dreams of galloping a thousand miles.

3. 生当作人杰，死亦为鬼雄。

Be a hero among men while you are alive;

Be a hero among spirits even after you are dead.

4. 千里之行，始于足下。

A journey of a thousand miles begins with one step.